WHAT YOUR COLLEAGUES ARE S___

"This is a knock-your-socks-off, why-didn't-I-think-of-that, yes-of-course-that-makes-sense read! Both students and teachers across the country need a little pick-me-up—and this is it! Inquiry as cognitive apprenticeship is going to transform the learning lives of students and teachers for generations! Bring the joy back to teaching and learning."

—Renee Houser, co-author of *What Do I Teach Readers Tomorrow* series and
Teacher's Toolkit for Independent Reading

"How do we empower our students as learners? How do we ensure that every teacher receives the guidance to deliver powerful instruction, particularly to the students who are most often underserved? These and other critical questions are addressed in this important new book. Under NCLB, we've spent too much time on testing and not enough time focused on how to provide all students with the opportunity to learn. Jeff's book moves us in this direction with thoughtful guidance and helpful strategies."

—Pedro A. Noguera, Distinguished Professor of Education and
Faculty Director of the Center for the Transformation of Schools, UCLA

"What a profound and daring aim: to help teachers transform their teaching so that they can, in turn, transform their students' lives—both in and out of school. *Planning Powerful Instruction, Grades 2–5: 7 Must-Make Moves to Transform How We Teach—and How Students Learn* provides a framework to help teachers across disciplines plan units and lessons that will make their classrooms places that they and their students will want to be: caring communities in which all of the members engage in the kind of thinking, talking, reading, and writing that motivates genuine engagement and that develops and rewards expert strategies and habits of mind. I'll admit to some acronym envy: Wilhelm, Miller, Butts, and Fachler demonstrate the power of EMPOWER, a model of instructional planning that will surely invigorate the work of any teacher."

—Michael Smith, co-author of *Developing Writers of Argument*

"We all want to teach in a way that goes beyond dispensing information to transforming learners' lives. The great thing about this book is that it shows us *how*—by EMPOWERing students (an acronym for seven practices that promote guided inquiry through apprenticeship). Choose this book as a source of personal reflection or professional study with colleagues. It's a treasure trove of clearly defined strategies easily adapted to any elementary classroom—along with real-world examples, planning protocols, rubrics, charts, templates, and more."

—Nancy Boyles, author and independent literacy consultant

"Educators know the practices they should be using—collaboration, think-alouds, questioning, deep discussion— but the work of integrating, aligning, and operationalizing it all can be daunting. *Planning Powerful Instruction* provides a framework for effective planning by taking theory and making it practical. This is a guidebook that can be internalized!"

—Lynn Angus Ramos, K–12 English Language Arts Curriculum Coordinator

PLANNING POWERFUL INSTRUCTION

GRADES 2-5

From Jeff:

I dedicate this book to my daughter, Jasmine Marie Wilhelm, who is just entering the exciting and empowering career of teaching, although she has already been my teacher since the day she was born!

From Jackie:

I dedicate this book to my parents, Monte and Maureen Miller—my original teachers, who have taught me to take risks, embrace challenges, stay curious, be a lifelong learner, and love deeply—and to my brother Marcus, who encourages me to live life with great passion and to enjoy its adventures. Thank you for always believing in me and for your constant love and support. I love you!

From Chris:

I dedicate this book to my wife, Emily Martha Joyce. She guides me like a dorsal fin.

From Adam:

I dedicate this book to my parents, Bonnie and Jeff, who always encouraged me to ask questions; to Brad and Amanda for showing me how writers get it done; and to my wife, Liz, the most compassionate, creative, and supportive partner I could ever ask for; thank you for your endless love. I love you all.

PLANNING POWERFUL INSTRUCTION

7 Must-Make Moves to Transform How We Teach—and How Students Learn

GRADES 2-5

Jeffrey D. Wilhelm, Jackie Miller, Christopher Butts, and Adam Fachler

FOR INFORMATION:

Corwin
A SAGE Company
2455 Teller Road
Thousand Oaks, California 91320
(800) 233-9936
www.corwin.com

SAGE Publications Ltd.
1 Oliver's Yard
55 City Road
London EC1Y 1SP
United Kingdom

SAGE Publications India Pvt. Ltd.
B 1/I 1 Mohan Cooperative Industrial Area
Mathura Road, New Delhi 110 044
India

SAGE Publications Asia-Pacific Pte. Ltd.
18 Cross Street #10-10/11/12
China Square Central
Singapore 048423

Printed in the United States of America

ISBN 978-1-5443-4281-8

Acquisitions Editor: Tori Bachman
Editorial Development Manager: Julie Nemer
Senior Editorial Assistant: Sharon Wu
Production Editor: Tori Mirsadjadi
Copy Editor: Jared Leighton
Typesetter: C&M Digitals (P) Ltd.
Proofreader: Liann Lech
Indexer: Integra
Cover and Interior Designer: Scott Van Atta
Marketing Manager: Deena Meyer

This book is printed on acid-free paper.

20 21 22 23 24 10 9 8 7 6 5 4 3 2 1

CONTENTS

Visit the companion website at
http://resources.corwin.com/EMPOWER-elementary
for downloadable resources.

ACKNOWLEDGMENTS

We all want to thank Lisa Luedeke, our longtime editor and supporter; Tori Bachman, our most dedicated and wonderful editor; and Chris Downey, our developmental editor. We are doing something totally new in this book, and this team helped us navigate that territory. Thanks, too, to the entire design team at Corwin for making our work look so good. Finally, a team of teacher reviewers provided very valuable feedback on our proposal as we were working on our final revisions. Thanks to all of you.

We tried our ideas in collaboration with the fellows of the Boise State Writing Project, in their classrooms, and through the Idaho Coaching Network, as well as through Jeff's work with the coaches from the American Reading Company. Our thanks to Scott Cook for all his support over many years.

Jeff would like to especially thank Chris, Jackie, and Adam for undertaking this significant and very exciting project as a true team of thinking partners. He appreciates their hard thinking, good humor, and constant collegiality. Jeff also wants to give a twenty-one-gun salute to his wife, Peggy Jo, and to all his colleagues and students with whom he has taught and learned over the course of his career. Thanks to so many Boise State Writing Project fellows for their collegiality and support over many years, especially Rachel Bear, Karen Miller, Cecilia Pattee, Laurie Roberts, Paula Uriarte, Ramey Uriarte, Jim Fredricksen, Amber Warrington, and so many more, too numerous to mention.

Jackie would like to thank all the students and teachers she has had the privilege of teaching and learning with and from throughout her career—all of whom have had a significant impact on her life. Jackie would also like to offer a special thanks to all her family and friends, who are quite simply the best and mean the world to her. She would like to thank Jeff for his ongoing mentorship and for inviting her to partner with him on this book. Jackie also offers her sincere thanks to her co-authors, Chris, for his thoughtful, innovative, and fun-loving nature, and Adam, for his visionary thinking and work in developing the EMPOWER mental model. She would also like to thank all the thinking partners who support and challenge her as an educator, both in and beyond the classroom, especially Katy Shea, Carissa Hale, Steve McConnel, Jennifer Varner, Lisa Martell, Brieann Trueblood, Ramey Uriarte, Rachel Bear, Scott Cook, Brandon Bolyard, Amy Brownlee, Jayna Eichelberger, Emily Morgan, and all her colleagues in the Idaho Coaching Network.

Chris would like to thank Jeff for his mentorship and friendship, Jackie for her drive for awesomeness, and Adam for making the complex comprehensible. Thanks to my fellows at the Boise State Writing Project for creating a vibrant culture that supports joy, deep thinking, and writing. Thanks to the people that make up the Idaho Coaching Network for promoting teacher leadership across our great state. Finally, thanks to my colleagues and friends at Frank Church High School for your trust and loyalty.

Adam would like to thank Chris and Jackie for being tireless thought partners and connecting so many dots for our elementary colleagues. He would also like to thank Jeff for answering a random e-mail from a reader in 2014, leading to all this happening.

PUBLISHER'S ACKNOWLEDGMENTS

Corwin gratefully acknowledges the contributions of the following reviewer:

Lynn Angus Ramos
English Language Arts Coordinator
DeKalb County School District
DeKalb County, GA

ABOUT THE AUTHORS

Jeffrey D. Wilhelm is distinguished professor of English education at Boise State University. He is the founding director of the Maine and Boise State Writing Projects. He is the author or co-author of thirty-nine books about literacy teaching and learning, and he has won NCTE's Promising Research Award for *You Gotta BE the Book* (1997) and the David H. Russell Award for Distinguished Research in the Teaching of English for *"Reading Don't Fix No Chevys"* (2003) and for *Reading Unbound* (2016). Jeff has devoted his professional career to helping teachers help their students. He is particularly devoted to assisting students who are considered to be reluctant, struggling, or at risk. He is a passionate advocate for teachers and for students. He is committed to teaching for wholeness and well-being. He is an ardent Nordic marathon skier, mountain biker, and backpacker. He lives with his wife, Peggy, in Boise, Idaho.

Jackie Miller is a respected educator and instructional coach in the state of Idaho. She previously taught elementary school for seven years and now facilitates professional development and coaching support for teachers across the state of Idaho through the Idaho Coaching Network. This network adopts the National Writing Project premise that teachers are the best teachers of teachers because they can and do speak from the authority of their practice. In this network, Jackie helps to cultivate teacher leaders who grapple with and embrace best instructional practices and extend their learning by sharing with colleagues in their schools and districts. Through this pay-it-forward approach, teacher leaders in this network provide thousands of hours of professional development that impacts every district in the state. Jackie also co-teaches classes for educators through the Boise State Writing Project and works diligently to help teachers to transfer and apply their learning in their contexts. Throughout her career, Jackie has worked with both students and teachers, empowering them to grow their self-efficacy and rise to their highest potential. She is a strong advocate of inquiry as cognitive apprenticeship and has employed this in her classroom across all disciplines. Beyond teaching, Jackie enjoys spending time with family and friends and doing all things outdoors.

Christopher Butts is a Title I coach at Frank Church High School in the Boise School District, co-teaching in English and math classrooms. Additionally, he spent ten years at the elementary level as a paraprofessional for English language learners and then as a third-grade teacher. He has been a teacher-consultant with the Boise State Writing Project since 2012. He has designed and facilitated online courses about teaching informational and argument writing. As a coach and co-director for the Idaho Coaching Network, he assisted teachers in the creation of their own inquiry as cognitive apprenticeship units and trained teachers in how to lead professional development at their respective sites. He is passionate about working with marginalized learners of any age.

Adam Fachler is a strategist, coach, and consultant for preK–12 teachers and educational leaders throughout New York. Formerly a middle school teacher, staff developer, and intern principal, he left the classroom in 2014 to co-found the School in the Square, a public charter school in Washington Heights. Adam believes all educators deserve a coach in their corner and strives to provide them with the highest caliber of professional support they have ever received. In addition to creating the EMPOWER framework, Adam is a leading expert in Thinking Maps®—a visual language for learning—and a StoryBrand Certified Marketing Guide. Adam lives with his wife, Liz, in Brooklyn, New York.

Introduction

"Education is an act of love, and thus an act of courage."
—Paulo Freire (2013, p. 34)

Teaching well is an act of love for our learners. It is also an act of love and respect for ourselves; for knowledge that has been developed over time in the disciplines; for reading, composing, and problem solving; and for all significant learning that makes a difference to the quality of our personal and shared human experiences. It is an act of love for the world and for the future and an act of faith in our capacity to better ourselves and our world. Teaching well is often a kind of loving rebellion because it requires going beyond the status quo, of caring for what is yet uncared for, of working for justice, for new ways of knowing and being, for what is in the act of becoming and yet to be (Wilhelm & Novak, 2011). Teaching well is all about *transformation*.

Teaching well is an act of social justice. In America today, demographics often determine destiny. Parents' socioeconomic status and educational attainment are the primary predictors of a learner's later success. But it does not have to be this way. When we *cognitively apprentice* learners into the joy and capacity of greater expertise, social barriers to success can be overcome. Research on human potential stretching, from Vygotsky (1978) in the 1920s to Benjamin Bloom (1976) to the recent work of Anders Ericsson and Robert Pool (2016), demonstrates the liberating finding that *everyone* is capable of learning the next available concept or process if they get the proper assistance in a meaningful context of use—in other words, if they are apprenticed.

Teaching—as an act of love and for social justice—is the most noble calling and transformative pursuit that exists in the world!

Teaching for deep understanding and growth requires passion, purpose, and dedication, but more than that, teaching well requires expert practice in the use of scaffolds, structures, and strategies to activate and enliven the passion and purpose, to operationalize the dedication, and to make the learning happen, now and into the future. These scaffolds, structures, and strategies move from providing models and guided support to promoting self-regulation and self-direction and move the learners into independence, into the full flowering of their human potential. Teaching well is about inducting learners into meaning-making power; it is about sharing the persuasive power of expertise *with* learners, not having authoritative power *over* learners.

THE TRANSFORMATIVE POWER OF GUIDED INQUIRY

This book is about using a specific form of guided inquiry (known as **inquiry as cognitive apprenticeship**, or **ICA**) to teach in ways that develop passion and purpose and that lead to independent and increasing expertise in learners. When we use guided inquiry, we teach for possibility, deepen learning, and help our learners actualize their potential, thus transforming the lives of individuals and leading to a better tomorrow.

The EMPOWER model we introduce in this book is a map for instructional planning of guided inquiry at both the unit and lesson instructional levels. EMPOWER names the *must-make moves* of teaching through guided inquiry and apprenticeship:

E	Envision a lesson's or unit's bottom-line goals for student learning
M	Map out the steps of the learning journey for moving toward a new destination
P	Prime learners by activating their prior knowledge and interests
O	Orient learners to the goals, purposes, and payoffs of the learning
W	Walk through the skills and processes that move learners to increasing expertise by modeling, mentoring, and monitoring learner performance, gradually releasing responsibility to them through the process of apprenticeship
E	Explore new territory as learners personalize and transfer what has been learned
R	Reflect throughout the process to name what was learned; how it was learned; and ways to continue thinking about, growing, applying, and transferring what has been learned

EMPOWER is a model for systematic instructional planning that uses backward design and captures current research across the learning sciences into motivation, engagement, optimal experience, cognition, development of expertise, understanding and transfer, and more. This kind of planning is the central domain of a teacher's professional knowledge. In the chapters that follow, we will first share the research and general principles behind EMPOWER and then proceed to the specific must-make moves necessary to enact the transformational teaching of guided inquiry as we plan units, plan lessons, and then implement and hone them with our learners. The strategies in this book are the concrete practices that put the must-make moves of the EMPOWER model into our teaching practice.

When we learn how to plan and then teach with EMPOWER, we focus on learners and the highest goals we have for them. We use and adapt the must-make moves flexibly and in service of learners' deepened engagement. Teaching begins and ends with attentiveness and responsiveness to learners and to their learning: teaching them from where they are and moving them toward where they could be. The teaching itself requires knowledge of planning and the use of strategies that scaffold and support learners to increase expertise as they practice, perform, and transfer their learning.

If we have a planning process and a repertoire of strategies to model reading, composing, and problem solving in new ways *for* learners, then we can ask them to use these processes *with* us, then *with* each other, and, finally, *by* themselves. This is the process of cognitive apprenticeship, also known as the **gradual release of responsibility**. Our approach works toward *total engagement and participation* on the part of each learner and in ways that develop conceptual expertise that can be used and honed throughout a lifetime.

Our colleague Pedro Noguera (2018) has stressed that as a culture we typically ask the wrong question, which is, *How can we raise achievement?* What we should ask is this: *How can we engage, challenge, stimulate, and deepen the learning of our learners, those specific human beings who enter into our learning environments?*

Noguera's question is one we try to answer in this book. To undertake it, courage will be more important than caution. Improvement requires building on what we already know and do to move into new ways of knowing and doing. This book is about transforming how we teach so we can transform why, and how, and what our learners learn. The ultimate goal is for learners to be transformed through **deep understanding** and the achievement of **conscious competence**—the capacity to monitor, justify, reflect on, and **transfer** what they've learned, and to extend and adapt their knowledge to solve future problems. This kind of 3-D teaching and learning requires knowing, doing, and thinking. But how do you *do* it? What is the *process* for getting the results you're seeking in your classroom?

Before we move further, let's be clear: *Guided inquiry is neither an extra nor an option.* It is the work of truly teaching. It is the necessary process for achieving motivation, engagement, deep learning, practical and usable disciplinary expertise, and the capacity to meet all next-generation standards and assessments. It is a way to make your classroom into a caring community of practice, where everyone works together on common projects that mirror real-world expertise. It is what is necessary to move away from the shallowness of information-driven teaching with its recitation and retrieval and move toward deeper learning, critical thinking, learner ownership in the process, and transfer of knowledge and skills to the world beyond the classroom. We are devoted to guided inquiry and our EMPOWER model for planning and teaching with it, because this process

1. promotes, increases, and leverages the motivation, engagement, and even joy of learners (Smith & Wilhelm, 2002, 2006);

2. prepares learners for the intellectual and problem-solving demands of future education, work, citizenry, and personal affairs (Newmann, Carmichael, & King, 2016);

3. significantly boosts achievement, understanding, and transfer of learning, including achievement on standardized tests (McTighe, Seif, & Wiggins, 2004; Newmann & Associates, 1996; Newmann & Wehlage, 1995; Smith & Wilhelm, 2006; Weglinsky, 2004);

4. strengthens a sense of belonging and community on many levels: the community of the classroom; the connection between learners, between learners and teacher, and from the classroom to real-world communities of practice; and the collaborative culture and powerful professional community among teachers (Wilhelm, 2012b); and

5. is consistent with and extends all other proven methods of guided inquiry, as shown in Figure I.1.

■ FIGURE I.1: CHART COMPARING EMPOWER TO DIFFERENT GUIDED INQUIRY MODELS

EMPOWER	SYSTEMS CONNECT	PROJECT-BASED LEARNING (PBL)	INTEGRATED INQUIRY (INTERNATIONAL BACCALAUREATE)	UNDERSTANDING BY DESIGN (UBD)	VESTED	SHELTERED INSTRUCTION OBSERVATION PROTOCOL (SIOP)	6 E'S	TEACHING FOR UNDERSTANDING
Envision	Topic selection and learning objectives	Key knowledge	Transdisciplinary theme	Stage 1: What is worthy and requiring of understanding?		Lesson prep	Engage	Use topics that engage and connect to other subjects
Map	Essential/driving questions; context; define issues and measurable changes	Challenging problem or question and student voice	Tuning in	Stage 3: What learning, experiences, and teaching promote understanding, interest, and excellence?	View	Building background		Create coherent goals
Prime								
Orient								
Walk Through	Plan and conduct investigations; analyze and interpret data; construct explanations; develop claims, informed action	Sustained inquiry, authenticity	Finding out; sorting out; going further; making conclusions		Experience / Speak	Comp. input strategies / Interaction	Explore / Explain	Create engaging learning experiences
Extend and Explore		Public product	Going further; taking action	Stage 2: What is the evidence for understanding?	Transform / Extend / Deliver / Perform	Practice/application / Lesson delivery / Review and assessment	Elaborate / Extend	
Reflect		Reflect					Evaluate	Develop formative and summative assessments that deepen understanding

MOVING FORWARD: THE JOURNEY OF EMPOWERMENT

Be aware that this process is not DFY (done for you) but, instead, DIY (you will learn how to do it for yourself and to adapt and extend the model for your purposes with your learners throughout the evolving challenges of your career). EMPOWER is not a script; it is a flexible framework and mental model of expert teaching. Your vision, energy, and commitment to improving your teaching and helping your learners play a major role in this process. If you're bringing the *passion*, we're bringing the *process* and *teaching strategies* to implement expert planning and teaching—a process that you will soon make your own. You will be able to adapt our high-leverage apprenticeship strategies, extend them, and understand the principles behind each must-make move so you can come up with lessons and activities of your own.

As Jeff's dad used to say, "If you always do what you've always done, then you'll always get what you always got." Our approach rejects the traditional and typical (so embedded in educational practice) and champions more progressive ways of teaching to achieve deep engagement and usable understanding, to help ourselves and our learners become our best and most powerful selves.

Teaching well is an act of love. And with love—and a teacher's mindful instruction and support—all potential can be brought into being; all things can become possible.

An Introductory Activity: Getting in the Game of Guided Inquiry

What teacher has not struggled with planning curriculum that works for learners? Or felt perplexed by how to help learners develop the skills they need while keeping the learning joyful? Maybe you know the feeling of giving up on a new unit of study (or even a lesson) because the task of creating it without even knowing if it would work was too daunting. Perhaps, like your fellow teachers nationwide, you face a new set of standards requiring that learners think at a deeper level than has been expected in the past. Or maybe you've just grown tired of searching online for the "perfect" lesson or unit for your learners only to be disappointed by the results. If any of this sounds familiar, this book is for you. We intend it as a practical guide to creating curriculum and facilitating instruction—units and lessons—to achieve four goals:

1. Unlock the motivation and engagement in classrooms of diverse learners

2. Maximize your learners' chances of mastering desired learning outcomes

3. Position and help learners to think, understand, and act more like disciplinary experts and democratic citizens

4. Access your fullest potential as an instructional leader

(Continued)

We all want to make a positive impact in the lives of our learners and in the classrooms of our colleagues. In order to do that, we need a consistent, reliable way to design and deliver instruction that works. But that leads to another question: *What works?* Consider the four teaching vignettes that follow. Because we want the focus to remain on the pedagogy—the teaching moves, not the subject area— we've designed scenarios around a subject we are fairly confident few of our readers teach: rock climbing. After reading the scenarios, try to determine which one will most likely lead to the highest degree of climbing independence and expertise and be able to explain why you think so.

Vignette 1: The unit begins with the teacher explaining why people climb mountains and how the class will climb one. Every day, the teacher models a new skill on a section of terrain for learners, briefly guides the practice of the new skill, and then facilitates the learners' independent practice. "I do, we do, you do" is practiced with every new skill each day, until the class collectively reaches the top of the mountain, with the teacher providing copious feedback along the way. At the end of the unit, learners put all the skills together and climb a new mountain independently. After the climb is complete, the teacher creates a gallery of photos from individual learners' climbs and writes *a glow and a grow*—a point of praise and a suggestion for improvement—next to each photo.

Vignette 2: "How do *you* think we should climb this mountain?" Not wanting to stifle learners' creativity, the teacher invites learners to discover their own strategies for climbing and presents them with various tools they might need. Documenting their own trial and error, learners create a notebook full of personal climbing strategies. Not only do they create their own styles of climbing, but they all climb different mountains tailored to their interests. The more naturally gifted climbers help and give feedback to the less gifted climbers during group work. At the end, the learners all climb different mountains independently using their own unique styles and give a presentation to the community based on their climb.

Vignette 3: The teacher opens the unit by asking learners what strategies they already know for climbing and then assesses their use of these strategies on a climbing wall. The teacher identifies a mountain in the distance as the destination of the unit and poses a guiding question: *Why and how do experts climb mountains?* After exploring a few stories and strategies of expert climbers, the learners create a basic checklist of moves for their first climb, a molehill. With a "quick win" under their belts, the learners scale two progressively higher mountains with the teacher's coaching, using and extending their *expert-move checklist* after each climb. They then tackle two even higher mountains in groups, relying almost entirely on their peers' feedback and support. By now, they have outgrown the checklists; they are using more developed scorecards and keeping process journals. The learners' final task is twofold: (1) climb a new mountain independently and (2) teach a group of local kids who have never climbed before how to tackle their first mountain. Afterward, there is a debrief where learners share their experiences and brainstorm a plan to climb another mountain or a way to transfer their skills to a new pursuit.

Vignette 4: A new unit called "Mountains and Molehills" begins. The teacher assigns worksheets about the process of climbing, multiple-choice questions about different kinds of mountains, and matching tasks to relate climbing tools to their purpose. Sometime toward the end of the year, learners climb a mountain on the same day as all the other kids in their state. Afterward, learners watch several movies about climbing.

ANALYSIS OF THE VIGNETTES

Vignette 4: Educational malpractice

The learning activities in the worksheet-driven classroom do not correspond to how real-world climbing experts train, plan, or climb, so this approach fails to translate into gains in rock-climbing expertise. Nobody argues for teaching this way, but it still tends to dominate American education (see Chapter 2). Learners in classrooms like these feel disengaged and grossly unprepared for their state test on "climbing" as well as for real-world applications.

Vignette 1: Skill-a-day learning

Although this vignette presents many elements that *appear* sound, upon closer inspection, it's clear that the teacher misunderstands the gradual release of responsibility—the process of transferring ownership of a task from the expert to the learner over time—as something that happens over a day instead of over weeks, months, or even years. This teacher values the consistency and structure of having an "I do, we do, you do" element in every lesson, but the unintended consequence of this is learners becoming dependent on *daily teacher assistance*. There is always a "we do" and never a period for learners to consolidate and extend their previous learning. The teacher's removal of all scaffolding for the final task can be abrupt and jarring for learners as well. Here's one final point: By breaking down the climbing into a series of subskills and only focusing on one at a time, learners never get the experience of linking moves to climb a whole mountain, making success on the final task highly unlikely for many of them.

Vignette 2: Discovery-based—or "choose your own adventure"—learning

Allowing learners to wrestle with open-ended challenges has its place (and generally this place is *after* learners have been supported to learn something new); however, reliance on this strategy is unsound pedagogy because it abruptly releases responsibility to unprepared learners. In this totally unscaffolded, discovery-based environment, the climbers climb and the nonclimbers roll down the mountain, often getting hurt in the process. Learners almost certainly will not develop real expertise because real expertise is passed down through communities of practitioners who study their predecessors, compare notes, and make connections to new challenges, not by simply holing oneself off and tinkering. This vignette does present a rosy, if not romantic, vision of learning, but ultimately, it's a misguided and unrealistic one. Furthermore, as the description of the final task suggests, learners in classrooms like these end up "all over the map" (in this case, both literally and figuratively) as a result of uneven skill development and unclear direction. Learners who never learn the practices of experts cannot be expected to independently navigate an open-ended challenge.

ANOTHER WAY?

Insightful readers may notice somewhat exaggerated parallels (though not by much) between the vignettes provided here and the most common instructional approaches employed by schools nationwide. The pedagogical issues just enumerated abound in even the most popular publishers' curricula. So, if Vignette 1 is too scaffolded and Vignette 2 is too unscaffolded, what is the alternative? What would such a pedagogy present? Ideally, such an approach would balance the need for explicit instruction with the need for learner autonomy, infuse rigor with meaning, and serve learners now and in the future.

(Continued)

(Continued)

VIGNETTE 3: EMPOWERMENT PEDAGOGY

In this vignette, the teacher *primes* learners for the new challenge by tapping into their prior knowledge and skill. She then *orients* them toward a new destination and asks a compelling framing question. From there, it's classic apprenticeship: She *walks through* some expert approaches to the task, inviting learners into a community of experts, and helps learners get a quick win. Over time, the teacher *extends expertise* by challenging learners to take on progressively harder climbs with less assistance from her and more assistance from peers. Finally, the teacher calls on learners to *explore* new territory, climbing the mountain independently and then teaching someone else. Both the teaching task and future climbs are made possible by learners having developed an evolved mental model of climbing expertise from ongoing opportunities to *reflect* on their process through checklists, scorecards, and process journals.

These five elements (whose initial letters spell P-O-W-E-R), in addition to two behind-the-scenes teacher moves, *envision* and *map* (giving us E-M), "spell out" the pedagogy of EMPOWERment: the subject of this book.

While other pedagogies impose artificial form and vocabulary onto learning, EMPOWER does the opposite: It distills the elements of real-world teaching and learning and codifies them into a replicable process. Far from formulaic, EMPOWER merely *describes* what happens when learners and teachers engage together in highly relevant, highly authentic teaching and learning. EMPOWER leverages the power of two schools of thought:

1. Expert inquiry—the recursive process of developing and performing knowledge the way real-world experts do

2. Apprenticeship—the art of gradually releasing responsibility for task performance to learners by building their capabilities until they can "own" the whole endeavor themselves

Instead of treating relevance and authenticity as an afterthought, EMPOWER uses them as a starting place to explain real-world learning better than any existing paradigms. Learners achieve 3-D learning as they are helped to know, do, and think: reflecting on, justifying, and managing their learning.

A MAP OF THIS BOOK

These vignettes attempt to answer timeless questions about teaching: *What kind of teaching can actually achieve transformations in understanding, performance, and ways of being? Under what conditions are people guided to inquire and develop expertise that can be applied in the real world? In light of that, what defines excellent instructional design? What moves must educators make to guarantee that learners develop expertise, insight, and independence?*

Like the learners in our vignettes, you too will begin a journey—surveying your methods and engaging in reflective practice. If you put in the work, your destination is assured: You will reach new heights as an educator. You may find, too, that you'll take on a new role as an instructional leader.

We frame each chapter with a guiding question and include illustrative examples, stories from the field, and actionable insights. Chapters 1 and 2 provide a "map of the territory" and necessary background for the EMPOWER framework. Chapter 1 explores how EMPOWER works as a model of guided inquiry and apprenticeship to help people achieve the capacity of experts. Chapter 2 looks at how to make the shift from informational to transformational teaching. We'll describe the differences so you can monitor your own shift, and we'll explain why even very accomplished and progressive teachers can often revert to the "salience of the traditional" (Zeichner & Tabachnick, 1981).

Then, we get practical. Chapters 3 through 5 explore how to work offstage to plan your units and individual lessons through the techniques of *envisioning* and *mapping* (the E-M of EMPOWER). Chapter 6 is about how to prime the classroom culture and community necessary for guided inquiry. In Chapters 7 and 8, we examine how to prepare learners for success with specific conceptual and procedural learning targets through *priming* and *orienting* (the P-O of EMPOWER). Chapters 9 through 13 focus on how to use various scaffolds and supports to actually apprentice, or *walk through*, new complex learning with learners in order to develop and then *explore* and *extend* independent expertise (the W-E of EMPOWER). Chapters 14 and 15 look at techniques and assessments to help learners *reflect* (the R of EMPOWER) on, name, transfer, apply, and move consciously into the future with their newfound expertise.

We've included a throughline unit in each of the chapters so that you can see how each must-make move of guided inquiry can be used as a lesson that is part of an actual unit. The first strategy and the accompanying lesson canvas in each chapter will come directly from this unit. The strategies that follow in each chapter will demonstrate how the featured must-make move can work in other ways in the throughline unit or in units from different subjects across the curriculum.

There are two websites to support the work started in this book. The Online Companion site at **resources.corwin.com/empower-elementary** contains pieces that match directly with strategies you'll find in the book. This website is hosted by Corwin, our publisher.

To further support you, we have created a website that we maintain on our own, **empoweryourteaching.com**. Here you will find ongoing updates, an online glossary of terms to support PLC work, and resources that complement and extend those from this book.

PART 1: TRANSFORMATIVE PLANNING AND INSTRUCTION

ENVISION   MAP   PRIME   ORIENT   WALK THROUGH   EXTEND/EXPLORE   REFLECT

Chapter 1

WHAT'S AT STAKE? TEACHING TOWARD EXPERTISE WITH A SENSE OF URGENCY

> **ESSENTIAL QUESTION**
> What's the best way to prepare learners
> for real-world expertise?

If the goal of K–12 education is to ensure that our learners are ready for the next learning challenge—and eventually for college and careers and everything their futures hold—*then we must transform learners' motivation and capacity in ways that correspond to those of experts before they finish school.* We accomplish this when we motivate learners with authentic tasks learners find interesting, meaningful, and usable. Deliberate practice with strategies necessary to completing real-world tasks will develop the same mental models that experts use, which means learners will be able to transfer those skills and ways of thinking to new tasks and problems throughout their lifetime.

The most effective way to achieve this kind of transformational teaching and learning is by using the mental model of EMPOWER. In this chapter, we explain the EMPOWER framework more fully and show how it captures the research on creating the conditions of motivation, developing expertise (especially through the use of deliberate practice), and achieving transfer. The process in which learners come to **know** (understand conceptually like an expert); **do** (perform and use knowledge like an expert to get things done); and **think** (justify and explain what and how they know, monitor and self-correct performance, and adapt what has been learned for use in new situations) is called *3D teaching and learning.* This promotion of expert knowing, doing, and thinking mirrors what cognitive scientists call *understanding.*

What's in this shift in practice for you? Becoming a highly competent professional teacher who can more expertly motivate and assist your learners towards real-world expertise and application. What's in it for the kids? Everything! EMPOWER moves learners into the future with purpose, motivation, and expert tools that provide them with the deep understanding to make their way in the world as learners and community members in ways rarely achieved by traditional instruction.

The EMPOWER model, which helps teachers enact the design and delivery of teaching through the lens of guided inquiry, aligns with the cognitive science of *improving*. At every stage in the process, learners actively engage in the "hard fun" of mastering new learning. There is explicit and active teaching throughout, punctuated by periods of learners' deliberate practice, and then time to use and enjoy, consolidate, personalize, and extend their new competence. In other words, there is a balance of instructional and independent work—of apprenticeship, practice, and use—in a process of continuous and ongoing improvement.

***

Teaching requires intentional design and adept decision making. Every day, there are multiple decisions to make about how to plan, design, revise, differentiate, and implement instruction, not to mention managing learners' energy—which is best done through both caring relationships and engaging and assistive instruction. In our work with teachers, we found that deciding on the first instructional move—or just getting *started* with planning—can provide the biggest challenge. As a result, teachers often rely on textbook questions or turn to Pinterest or Teachers Pay Teachers to grab a lesson plan. Such lessons may engage learners in the moment, but they were neither designed nor differentiated for your classroom's deepest-felt needs and current challenges. These canned approaches prevent learners from developing to their full capacity and do not build the professional knowledge of the teacher.

Expert teaching and deep learning do not happen by accident; they happen *by design*, through mindful planning and implementation based on what you know about your own learners and their needs. We design learning experiences not just for our learners but for ourselves and even our schools and local communities. We also design the classroom culture that allows these learning experiences to be especially powerful and fruitful. We ask ourselves, *What kinds of experiences do we want learners to have and do we want to have **with** learners? What kinds of writing do we want to read? What kinds of projects do we want to collaborate on and share with the community?*

TEACHING TOWARD EXPERTISE

Expertise in teaching is knowing how to teach people how to do new, complex tasks: to pursue ever more complex reading, writing, problem solving, math, and science in more reflective and wide-awake ways that correspond ever more closely to the knowing, doing, and thinking of experts. We want our learners to develop authentic, applicable, real-world expertise across all content areas and human pursuits. This is usable expertise that is "tool-ish" instead of "school-ish" (Newmann et al., 2016; Smith & Wilhelm, 2002, 2006); it is learning that is authentic because it has value outside of school in a variety of contexts.

For example, when learners truly master how to share and support their opinions, it helps them in myriad ways: They can advocate for themselves, organize their ideas, provide reasons for their solution to a problem, listen more attentively, more peacefully resolve conflict, and so on. Every part of the opinion-sharing process—reaching a decision, considering how they reached that decision, and clearly sharing why they think the way they do—represents the kind of "tool-ish" learning we're talking about throughout this book. If our teaching does not lead learners toward consciously held and applicable expert practice, we are not teaching for understanding and use; we are in the realm of the "school-ish," and kids are merely "doing school." Cognitive scientists call the authentic application of expertise "meeting the correspondence concept" (Bereiter, 2004). All learning activities should move learners in the direction of expertise, along what is called the **correspondence continuum**. In other words, good teaching corresponds to what actual experts do. Instruction should meet the real-reader test, the real-writer test, the real-scientist test, and the real-mathematician test.

Since the 1980s, data from the United States demonstrate low average learner competence in academic subjects, analysis, problem-solving skills, interpersonal relations, communication, technology use, and a wide variety of occupational skills (see, e.g., Autor & Price, 2013; Newmann et al., 2016). Further, there are major disparities in achievement along racial and ethnic lines and by economic and disability status. The latest National Assessments of Educational Progress (NAEPs) show that the problem is not going away and is probably getting worse (NAEP, 2019). The takeaway is this: We're generally not teaching for real-world expertise, and learners who are marginalized in any way are especially endangered by standard teaching approaches. Shifting our practice begins to address these high-stakes issues for our learners and our world.

When we think of how little time during any given year we have to spend with our own learners and of the momentous task of helping diverse learners to become more engaged and expert and to overcome social inequities, we feel a profound sense of urgency. After all, which of our learners doesn't need to be more literate, more wide awake and aware, and more expert at reading, composing, critical thinking, and problem solving in every subject? Who does not need to be prepared to meet new and nonroutine challenges by drawing flexibly on what they learned? We want our learners to be consciously competent, and consciously competent students learn from consciously competent teachers. This necessitates that everyone in the classroom focuses on improving and deepening their understanding about the subject at hand.

WHAT ARE THE PREREQUISITES FOR ALL LEARNING?

The research is abundantly clear that motivation and engagement are necessary for learning. In other words, we need to develop both motivation (the impulse) and engagement (the behavioral and cognitive tools) to do something new. When we achieve both parts, we enter a state of flow (Csikszentmihalyi, 1990). The research is also clear on the conditions that promote motivation and deep engagement toward expertise (Csikszentmihalyi, 1990; Ericsson & Pool, 2016; Smith & Wilhelm, 2002, 2006). *Meeting these conditions is the responsibility of the teacher.* Here's how: First, we must plan instruction that meets the conditions of flow experience. We must then plan for learners to deliberately practice the strategies of experts over time until they achieve independence and have a mental model they can use to think about, reflect on, and adapt to new situations. These research findings explain why those one-and-done activities from textbooks or the Internet fall woefully short for developing expertise and understanding in any area.

What kind of teaching and learning approach does meet these demands? *Only* guided inquiry through cognitive apprenticeship: a learning-centered curricular structure that assists learners to ask their own questions, solve problems, and create projects. These projects must be knowledge artifacts that do "social work," that are usable by others to learn or solve problems (Csikszentmihalyi, 1990; Smith & Wilhelm, 2002, 2006). We developed the EMPOWER framework to help teachers intentionally think through the process of apprenticing learners toward expertise. Figure 1.1 shows what the EMPOWER framework looks like in the classroom and how it meets the conditions of flow.

■ FIGURE 1.1: THE CONDITIONS OF FLOW EXPERIENCE IN AN EMPOWER CLASSROOM

FLOW CONDITION	WHERE IT CONNECTS TO EMPOWER	WHAT IT LOOKS LIKE
A clear purpose, payoffs, goals, and immediate feedback	Envisioning Mapping	Learning framed as a problem to be solved (e.g., with an essential question); goals clear to all; culminating projects identified that require meeting the goals; an instructional path to develop learner capacity in meeting goals is clear and available to all
A focus on immediate experience	Priming Orienting	Prepare for success through frontloading; elicit preexisting interests and background knowledge that relate to the learning; focus on current relevance; active involvement: making and doing; immediate function and applications; fun and humor; edginess and debatability
A challenge that requires an appropriate level of skill and active assistance to be successful	Priming Orienting Walking through Extending expertise	Guided assistance and apprenticeship in the strategies of experts; plenty of time for deliberate practice and ongoing procedural feedback
A sense of control and developing competence	Walking through Extending expertise	Use of one's voice and cultural resources; justifying one's practice; the opportunity to stake and defend points of view; the opportunity for meaningful choice; naming growing competence and ways forward
The importance of the social and reflection	Walking through Extending expertise Reflecting	Collaborative group work; peer assistance, including reflecting together and providing feedback to each other; having a social purpose for all learning and use of learning; engaging in social reflection on how the purposes are being met and used; negotiating and sharing what is learned; reflecting on learning

HOW DOES SOMEONE BECOME AN EXPERT?

Expert teachers teach for **conscious competence** and **high-road transfer**, for the flexible application of what is learned in different situations. They teach for transformational change as learners move into the future.

But how do we start to teach the *how* of becoming more expert with any learning process or performance?

Let's do a thought experiment. Think of something significant that you learned to do, either in school or out. How did you progress toward and achieve competence and then expertise? How were other people involved in and affected by your learning? Also consider this: *Was there something at stake?* As in, why did you care about the learning in the first place? Did you learn to more efficiently exercise to lose weight, promote fitness, or finish a race? Did you pick up a new language because you planned to visit a different culture? Did you develop a new teaching strategy to solve a learning challenge, engage learners, or stay current in our profession? Or did you simply have a deeply *felt need* to explore some topic out of pure personal interest?

As a lifetime endurance athlete and outdoorsperson living in beautiful Maine, learning how to white-water kayak was a natural fit for Jeff. He was motivated to try a new sport, to go down rivers enjoying the outdoors, to paddle with friends, and to enjoy the excitement of white water. When he started, he spent a lot of time learning how to roll his boat, a prerequisite skill for white-water kayaking. As Jeff improved, he watched kayakers roll in different situations (e.g., in giant side waves or river holes) and tried to emulate them. He also watched slow-motion videos as an expert kayaker narrated her thought process while conducting an advanced rolling strategy, naming the moves and using prompts to guide practice, such as "Hand on your butt to save your butt!" when setting up to roll a boat in heavy roiling white water. While practicing how to roll, a teacher helped Jeff place his hands (*One hand on the butt!*) and paddle in the right way (*Curl that wrist!*), guiding his movements until he could execute the maneuver on his own. Jeff practiced another foundational move of rolling, the hip snap, while leaning against the side of the pool as well as in the gym with weights, ironing these muscular firing patterns into his mind until he mastered them. When he was competent enough, he went to increasingly challenging places in the river to practice rolling, using the cues and moves he learned from his teachers and paddling partners.

Over time, his confidence—and, more importantly, his *competence*—grew. Beyond that, Jeff grew increasingly conscious of *why* he was successful (or not), able to explain what contributed to his performance and to reflect on how he could improve. He became a **consciously competent** kayaker who understood the principles behind important practices, possessed **executive function**, and could **self-regulate** and self-correct his performance—and, therefore, teach others. From point zero (at first, he did not even know how to get into a kayak), the process of apprenticeship is what helped Jeff become an accomplished kayaker who has twice kayaked the Grand Canyon and even rolled his boat in the famous Lava Falls—and most definitely not on purpose!

We wonder: How often do teaching and learning through this kind of apprenticeship happen in ELA, math, science, or social studies class? How can we more mindfully enact this time-honored process of apprenticing learners into developing expertise in our own teaching?

HOW DOES SOMEONE IMPROVE?

This is the age-old question at the heart of the teaching profession: How does anyone get better at anything? How do people become competent and then truly expert, especially with complex processes like those required by reading, composing, and doing math or science? What role does an educator, a coach, or a mentor play in that process?

Cognitive science provides us with a clear answer (Ericsson & Pool, 2016): Like Jeff in his kayak, experts are those who have been apprenticed and mentored into **deliberately practicing** to approximate and then master the stances, thinking, problem solving, and performance activities of established experts. This deliberate practice can be playful and involve a great deal of experimentation. Those who have achieved expertise use mindful practice over time to develop a rich **mental model** of the specific tasks they must navigate. This mental model is a kind of **map**, typically including rich visualizations (like an illustrated flow chart), that guides and then extends continued development of expertise. *Possession of such a mental model is considered to be the hallmark of expertise* (Ericsson & Pool, 2016). This book is filled with such mental models for teaching specific tasks. EMPOWER is our mental map for planning, and the practice chapters (6–15) contain a variety of mental maps for pursuing specific kinds of teaching and learning, such as questioning to develop understanding or collaborating to socially construct knowledge.

Our careers as teachers and researchers have been about articulating mental models: making the stances, strategies, and processes of expert performances visible and available to teachers and learners. Visible representations of expertise make critical standards clear, providing both a mirror and a measure of success. The possession of a mental model is essential to expertise, to transfer and application, and to the creation of new knowledge. Meeting any standard—such as inferencing, analyzing, or understanding how authors achieve meanings and effects or sharing and supporting an opinion—requires a rich mental model of how the task is pursued. This is a major takeaway of cognitive science: Without a mental model of a task, you cannot get better at that task.

Without evolving mental models, we would have to start from square one every time we want to solve a problem. Scientists would argue about how to conduct fair experiments every time they want to test something instead of applying the scientific method. First responders would lose precious seconds during emergencies instead of performing life-saving assessment and action protocols. Doctors would not know what tests to use for a particular complaint, nor how to analyze the results to inform a treatment. And the list could go on and on. When we teach, we need to plan for how we will induct learners into competence and expertise, helping them develop the mental models used by experts. In other words, we are apprenticing our learners down the correspondence continuum toward mastery, deep knowledge, and high-road transfer. Cognitive scientists call this process **cognitive apprenticeship** (Collins, Brown, & Newman, 1992), and this is the basis of the guided inquiry introduced in this book.

In the real world, experts do not act alone. Instead, they interact with others in what are known as **communities of practice**, defined by Lave and Wenger (1991) as groups of people who share a concern or a passion for something they do and learn how to do it better as they regularly interact. When we inquire about a common topic and help each other to understand in a professional learning community (PLC) or a professional learning network (PLN), we participate in a community of practice. We ask questions about learning and teaching as we engage in guided inquiry that continues to apprentice us into an *expert* community of practice.

Vygotsky (1978) portrays learning as a form of cognitive apprenticeship that moves learners from their **zone of actual development** (ZAD) with a strategy or task through their **zone of proximal development** (ZPD). This means that learners are taken from where they currently are and what they can currently do independently and without help (ZAD) and are assisted and supported to do what they *cannot yet* do alone and without support (moving through the ZPD). This process helps learners understand the mental models that are currently shared by experts within a community of practice. Vygotsky considered the help we give learners to do what they cannot yet do alone—but could do with support—*the very act of teaching*. Let's put it this way: School is where you go to learn what you don't *yet* know how to do. Otherwise, what's the point? One of the great motivations and joys of being human is transformation: outgrowing ourselves and developing new competencies (Seligman, 2002).

No one was ever motivated to read by learning the *cr-* blend or how to infer, but kids will learn such things with joy in support of learning something they care about. Unfortunately, many students—boys, in particular—tend to view school learning as separate from real life; they are not typically taught new concepts or strategies in a context of use but rather through decontextualized readings and worksheets. This powerfully undermines motivation and learning (Smith & Wilhelm, 2002). So it's important to remember the following:

- The linchpin of motivation is developing usable competence.

- In order to be engaged, kids (1) need to see the value/usefulness of what they are learning and (2) need to feel assured they'll get the support needed to be successful.

- Engagement is necessary to the development of competence, and competence is necessary to staking identity—the central task of human development.

- Teachers need a growth mindset *about* their learners, as well as to develop this mindset *in* their learners (Smith & Wilhelm, 2002, 2006).

GUIDED INQUIRY: WHY THE BIG SHIFT IS NECESSARY

Guided inquiry as cognitive apprenticeship (ICA) is the rigorous mentoring of learners into the ways of thinking and doing that are required to become more expert and to address real-world problems. Guided inquiry involves framing what is to be learned—the objective of the apprenticeship—as a problem to be addressed and perhaps solved. For example, instead of teaching *Charlotte's Web*, you might use the novel to explore the question, *What makes a true friend?* Instead of teaching Rosa Parks as an important person in history, you could reframe the learning as a social issue using the question, *How can we best protect and promote civil rights in our school and community?* Instead of teaching the water cycle, you might ask the question, *What are the water problems in our community, and how can we help to address them?*

It's important to note that guided inquiry is *not* student-centered discovery learning, where learners simply find their own way. Instead, we explicitly invite learners into a community of expert practice, provide them with models of expertise, give assistance, and offer guided and deliberate practice over time. We support learners in applying what they have learned to solve real-world problems in the ways experts do and in reflecting on and honing expert processes. Over time, learners come to practice and use what they learned on their own as they explore and extend their newly developed expertise. In this exploration and extension phase, learning may look like discovery, but learners are making use of newly developed capacities achieved through apprenticeship. At the same time, the teacher observes, provides procedural feedback that makes expertise and ways forward more visible and conscious, and points learners in new directions.

Though there are many large-scale studies demonstrating the unique power of guided inquiry and apprenticeship approaches, our favorites include the Fred Newmann Restructuring Schools and Authentic Intellectual Work studies (Newmann & Associates, 1996; Newmann et al., 2016; Newmann & Wehlage, 1995) because they show how this approach engages learners, helps them understand and develop expertise with value beyond school, and enables them to retain gains over time. Literacy researcher George Hillocks made a career of showing that guided inquiry is the way to most effectively teach writing (1986a, 1986b) and language use/grammar (1995), as well as to promote engagement and conceptual learning generally (1999). He found that for deep learning to occur, learners need to be positioned as inquirers and assisted to explore how texts and language work for meaning and effect.

John Hattie's influential review (2008) conflates inquiry as student-centered discovery learning with guided inquiry approaches such as cognitive apprenticeship, which accounts for the diminished effect size he reports. With data exclusively about guided inquiry as cognitive apprenticeship, this approach is shown to be, by far, the superior approach to teaching for engagement, understanding, and application.

We must also acknowledge the elephant in the room: next-generation standards and assessments. The model we propose is the most effective teaching model for the goals of achieving higher scores and meeting standards, as evidenced by standardized test data like the NAEPs, TIMMS, and PISA (see, e.g., Wiggins & McTighe, 2005). And we want to make this point clear: **Guided inquiry as cognitive apprenticeship can be used with any kind of curriculum, material, or text to deepen the teaching and learning.**

Perhaps most crucial, meeting the demands of—and solving the problems that face—our local and global communities will require new kinds of knowledge. In other words, traditional methods and rote learning of established information are woefully insufficient to our current and future challenges and needs. Not only is current knowledge insufficient to solve current problems, but new problems continue to emerge. *Only learning **how** to learn, inquire, and problem-solve will suffice.*

THE EMPOWER MODEL: A FRAMEWORK FOR PLANNING AND TEACHING THROUGH GUIDED INQUIRY

We've been arguing that (1) we need to teach toward real-world expertise, which is captured by mental models, and (2) guided inquiry is the way to motivate and apprentice learners into such expertise. Now we want to share a framework—the EMPOWER model—as a highly effective model for planning and teaching through guided inquiry. Figure 1.2 shows the steps of EMPOWER at a glance.

■ FIGURE 1.2: THE EMPOWER MODEL

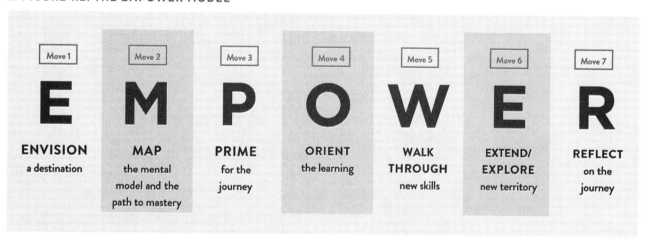

EMPOWER is *not* a formula; it is a **mental model** or **map**—a representation of the framework that informs and the process an expert teacher takes to perform the complex tasks of teaching. **The possession of a complex mental model or map for complex task completion is considered to be the hallmark of expertise** (Ericsson & Pool, 2016). This is why using EMPOWER helps you map your journey toward expert teaching. According to Ericsson and Pool's seminal research (2016), becoming expert at anything requires **deliberate practice** using and developing the processes of experts with the support of apprenticeship. Deliberate practice involves all of the following six elements highlighted by EMPOWER, as shown in Figure 1.3:

- Clear and specific goals (*envision* and *map*)
- Preparation for success (*prime* and *orient*)
- Focused practice (*walk through* and *extend and explore*)
- Pushing beyond one's comfort zone (*walk through* and *extend and explore*)
- Receiving high-quality feedback (*reflect*)
- Developing a mental model of the expert task (*reflect*)

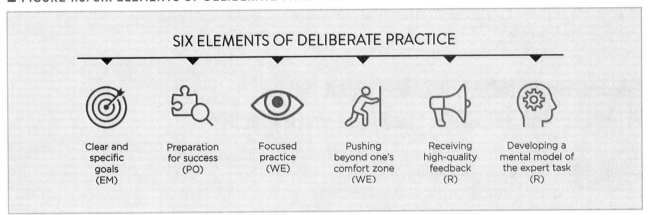

EMPOWER provides a map for teachers to follow as they plan and then apprentice learners through navigating and completing a complex task using expert stances, concepts, and strategies. As we will explain, EMPOWER provides a process for planning and implementing instruction—and for learning itself—that reflects the expert knowledge and research in a wide variety of areas from various learning sciences. Here's how the stages of EMPOWER unfold:

EM: "Offstage," before we engage with learners, expert educators first *envision* (E) a destination for learners and then *map* (M) out each step of the journey necessary to achieving that destination, including how to develop the knowledge, tools, and mental models required for achievement of mastery. This is often known as **backward planning**, mapping out instruction with the end goals and deliverables in mind.

PO: Once in front of learners, educators build motivation and personal connection as they *prime* (P) learners by activating and building their background knowledge and preexisting interests so these can be used as resources for the new learning; they also *orient* (O) learners toward the new destination and the purpose and payoff of reaching it. Orienting identifies learning targets and success criteria in terms of what learners will be able to do and create *independently* by the close of the unit, and learning outcomes that explain how they will use their new capacities now and in the future. Orienting means learners understand the purpose and payoffs of the new learning.

WE: Learners now require explicit instruction and active apprenticeship in developing new ways of understanding and performing knowledge that are required to meet the goals. Educators model the use of new strategies and concepts for learners and support them in deliberately practicing their use. This walk-through (W), or explicit instructional modeling and deliberate practice, develops and extends the expertise of learners through a variety of guided and collaborative tasks. These tasks increase in challenge/complexity and decrease in scaffolding/support over time, embodying a **gradual release of responsibility** to achieve independence. This is the time for modeling, coaching, and feedback as learners rehearse, practice, and approximate the robust understandings and practices of experts. These activities are purposeful, contextualized, low-stakes learning experiences that prepare learners for success on higher-stakes tasks. The walk-through is robust Tier 1 instruction.

With their skills and knowledge built, it is then time for learners to put their learning to the ultimate test. Educators challenge learners to *extend* their learning. This is where various kinds of differentiation and robust Tier 2 and Tier 3 instruction take place. Those who need more help get it in different forms. Those ready to move forward get support to further develop their mental model and its application. Soon, instruction moves to *explore* (E) new territory: to apply their knowledge more independently, transferring skills and ideas into novel situations that present the possibility of failure and the need to consolidate, revise, and improve on what they learned. This is very much like the "call to action" found in the hero's journey, the build-up to the "big game" in sports, or an opening-night performance in the arts. At this point, the mentor has moved mostly to the sidelines. The teacher's job now is to step back and let learners create new meanings and navigate trouble with one another so that learners become ever more independent. Teachers intervene only as necessary to keep the learning moving forward and focus their energy on encouraging and celebrating their learners and their journeys. This is where high-road transfer is put into play.

R: Throughout this entire process—each and every day but particularly near the end of a learning sequence—with the big game, opening-night performance, culminating project, and general dragon slaying behind us, we—as teachers and learners—collectively *reflect* (R). What was learned, and how? Why is it important, and how does it connect to our current and future goals? How can we use it now and in the future? What are our individual and collective strengths and struggles? How did we navigate trouble? What will we change and do next time we meet this kind of challenge? What opportunities do we foresee for using and further developing this knowledge now and in the future? What are our next steps?

When you teach via EMPOWER, learners do and make things every day (**daily deliverables**) that engage them; promote learning; involve deliberate practice; and provide the learner and teacher with opportunities to reflect on and name what's been learned, as well as possibilities for moving forward. This kind of reflection is **formative assessment** *as* and *for* **learning**.

THE PRIMACY OF PLANNING

Planning instruction for your specific learners in your particular context at this moment in time (something that you are the world's only expert on), at the unit and lesson level, *is* the *central challenge of teaching.*

Professions are defined by knowledge creation, and planning instructional practice is a central piece of teacher professional knowledge. At first glance, planning might seem like a fairly simple and even mundane task. It is neither. Planning is essential to becoming an expert teacher and also provides an opportunity for creative expression. The EMPOWER model helps us answer the big questions of teaching: *Why* do we choose to teach? *Why* do we teach *what* we teach in the ways that we do? *What* should be our major goals, and *why* are these goals worth achieving? *How* can we most effectively assist learners toward motivation and even joy and then into deep understanding and application of their learning? *When*, *where*, and under *what* conditions are teaching and learning most engaging, joyful, and effective?

All of these questions are in service of becoming more expert teachers and making our learners more expert readers, writers, and knowledge creators. Being flexible and responsive to the specific learners and learning needs in the room is one of the most challenging aspects of teaching and a distinguished indicator of teacher expertise.

TEACHING FOR TRANSFER

EMPOWER captures the "must-make moves" of planning and implementing guided inquiry. It also cultivates a spirit of high-road transfer, which is the crux goal of inquiry as cognitive apprenticeship.

A focus on transfer may seem obvious, but research shows that transfer rarely occurs in school (Haskell, 2000; Perkins & Salomon, 1988). When it does, it's usually *low-road transfer*, where two tasks so closely resemble each other that learners automatically use the same strategies. For example, if you rent a car, you transfer what you know about driving your own car to driving the rental. *High-road transfer*, on the other hand, requires "mindful abstraction of skill or knowledge from one context to another" (Perkins & Salomon, 1988, p. 25). For example, if you suddenly had to drive a forklift or a school bus, you'd have to ask yourself, "What do I do first?" This mindful abstraction constitutes what Haskell calls *theoretical understanding*—that is, to transfer knowledge from a familiar context to an unfamiliar one requires you to possess **conscious competence** with **principles of practice**. You need to know what you do, why you do it that way, how you do it, how you know it works, in what kinds of situations you might use the knowledge, and how to self-correct and think through problems.

Again, research shows that this kind of transfer rarely occurs in school—for example, learners don't automatically apply strategies required for one reading to subsequent readings or from one writing assignment to the next one. The good news is that learners can and do transfer new strategies if particular conditions are met. Haskell (2000) presents eleven of those conditions, which we have collapsed to four:

1. Learners must deeply understand the knowledge that is to be transferred and the purposes served by using this knowledge; that is, the conceptual principles and the payoffs of using that knowledge must be clear. (*Knowing*)

2. Learners must deliberately and repeatedly practice applying the meaning-making and problem-solving principles to new situations. (*Doing*)

3. Learners must understand the principles and processes of practice to be transferred; learners must have a mental model and map for applying the principles, reflecting on them and revising them for new situations and demands. (*Thinking*)

4. The classroom culture must cultivate a spirit of connection making and intellectual risk-taking; learners must continually consider and rehearse how to use and adapt their knowledge immediately and in the future. (*Thinking*)

Based on our work as thinking partners with thousands of teachers over the years, we know that EMPOWER helps teachers know *how* to teach learners *how* to develop and use expert strategies as readers, writers, and problem solvers.

DEVELOPING CONSCIOUS COMPETENCE (AS TEACHERS AND IN LEARNERS)

Here's a big, itchy problem: Teachers, even those who have a repertoire for transformational teaching, often revert to traditional practices due to the pressures of curriculum, school structures and schedules, parental/learner/colleague expectations, standard assessments, and so on. EMPOWER is a powerful solution because it provides a coherent and research-proven response to "But we've always done it this way." It also provides educators with a common language for thinking and talking about teaching and learning.

The hallmark of expertise—and the goal of all teaching and learning—is the achievement of conscious competence. Conscious competence in teaching occurs when you achieve a level of mindful awareness and the necessary tools to successfully identify a group of interrelated learning targets, monitor progress toward them, productively struggle through challenges along the way, reflect to understand and explain student learning, and move forward. When we proceed with conscious competence as teachers, we can assist learners to conscious competence as well.

With the achievement of conscious competence in learners, a room full of teachers and thinking partners is created. Conscious competence does not mean that solving any problem at hand will run smoothly. What it does mean is that the teacher and/or learners have a sense of when things go awry, can explain why that might be, and can develop a path of action for what to do about it. They have the capacity to monitor, reframe, develop, and draw on a repertoire for moving forward. This kind of expertise can eventually be internalized and might look like *unconscious* competence, but the expert can return to the map and make it conscious again when needed. Figure 1.4 details the progression from unconscious incompetence to conscious competence.

■ FIGURE 1.4: CONSCIOUS COMPETENCE CONTINUUM

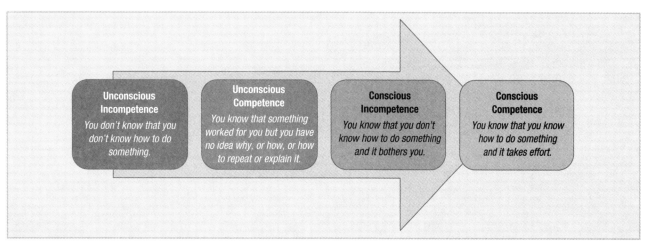

Note: We align ourselves with researchers who see an advanced form of unconscious competence as a potential stage 5, when the competence is so internalized and automatized that it has become second nature. In this case, the competence can be retrieved, extended, or revised as needed as problems arise.

POWERFUL PLANNING WITH SO MUCH AT STAKE

There is much at stake when we consider how to most effectively teach. *For teachers*, this is about achieving higher purpose and a higher level of professionalism, developing **conscious competence**, possessing the capacity to develop knowledge about teaching and our subjects, experiencing joy as a teacher—and working to develop the fullest capacity of each and every learner. *For learners*, it's about finding engagement and joy through learning, understanding, and conscious competence, as well as discovering and forging an evolving identity as a learner, reader, scientist, mathematician, and so on. Most of all, it's about achieving transfer of learning toward the next task and into the future. *For teachers and learners*, it's about creating a collaborative and supportive classroom community that is a disciplinary **community of practice** and that meets the deepest needs and expresses the deepest hopes, aspirations, values, and commitments of all its members. EMPOWER assists in meeting all of these goals.

Bottom line: What is at stake is whether we truly *teach* and learners really *learn*.

Teaching well means that learners and their understandings are transformed—that they achieve transferable ways of knowing, doing, thinking, and being—and conscious competence that justifies what they know, how they know it, and how they will use it. So yes, there is very much at stake.

Chapter 2

MAKING THE SHIFT FROM INFORMATIONAL TO TRANSFORMATIONAL TEACHING

ESSENTIAL QUESTION
How do we teach for transformation?

We all want our teaching to matter and to make the biggest possible difference in our learners' lives. This requires a momentous shift away from traditional teaching practices: moving from providing information to teaching for transformation—moving away from lecturing, reading textbooks, doing worksheets, and teacher-led discussions and toward collaborative inquiry and apprenticeship into expert practice in partnership with learners. We want our teaching and all learning activities to mirror what experts do in the real world and to encourage the kinds of knowing, doing, and thinking that lead to deep and usable understandings.

There is a gap between what is known about transformational teaching and what teachers typically do, despite the best of intentions. Part of the problem is the old dilemma: We don't know what we don't know. Teachers are not always aware of consensus understandings from cognitive science, educational research, human development, and other fields, so they don't know how to put these insights into practice. Even when we *do* know the research and best practices, we often suffer from the knowing–doing gap. Research shows that teachers tend to default to traditional, informational forms of teaching, which are encouraged by many traditional school structures—student, parent, and even colleague expectations, as well as textbooks and traditional boilerplate curricula. Even when we know what to do, we often don't do it as individuals or as systems (see, e.g., Bryk, Gomez, Grunow, & LeMahieu, 2015; Zeichner & Tabachnick, 1981). Teachers who think they are making the necessary shifts may not be doing so—or they may be doing so inconsistently. It's a bit like knowing you should floss your teeth every day or that you should start off your morning with guided meditation. We know we *should* do it, but we often don't for various reasons. Sometimes, the reason is that we need to break old habits and form new ones. Sometimes, the problem is that we don't know how to start moving in a new direction.

In these pages, we will name the necessary moves for the shift to transformational teaching so that we can be more aware of possibilities and monitor ongoing progress.

The stakes are high because our educational practices are not yet meeting the demands of the present moment, nor those of the future. Many of the problems our learners face are evolving, and many of our most pressing challenges do not yet have solutions. Social agreements about knowledge are constantly changing—did you notice that Pluto is no longer a planet?—and the job market is rapidly changing, too. The World Economic Forum (2016) estimates that more than two-thirds of today's kindergartners will enter fields that do not yet exist. Likewise, with increasing use of artificial intelligence, many jobs are becoming automated. This means the most important skills we can teach our learners are nonroutine problem-solving skills—those uniquely human areas of expertise that cannot be taken over by robots.

Studies by Autor, Levy, and Murnane (2003) and Autor and Price (2013) explore the changing demand for skills in the U.S. workplace. The *only* jobs that are growing—and they are growing exponentially—are *nonroutine* analytical and *nonroutine* interactive. For example, managing both projects and people involves nonroutine analysis of ever-changing factors as well as nonroutine interactions with different groups of workers and clients. Teaching is a classic example of this type of job. Routine jobs (e.g., mining, agriculture, manufacturing) that do not require creative communication, analysis, and on-the-spot problem solving are all but disappearing. In other words, our learners need to *learn how to learn*, how to relate and empathize, and how to collaborate and communicate to solve new problems and create new knowledge.

Here's the gist: The way American schools have traditionally taught—and, typically, still teach—does not help learners meet the demands of next-generation standards and assessments or the demands for real-world expertise and learning how to meet new challenges. Yet, as various studies show (e.g., The New Teacher Project [TNTP], 2018; Newmann et al., 2016), authoritative and informational teaching practices still dominate American teaching. This kind of teaching hurts all learners, but those learners who are minorities, living in poverty, or marginalized in any way are especially at risk. (This authoritative, information-driven teaching is what Martin Haberman refers to as *the pedagogy of poverty*, which we'll discuss in more depth later in this chapter.)

Guided inquiry through EMPOWER directly addresses the most significant problems with traditional schooling. For example, nearly 50 percent of high school dropouts reveal that they left school because it was neither interesting nor authentic, and 70 percent disclose that they were neither motivated nor assisted to work hard by typical school assignments and structures (Bridgeland, DiIulio, & Morison, 2006). In contrast, we have found that nearly all learners, especially learners who often struggle or are considered at-risk, will enthusiastically embrace guided-inquiry approaches (Smith & Wilhelm, 2002, 2006). School suddenly makes sense; is purposeful and usable; is culturally relevant; promotes competence and personal power; and enables learners to get the help they need, when they need it.

The Knowing–Doing Divide: A Real-World Story

Thirteen years ago, Jeff's wife, Peggy, collapsed as a result of what was thought to be brain cancer but turned out to be a massive cerebral hemorrhage. Jeff was told that Peggy was terminal on four different occasions over the course of the next six years. In year five, Peggy spent two months in a coma. The doctors could not explain her fluctuating blood counts. Because they did not know the *why* behind her condition, they did not know what to do. Their lack of a mental model meant they could not articulate and pursue a theory of action. For the first few years, there was no diagnosis and no viable treatment plan.

How did Jeff and Peggy succeed in meeting Peggy's medical challenge? Of course, Peggy is a woman of immense grit and grace. But there is also this: The two were thinking partners and teachers for each other throughout this health journey. They never gave up in the face of dire diagnoses. They tirelessly researched medical options and kept open minds toward all perspectives and possibilities. They had friends and family to support them (including everyone on this author team).

The turning point came when Jeff and Peggy were referred to the Mayo Clinic (a research hospital) and, from there, to the National Institutes of Health Undiagnosed Disease Program (a research program) and, from there, to the Hai-Shan Eastern Medicine Research Clinic. Up to that point, the doctors had focused primarily on information and algorithms. This kind of "one-size-fits-all" thinking suffices if you have a condition that is already understood. It did not, however, suffice for Peggy. It was not until she entered a research hospital that the doctors thought with mental models and maps, working together on the unsolved problem using the strategies of inquiry and apprenticing one another through multiple perspectives into not just deeper understanding but into new kinds of knowledge and understanding.

Jeff can assure you of this: When someone you love is dying of an undiagnosed disease, you will get on your knees and thank the animating spirit of the universe when you find a doctor who knows how to inquire and work with a community of practice. Ill-formed and unsolved problems like these are what Autor and colleagues (2003, 2013) mean when they talk about "nonroutine analytic and interactive tasks"—and these are the jobs that are coming to dominate the American workplace. So we ask, *What kind of learner do you want your teaching to produce?* We know our answer.

BRIDGING THE KNOWING-DOING DIVIDE IN SCHOOL

The real challenge of improving teaching and learning is not a lack of knowledge. *We know what works* to engage learners and to develop learner capacity. We know it from robust research into motivation and engagement, optimal experience, human development, educational psychology, cognitive science, development of expertise, social-emotional learning, and many other fields (see Chapter 1). The challenge is translating what we know into practice (Bryk et al., 2015; Newmann et al., 2016). The EMPOWER model is effective because it captures the central insights from all of these research areas and puts them into practice. EMPOWER helps us plan instruction, do the teaching, study and reflect on learning, and revise our instruction in a focused process of continuous improvement supported by robust research from across the learning sciences.

EMPOWER is also effective because it naturally integrates many diverse goals into our instruction. It allows us to put things together that actually go together, like having learners read about topics that they will write about. Learning how to navigate complex tasks through guided inquiry requires executive functioning and the use of mental models. EMPOWER is about learning through relationship, dialogue, sharing, and procedural feedback. Engaging in all of these activities requires us to develop social-emotional learning. We use EMPOWER to improve teaching because it bridges the knowing–doing divide. It provides a context and a focus for *all that we do* in schools, from professional development to lesson planning and instruction.

THE SHIFT FROM A PEDAGOGY OF POVERTY TO ONE OF EMPOWERMENT

The shifts necessary to move to teaching for transformation (i.e., for deep understanding, application, and transfer) (knowing–doing–thinking) are captured by the lifetime research of Martin Haberman (e.g., 2010); he argues that purely informational teaching, or *the pedagogy of poverty*, does not work to build engagement or expertise and is particularly harmful to children in poverty or otherwise marginalized. Haberman has shown that this approach keeps learners in poverty (intellectual as well as economic) because it does not engage them or develop usable expertise. This kind of traditional teaching is curriculum centered, focusing almost solely on the content or *what* is to be learned, with the teacher controlling everything, whereas transformational teaching is learning-centered, focuses on the *why and how* of learning (which cannot be practiced without the *what* of deep content understanding), and supports learners to gradually take independent ownership over their learning. Haberman demonstrates that the traditional approach to teaching is deeply embedded in American schooling and that it requires conscious and deliberate effort to change.

The recent "Opportunity Myth" study (TNTP, 2018) shows that American schools continue to fail at promoting deep learner engagement and capacity. The study found that the vast majority of work required of American students is unengaging and below grade level, involves passive reception versus active participation, and does not reflect expert practice. Even if learners do the work, they don't have access to future growth or opportunity.

Haberman contrasts the pedagogy of poverty with what he calls *good* or *effective* teaching. We call this the **pedagogy of EMPOWERment** because research shows that this kind of transformational teaching is highly effective, internally persuasive to learners, inductive/restorative to a community of practice, pegged to expert practice, and empowering for both teachers and learners. Learning-centered instruction, when planned using the EMPOWER model, is both culturally relevant and in service of social justice; all learners have more control over their learning, use their personal and cultural resources, and are apprenticed toward learning that can actually solve real-world problems.

SHIFTING FROM INFORMATION TO TRANSFORMATION

The contrasts between informational teaching, or the pedagogy of poverty, and learning-centered transformational teaching, or the pedagogy of EMPOWERment, mirror the differences cognitive science describes between information, which is inert, and knowledge, which is dynamic, generative, usable, revisable, and extensible (see Figure 2.1). This conception of knowledge is consistent with 3-D learning. The focus is not on knowing information but on *knowing and understanding* conceptually; *doing* by putting the concepts into use; and *thinking* through naming what was learned, justifying the learning like an expert, reflecting on the learning, rehearsing future uses, continually extending what has been learned, and achieving high-road transfer.

■ FIGURE 2.1: PEDAGOGY OF POVERTY VERSUS PEDAGOGY OF EMPOWERMENT

PEDAGOGY OF POVERTY *Traditional informational teaching and learning* *Curriculum and teacher centered (authoritatively imposed on learners)*	PEDAGOGY OF EMPOWERMENT *Authentic and transformational teaching and learning* *Learner and learning centered (internally persuasive to learners)*
Learners learn something because it is in the curriculum or on the test; the curriculum determines the content and timing of the learning. Knowing is focused on the *what*.	**Envision:** Learning is intentionally designed with clear purposes, goals, and payoffs. **Prime and Orient:** Learners understand the purpose and payoff of learning, both immediately and in the future. The curriculum is responsive to learner interest and capacities, and learners understand how and why experts use the knowledge. Knowing involves the *why*, *how*, and *what*, in that order. Knowing also considers the *when* and *where* of application. Human purposes for the knowledge and knowledge use are foregrounded. **Teaching and learning are 3-D: about knowing, doing, and thinking: reflecting/ metacognating/rehearsing for transfer.**
Learning is primarily focused on rote skills and memorization.	**Map:** Learning involves creating a new (to the learner) mental model or map for understanding and making use of a concept or process.
Learning is linear and sometimes fragmented.	**Map:** Learning is structured, systematic, and weblike—concepts and processes are interconnected, and there is a clear relationship and interplay among structure, details, meaning, and use. Learning activities are carefully sequenced to demonstrate and build these connections.

(Continued)

PEDAGOGY OF POVERTY *Traditional informational teaching and learning* *Curriculum and teacher centered (authoritatively imposed on learners)*	PEDAGOGY OF EMPOWERMENT *Authentic and transformational teaching and learning* *Learner and learning centered (internally persuasive to learners)*
Learning is often decontextualized (taught separately from use), although concepts or problems may have classroom applications; they rarely extend beyond this. (We call this "school-ish," as the learning only counts in school contexts.)	**Prime and Orient:** Learning is authentic and contextualized: learned and applied in a situation (or simulated context) in which the knowledge is required to respond to real-world questions and needs. (We call this "tool-ish," as the learning extends human abilities to perform tasks of value in the world outside of school. This tool-ishness meets the conditions of what researchers call *situated cognition*.)
Knowledge and practice are static: *presented* as established and unquestioned facts; learners have no role except to accept and repeat. Teachers provide directions, assign worksheets, ask factual questions, and give tests and grades.	**Walk through and Extend and explore:** Knowledge and practice are dynamic: *understood* to be context dependent, evolving, extensible, and revisable. Knowledge is socially constructed, negotiated, and justified based on disciplinary standards, meaning that competing viewpoints are honored and considered; learners play an integral role in knowledge creation, crafting explanations of phenomena and processes, solving real-world questions and problems, and creating deliverables to show their progress or productive struggle.
Learning is received from outside sources (like textbooks or curriculum makers) and often constrained (not extensible or generative of other ideas and strategies); it is authoritatively imposed and requires learner acceptance and compliance.	**Walk through and Extend and explore:** Learning is constructivist and unconstrained because it can be built on throughout a lifetime. Learning must involve personal effort, contributions, and connection making to be personalized and internalized by an individual; learning is internally persuasive because it is convincing to the learner and it is understood why and how the process or concept works.
Learning is *receptive* and isolated. Finding out new information is often the end of learning.	**Walk through and Extend and explore:** Learning is *active*, productive, and generative and occurs while doing the discipline and collaborating in diverse groups; learners receive proper guidance and learn how to collaborate effectively. Finding new information is often the beginning of learning.
Teaching is considered the donation of information to learners: Learners *listen* to a teacher or read a textbook.	**Walk through and Extend and explore:** Teaching helps learners transform their capacity to participate in learning and problem solving by gaining knowledge, constructing deep understandings, and developing strategies that promote independence and new ways of being—now and in the future. Learners *do* the discipline in order to master major concepts and expert strategies of learning (i.e., threshold knowledge) through meaningful use and deliberate practice.
Learners may *hear* about communities of practice.	**Walk through and Extend and explore:** Learners *participate* in a community of practice.
Work is typically discarded once completed and submitted for a grade (e.g., term papers, tests, homework).	**Extend and explore:** Learning and creations are archival and extensible over time, by the creator and others, and can be continually revised and built on by the self and others, now and in the future, as well as adapted and transferred to new situations.
Learning is recapitulated.	**Extend and explore:** Learning is transformed, transmediated, re-represented, and used in new and multimodal ways.
The end of learning is repeating information in some form and receiving back an assignment with a teacher grade. Learners rarely reflect on and justify their learning.	**Reflect:** Learners are presented with ongoing daily opportunities and support to reflect on learning; self-assess; and justify what, how, and why they know according to critical standards (i.e., learners develop conscious competence). Learners reflect on their lives and consider immediate and future applications of their learning, as well as how they have come to know, do, think, believe, and feel as they do.

Source: Adapted from Barab and Hay (2001), Moore (2016), and Wilhelm (2012c).

You are already affected in some way by this shift from informational to transformational teaching. It is represented by the Common Core State Standards and the Next Generation Science Standards (NGSS) or by its correlates in states like ours, where the free and independent republic of Idaho has adopted the Idaho Content Standards for ELA/Literacy, Mathematics, and Science. Take a look at the new standards. You will see that they are expressed through higher-order thinking verbs such as *analyze, interpret, create,* and *revise.* The standards are now about *doing and thinking* as well as *knowing*: about *how* to read, compose, problem-solve, do science and math, and so on, and about dynamic ways of making meaning, as opposed to banking established information in learners' minds.

Using the EMPOWER framework does not require you to teach new texts or content. EMPOWER allows you to *reframe any lesson, unit, text, or topic in any subject* so the teaching and learning are more motivating and powerful. The next-generation standards worldwide provide the *what* (the descriptions of the processes, disciplinary practices, and cross-cutting concepts to be learned), but they do not provide the *how* for implementation. In this way, the standards are empowering because they honor teacher professionalism and expertise to determine the best way to teach, which we believe is clearly guided inquiry through cognitive apprenticeship (ICA).

When it comes to the challenges of teaching and learning, many of the solutions are hidden in plain sight in powerful examples of real-world teaching and learning. Whether it's a child being taught how to ride a bike, a hobbyist being taught to fly fish, or an intern being taught how to perform surgery, guided inquiry and mental mapping occur all around us. The materials and the standards are not the real challenge. The challenge is apprenticing learners toward expertise by teaching the skills and practices they need to solve real-world problems. Figure 2.2 shows what the shifts in teaching practice look like in our elementary throughline unit (featured throughout this book) that explores how expertise is developed in different domains like reading and math.

■ FIGURE 2.2: A TRADITIONAL UNIT VERSUS AN EMPOWER UNIT

	TRADITIONAL, INFORMATIONAL, AUTHORITATIVE INSTRUCTION	EMPOWER: COGNITIVE APPRENTICESHIP IN THE CONTEXT OF INQUIRY
Topic	Reading and math strategies	**Envision, Map, Prime, and Orient:** Learning is framed with an essential question and a problem to solve. For example: *How do I become an expert (in reading, in math)? What do experts do?*
Goals	Name and use essential reading strategies, such as predicting, visualizing, questioning, inferring, clarifying, and summarizing, to comprehend a complex text. In math, determine the appropriate computational method and use appropriate strategies to solve a problem.	**Envision and Map:** Goal is usable expert understanding and transfers to new situations. This requires apprenticeship into what readers and mathematicians do, in terms of the kind of mental models they use and the questions they ask; by learning from experts and seeing themselves as readers and mathematicians, learners develop more competence and confidence. This leads to threshold knowledge about how to approach different kinds of texts, problems, and tasks, as well as understanding the practices and strategies to employ. Learners enjoy reading and math and recognize the power of their current knowledge and developing capacities in tackling current and future reading and math challenges.
Frontloading	None, or pretest to see what learners already know	**Prime and Orient:** Consider the essential questions, *How do I become an expert (in a specific field or domain of knowledge)? What do experts do?* Brainstorm what defines someone as an expert in any field. Then, consider what good readers and mathematicians do, and make anchor charts of these strategies and practices. Complete a mindset opinionaire to share opinions about mindsets. Participate in a four-corners discussion to explore viewpoints about mindsets.

(Continued)

	TRADITIONAL, INFORMATIONAL, AUTHORITATIVE INSTRUCTION	EMPOWER: COGNITIVE APPRENTICESHIP IN THE CONTEXT OF INQUIRY
Organization	Teacher led; everyone does the same thing. Learners experience guided instruction and read or solve problems as a class and then independently.	**Walk through and Extend and explore:** Teacher-guided explorations of various topics. Robust Tier 1 instruction for all. Learners experience the gradual release of responsibility in which the teacher models, mentors, and monitors learners to independence. Instruction is differentiated through Tier 2 and Tier 3 instruction so every learner gets the extra challenge or help they need. Small groups eventually divide up and take ownership of various aspects of the inquiry; distributed expertise is achieved and shared.
Instructional Activities	Reading and math programs/textbooks, lecture, worksheets	**Walk through and Extend and explore:** Document-based inquiries where learners read a variety of texts about mindset, record what they notice and wonder, and share their knowledge with one another to deepen their understanding of the topic of inquiry and essential question. Learners are positioned as public intellectuals, evolving experts, and members of a community of practice. Jigsaw small-group inquiry discussions based on readings or direct experiences in which learners teach one another. Collection and analysis of data, creation of visual representations, and presentation of findings based on learners' passions. Drama/action strategies putting learners in the position of experts/famous people or putting learners in role as particular concepts or strategies to create a résumé and do a job talk about how useful they (the concept or strategy) would be to a certain group or for a certain task.
Questions	Factually oriented; primarily asked by the teacher	**Walk through and Extend and explore:** Questions are interpretive, synthetic, and applicative. Teachers ask questions of all types to model question generation and types for learners. Learners learn to generate questions of different types on their own as well as how to find the data to answer them.
Discussion Format	Teacher initiates, learners respond, teacher evaluates (I-R-E)	**Walk through and Extend and explore:** Learners collaborate in various groupings (small groups, think–pair–shares, and Socratic seminars) to discuss their learning, the inquiry question, and other questions of interest to the group. Discussions evolve to be mostly student run.
Reading Materials	Reading and math program textbooks and materials	**Prime, Orient, Walk through, and Extend and explore:** Reading and math program textbooks and materials may serve as a resource, but the teacher uses real-world problems and also pulls in a plethora of texts (children's books, excerpts, poetry, videos, interviews, complex math tasks/problems related to the real world, etc.). Learners conduct research and use resources of their choice to support their writing and presentation.
Assessment, Proof of Learning	Quizzes and tests, primarily on factual information (focused on reading comprehension and solving math problems)	**Extend and explore and Reflect:** Daily deliverables, formative assessments, observational notes, and procedural feedback. Living-museum exhibits and in-role speeches sharing findings about the expert they chose to research. Ongoing reflection focused on the essential question, learning growth, and deliverables. Learners reflect on the expert moves they are making independently in reading and math.

As we've stated, EMPOWER is a highly functional tool for planning and implementing inquiry-oriented units and lessons. Beyond this, however, EMPOWER inspires us because it helps us meet other related and deeply held commitments. EMPOWER captures six areas of research that mirror our commitments to addressing the needs of *all* learners and that provide a foundation for making the shifts from informational to transformational teaching (see Figure 2.3).

■ FIGURE 2.3: LEARNER NEEDS CAPTURED BY THE EMPOWER MODEL

1. ***Engagement:*** EMPOWER motivates learners by meeting the conditions of flow experience.

2. ***Personal connection and cultural relevance:*** EMPOWER makes a personal connection and connects to cultural relevance by starting with priming and orienting learner needs, concerns, lived experience, and cultural funds of knowledge.

3. ***Access to all, working for equity and social justice:*** EMPOWER creates access by differentiating so that all learners get the assistance they need to grow *at their point of need*.

4. ***A community of caring:*** EMPOWER creates community by meeting the social contract to care; by developing social-emotional learning through relational learning; and by fostering social connection and support to help manage relationships, emotions, and complex tasks (Smith & Wilhelm, 2002, 2006).

5. ***The knowing–doing divide:*** EMPOWER bridges this divide by teaching in a context of use and creating classroom communities of practice.

6. ***Growth mindset:*** EMPOWER promotes a growth mindset by supporting the development of learner identity as agents who can always learn how to get new things done.

Most importantly, EMPOWER works for *all* learners. By inducting learners into communities of caring and practice, making expertise visible and available, and providing appropriate and differentiated support, we assist all learners to explore and make progress toward this expertise, no matter their backgrounds and current capacities.

ACCESS AND DIFFERENTIATION

One of the many advantages of guided inquiry through EMPOWER is its flexibility. Teachers can differentiate elements of instruction at the point of need and use peers and groups to help teach, while all learners engage in a rigorous common classroom inquiry project. In fact, EMPOWER incorporates the features of Universal Design for Learning (UDL) through its basic processes and how these accommodate differentiation (see Figure 2.4). Differentiation is necessary to inductive and restorative practice because it provides access to all. It is a way to personalize and leverage learning for the benefit of every learner. EMPOWER and ICA also provide ways for learners to be restored to the community of caring and practice by teaching them to productively navigate struggle—whether behavioral, relational, or in terms of academic learning.

- *Different materials (levels of task or text complexity)*—learners read different materials written at different levels or read the same materials written at different levels.

- *Different time/pacing*—learning is scaffolded or extended based on learner needs to promote deep understanding; some learners receive more assistance or additional time on strategies.

- *Different methods and modalities*—various means of representation, expression, and engagement are used to support the unique learners and learning needs in the classroom; learners should be provided opportunities to use their own strengths but also be challenged to learn in ways that develop new strengths.

- *Different groupings*—learners engage in partnerships, triads, small groups, and whole group at different times and for different purposes (e.g., using centers, literature circles, inquiry teams, etc.).

- *Different levels of independence in task navigation*—different levels of teacher or peer assistance are utilized (e.g., through thinking partnerships, peer conferencing, and teacher conferencing and support).

- *Different levels of assistance*—scaffolds and differentiation are used to support learners in moving from their current level of understanding to a higher level of understanding and independence (e.g., gradual release of responsibility). (*Note:* Scaffolds should be removed as learners increase their level of independence.)

- *Different ways of demonstrating competence*—different kinds of assessment opportunities are provided throughout the unit (e.g., self-assessments, formative assessments, portfolios, and conferences); choice is provided in how learners share their learning (e.g., options for culminating project format).

- *Different levels of accomplishment criteria*—rubrics or progressions are used to show learners' varying levels of achievement and also to demonstrate growth toward goals.

POWERFUL PLANNING:
EMBRACING THE TRANSFORMATIVE POSSIBILITIES

These may seem like a lot of shifts. In our work, we promote the mantra "Eat your elephant one bite at a time." In other words, you can start with what feels accessible and keep making changes bit by bit. Making one shift naturally leads to other, related changes.

Informational teaching is like being a cook who warms up pre-prepared food. Transformational teaching is like being a chef who can create a meal specific to the guests and the occasion based on the available materials. A chef has conscious competence that can be creatively deployed to invent what is needed to meet the needs of the moment. When we embrace transformational teaching, we meet the conditions of flow (our basic motivational needs), the social contract to care and need for social connection (our basic human need to be recognized and belong), the conditions of social-emotional learning and inductive/restorative

practice, and the process of becoming more expert with complex tasks (our need to be assisted into expertise). All of those shifts are closely related, and focusing on one will make it easier to leverage the others. Transformational teaching and learning are achieved through guided inquiry by using the mental map of EMPOWER.

Chapters 1 and 2 focused on the theories and research underpinning the EMPOWER approach because when we understand the *why* behind our work, it makes our *how* and our *what* much clearer and more powerful. Only by understanding and articulating our theoretical orientation—our beliefs and philosophies about teaching and learning—can we consciously implement and reflect on a theory of action—our practices—to move forward. Next, we turn our attention to these practices of planning and teaching.

Chapter 3

INTRODUCING THE EMPOWER CANVAS

> **ESSENTIAL QUESTION**
> How do we empower our units and lessons for
> transformational teaching and learning?

Architects capture their art in blueprints, painters in sketches, composers in scores. On what "canvas" can teachers capture and express *their* art?

Usually, an educator's "canvas" is whatever unit or lesson plan template their district, school, or curriculum provides. This template, in theory, should line up with both the criteria for **flow** and the **mental models of teaching and learning** (see Chapters 1 and 2) that promote deep engagement and learning. Unfortunately, the traditional unit or lesson plan seldom meets these standards.

Various educational approaches, from project-based learning to balanced literacy to the workshop model, can all be supercharged by adding EMPOWER elements. However, collegial conversations around curriculum are hard to achieve when everyone has a different understanding of and language for their instructional designs. Since all of these pedagogies share a common goal—empowering learners to become expert thinkers and doers—then it follows that they should all contain the elements of EMPOWER, which represents a research-based "filter" for *all* teaching and learning (see introduction, Figure I.1).

For the sake of consistency, clarity, and ease across grade levels, subjects, and districts, we advocate that teachers use an **EMPOWER canvas**, a one-page form, to formally capture all the necessary elements of an effective teaching and learning design. This way everyone is on the same page, both literally and figuratively.

INTRODUCING THE EMPOWER CANVAS

The EMPOWER canvas is meant to serve as a convenient tool to reinforce the seven *must-make moves* that expert educators enact in designing effective and transformational instruction. The framework naturally organizes into two categories: behind-the-scenes, big-picture planning and learner-facing instructional implementation, as demonstrated in Figure 3.1. Digging one level deeper, Figure 3.2 breaks down what

PLC Connection

Use the EMPOWER canvas (see Figure 3.1) as a tool for designing quality professional development (PD). Just as with classroom instruction, when planning PD there is behind-the-scenes planning as well as learner-facing instructional planning. EMPOWER will help you to begin with the end in mind, considering the goals of the PD and the tools, questions, strategies, and mental models that will support your adult learners to succeed, as well as in planning a powerful sequence of learning events. As we explore in this chapter, the EMPOWER canvas can be used at the unit and lesson levels and, thus, works for long-term PD planning as well as planning individual PD experiences.

EMPOWER your TEACHING

ENVISION the destination
List 1–3 goals for learners to master.
Define the evidence and measures of success for each goal.
(If designing a unit, create a culminating task or portfolio piece.)

MAP the path to mastery
Do the culminating task and identify the mental models and skills required for the task.
Build quality assurance tools such as performance checklists and rubrics.
List key Tier 2 and Tier 3 vocabulary.

big-picture planning lays
the foundation for . . .

PRIME learners
Frontload vocabulary.
Activate prior knowledge.

ORIENT the learning
Help learners see the purpose and payoff of the future learning.

WALK THROUGH new strategies
Model, demonstrate, mentor.

EXTEND expertise
Deliberate practice.

EXPLORE new territory
Demonstrate mastery.

REFLECT on the journey
Summarize content and process.
Self-assess and set next steps.

a sequence of
learning events

we have briefly explained about each phase of the framework in previous chapters. (You'll find a downloadable EMPOWER canvas template on the companion website, resources.corwin.com/EMPOWER-elementary.)

■ FIGURE 3.2: PHASES OF THE EMPOWER FRAMEWORK

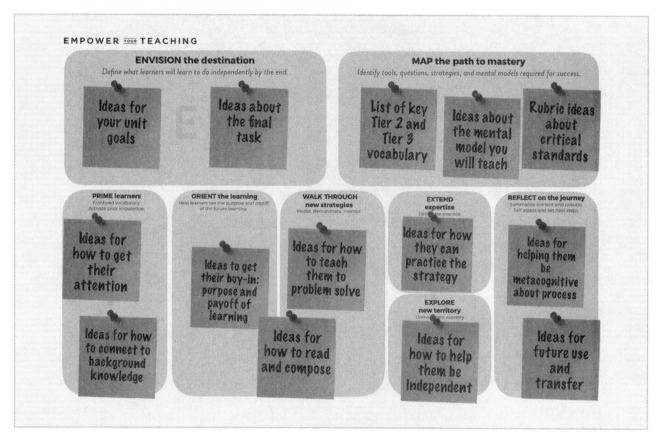

Educators often have personal approaches to planning and benefit from using different entry points that make sense to them. Of course, it's still important that we begin with the end in mind, because knowing our destination allows us to choose the best path for getting there. The EMPOWER tool is called a *canvas* instead of a template to emphasize its flexibility. Educators begin with the end in mind by *envisioning* and *mapping*, although they often bounce between these two "big-picture" planning pursuits that complement each other. As educators proceed with their planning, they consider lessons or events early in the unit to *prime* their learners and *orient* student thinking to the purposes, payoffs, and big ideas. For the remaining lessons in the unit, educators bounce back and forth between *walk-throughs* of new strategies and *extension* and *exploration* opportunities (real-world transfer and performance tasks) for learners. Ongoing *reflections* (after a lesson or series of lessons, for example) are strategically interwoven throughout the lesson for the teacher and learners to monitor their growth over time (see Figure 3.3). The following chapters provide many models of the EMPOWER canvas to help you think through the phases of EMPOWER as you begin to create your own.

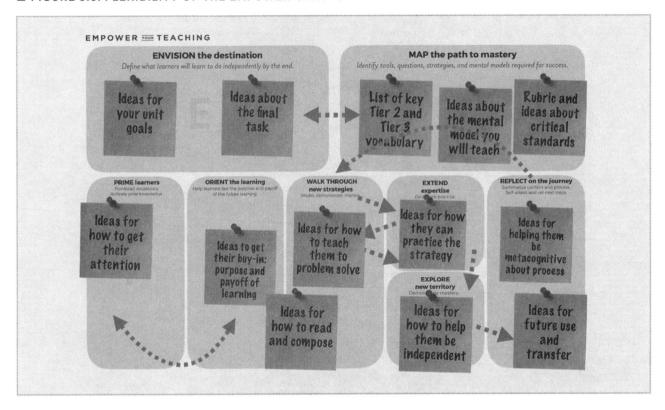

Educators who wish to build a new canvas work through each stage of the framework, populating it with ideas that can be captured via sticky notes or by writing on a physical or digital canvas.

UNDERSTANDING OUR THROUGHLINE UNIT

Throughout this book, we will refer to our *throughline unit*, organized to address an essential question, such as, *How do I become an expert?* Or, *What does it take to become an expert?* The unit focuses on apprenticing learners to greater expertise by helping them name and employ the skills and processes of different kinds of experts in the real world. The unit promotes the development of a growth mindset as learners move toward understanding how people become experts and move toward their own greater expertise, making and celebrating mistakes along the way. The lessons within the unit help learners develop the skills of expert readers such as visualization, questioning, and inferring, to name a few, and in math, we'll explore the Mathematical Practice Standards that highlight the processes, proficiencies, and dispositions of mathematicians outlined in the Common Core State Standards. It's a unit that is beneficial and can be adapted to any elementary grade as learners develop increasing knowledge and efficiency in using these skills in their everyday lives, both in and beyond school. Figure 3.4 shows our EMPOWER canvas for this unit.

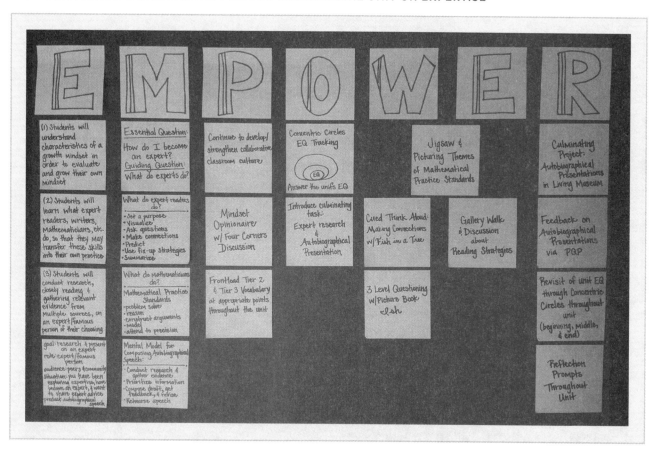

Each sticky note on the canvas serves as a placeholder and represents what will become a more evolved instructional activity or lesson, most of which we will explore throughout this book. For example, the "mindset opinionaire with four-corners discussion" sticky note is shown in expanded form in Chapter 8 on frontloading.

EMPOWER AT THE UNIT LEVEL

Using our throughline unit on expertise as an example, we first ENVISION the most significant **outcomes** for learners:

ENVISION THE DESTINATION

Define what learners will learn to do independently by the end.

- Learners will understand characteristics of a growth mindset in order to monitor and grow their own mindsets.

(Continued)

> - Learners will learn what expert readers, writers, mathematicians, and others know and do and how they think about this knowing and doing so that they may transfer and extend these skills independently to their own reading, writing, and mathematical thinking.
>
> - Learners will conduct research on an expert of their choosing, closely read and gather relevant evidence from multiple sources, and share learning about traits of experts and development of expertise.

As part of this stage, we create an authentic culminating task that positions learners in a **real-world role** and has them compose or design knowledge artifacts or services that address **real-world problems** for a **real-world audience**. In this case, in addition to rehearsing the skills and practices of readers, writers, and mathematicians throughout the unit, learners will transfer their knowledge and expertise about reading strategies as they conduct biographical research on an expert and then write and present about this person. Learners will gain information about real-world careers, skill sets, processes, mental models, and mindsets that lead to increased mastery, supporting continued future development.

Next, we *map* out the path to these outcomes in terms of the **conceptual understandings**, **strategies**, and **mental models** required to fulfill them.

MAP THE PATH TO MASTERY

Identify tools, questions, strategies, and mental models for success.

In the case of our unit, learners will become highly skilled at the following:

- Noticing and articulating what expert readers do (setting a purpose, forming predictions, visualizing, asking questions, making connections, inferencing, and using reading fix-up strategies) and transferring these skills to become more expert readers themselves.

- Noticing and articulating what expert mathematicians do (how they frame and approach problem solving, choose problem-solving strategies, use reasoning, construct arguments, create and use models, attend to precision, etc.) and emulating and practicing these skills to become more expert mathematical problem solvers.

- Understanding and using the process of conducting research and gathering evidence from sources, prioritizing this information, interpreting and reasoning from evidence, and composing and presenting an informational speech or a multimedia composition.

To frame the inquiry, we craft an essential question. (*Note:* We always begin with a tentative essential question. Depending on our learners' response to the *priming* and *orienting* activities, we may revise it with them in the early stages of the unit.) In our unit on expertise, we chose the essential question, *How do I become an expert?* because it gets at the heart of the unit's matter, is open ended, and will hopefully engage our learners in inquiry about experts, expert skill sets, and how they too can develop expertise.

With the behind-the-scenes planning complete, we turn our attention to how we will *prime* learners, or get their attention, activate prior knowledge and interests, and engage them through novelty and relevance triggers.

PRIME LEARNERS

Frontload vocabulary. Activate prior knowledge.

- To trigger **relevance**, we open the unit with our essential question, *How do I become an expert?*, ask learners to define the term *expert*, and then have learners consider what makes someone an expert at something. One way to do this is by having learners consider something they are an expert at and how they became an expert in that area. This can be a whole-class discussion, with common themes recorded on an anchor chart.

- To trigger **novelty**, we frontload conceptual Tier 2 and Tier 3 vocabulary and the strategy of reasoning from evidence that will support students' learning throughout the unit and, more importantly, extend beyond the classroom into their own vocabularies. For example, in our throughline unit, we'll help learners connect to Tier 2 vocabulary, such as *expert*, *expertise*, and *research*, and Tier 3 vocabulary, such as *inferencing, reasoning, fixed mindset*, and *growth mindset*, using a Frayer model or similar vocabulary activation activity.

- To trigger **prior knowledge and interests and build on them**, we administer a mindset opinionaire to probe learners' feelings and attitudes about the topic. We follow this up with a four-corners discussion, which gives us formative assessment data about what our learners already know and believe and are interested in as they share and argue their opinions. This type of discussion creates community in the room as learners exchange opinions and ideas to develop the class's collective knowledge.

Next, we *orient* learners toward the big-picture objectives, purposes, and payoffs: examining the skills and mindsets of experts; emulating them as they practice reading, writing, and solving math problems; and applying them to their own lives in and beyond the classroom. In this phase, we help learners comprehend what these outcomes mean and begin moving them forward by

- preassessing learners—having them answer the essential question (a task they'll repeat at several points throughout the unit, reflecting on new understandings and how their understandings have evolved over time);
- sharing learning goals; and
- using questioning tools to help learners develop and pursue their own related inquiries.

(Continued)

(Continued)

In addition, this is the time to *orient* learners to the culminating task to create engagement, buy-in, and excitement for the learning ahead. By introducing the culminating task early in the unit, learners develop a greater understanding of the payoffs of their learning as they see how they can apply it in a meaningful and authentic way.

ORIENT THE LEARNING

Help learners see the purpose and payoff of the future learning.

- Introduce the learning goals for the unit in student-friendly language, so learners understand what they will be learning. Have learners create "I will be able to . . . so I will be able to . . . and I will know I am able to when . . ." statements.

- Introduce the culminating task on biographical research and a public presentation of it, and help learners understand the purpose and payoff of completing this task. Provide a map or timeline of the steps of the process so learners understand the expectations, how they will organize their time to accomplish the task, and how the unit will help prepare them for success.

- Share the task description, carefully looking at its demands. Look at models.

- Introduce or collaboratively create success criteria, so you and your learners can articulate critical standards and assess progress toward learning goals.

- Examine the rubric for the culminating task and consider how this task will be assessed.

- Answer any questions learners have at this time about the culminating task.

The next components of the unit's instructional sequence focus on *walk-through*, *extension*, and *exploration* as learners increase their independence through modeling, mentoring, and monitoring (also known as model/mentor/monitor or for/with/by, or the gradual release of responsibility).

WALK THROUGH NEW STRATEGIES

Model/demonstrate, mentor, monitor.

- Explore and practice reading strategies (in particular, reading on, between, and beyond the lines; asking questions; clarifying; summarizing, etc.).

- Explore and employ the practices of mathematicians (the Mathematical Practice Standards) in the context of real-world problem solving.

EXTEND EXPERTISE

Practice deliberately.

- Apply reading stances and strategies as learners read various texts related to expertise (e.g., *Fish in a Tree* by Lynda Mullaly Hunt [2017]) and conduct research for the culminating task.

- Apply the math practices as learners solve increasingly complex problems and tasks.

EXPLORE NEW TERRITORY

Demonstrate mastery.

- Transfer knowledge and expertise about reading strategies as learners conduct biographical research on an expert and write and present about this person.

- Apply math practices in a real-world math performance task.

Reflection is the last box on the canvas, but let's be clear that informal and formal reflection should be ongoing in the way of daily, weekly, midpoint, and end-of-unit prompts and introspection. In particular, we frequently ask learners to refer to the essential question at specific points throughout the unit to build on their understanding and reflect on how their learning has grown or changed. We also ask learners to engage in self- and/or peer reflections on their culminating projects via assessment guidelines or a rubric. These formal and intentionally planned opportunities for reflection are critical for helping learners develop a deeper understanding of the processes, purposes, and payoffs of reflection. We continuously develop a culture and practice of reflection by asking learners to generalize what they have learned, to think about ways they could transfer knowledge or skills into new contexts, and to self-assess their level of effort and understanding. Unlike a traditional "exit ticket" that asks learners to perform a repetition of the target strategy or to demonstrate mastery via a quiz, ongoing daily reflection opportunities are designed to promote metacognition (thinking about their thinking), independence with the targeted concepts and strategies (knowing and doing), and a desire to learn and grow into their best possible selves.

(Continued)

(Continued)

REFLECT ON THE JOURNEY

Summarize content and process. Self-assess and set next steps.

- Reflect on the essential question *How do I become an expert?* multiple times throughout the unit (e.g., beginning, middle, and end), describing new insights and changes in understanding related to the question.

- Offer daily reflection prompts throughout the unit (for example, a confidence scale to show how comfortable learners feel using specific reading or math strategies).

- Have learners complete self- and peer assessments using the culminating project rubric prior to teacher assessment using this same rubric.

EMPOWERING YOUR CURRICULUM AT EVERY LEVEL

While most designs for learning allow you to design at only one level—either the lesson or the unit—EMPOWER works at every level of the instructional-design process. Through EMPOWER, global-level unit plans inform instructional sequencing and scaffolding within the unit, which informs micro-level lesson and activity planning. Each upcoming chapter will provide you with ideas to move from general concepts to concrete operations and from initial ideas to actualized lessons. As you progress through this book, you can internalize your big-picture thinking around the unit-level design (what's captured on sticky notes) before circling back to explore each strategy (the lesson-level canvases).

EMPOWER AT THE LESSON LEVEL

After completing the EMPOWER canvas at the macro-level (the unit), it's now time to turn our attention to micro-level planning (activities and lessons). The EMPOWER framework is set up to help you sequence the instructional activities throughout your unit. You will begin with lessons that *prime* and *orient* learners to the topic and significance of inquiry and then proceed to lessons that model, mentor, and monitor them toward increased independence and transfer of the new knowledge and strategies learned. Reflection opportunities will be included along the way, as components of daily lessons, as well as with more deliberate attention at certain points and at the end of the unit.

 A framework for planning at the lesson level is available for download at **resources.corwin.com/EMPOWER-elementary**.

To begin lesson planning, you will expand each of the components (sticky notes) of your unit canvas into one or more carefully crafted lessons. To see how EMPOWER works at the lesson level, let's look at one of the first lessons of our unit plan on expertise: the introduction and tracking of the essential question via concentric circles. For a quick sketch of our brainstorming, see Figure 3.5.

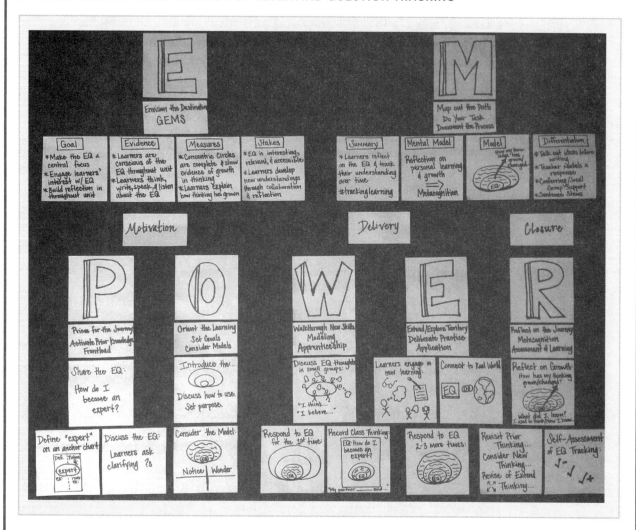

As with EMPOWER at the unit level, we begin by *envisioning* the destination and then *mapping* the path for this specific lesson plan. Again, this is the behind-the-scenes planning of consciously competent teachers. When we can name *what* we are doing, *how* we are doing it, and, most importantly, *why* we are doing it, we demonstrate our 3-D teaching (knowing, doing, and thinking capacity) and increase our competence and confidence as teachers. We also increase the likelihood of learner engagement, understanding, and success. Following this behind-the-scenes planning, we *power* our teaching by *priming* and *orienting* learners to the learning goals and plan for the lesson; *walking through*, *extending*, and *exploring*; and then ultimately *reflecting* on the learning achieved. You can see how this planning looks in our canvases of specific lessons throughout the book. See pages 124–126 for our canvas on essential-questions tracking.

GETTING TO YOUR FIRST DRAFT: A FEW TIPS

Like a painter who consciously considers every brush stroke of a new painting, educators engaged in the nitty-gritty work of curriculum design can find it takes time to truly nail down their learning plans. But in an environment where we often need our curricular solutions done yesterday, our processes must be ultraefficient. Therefore, we recommend the following tips:

1. **Sketch a canvas in one sitting.** Though a unit plan can take considerable time and iterations (often over many years of teaching it) to feel complete, your initial canvas should be sketched quickly—potentially in an hour or less. Yes, you read that right. *Set a timer, and get your first draft down in the space of one prep period.* (See one example in Figure 3.4.) You are going to come back to the document anyway, and as the saying goes, "Something is better than nothing." Having most of the canvas boxes completed with 50 percent detail beats one complete, thoroughly detailed box any day. You also don't have to work alone: If you have a thinking partner at school, planning your units together is very productive and can be lots of fun. As Vygotsky would say, we are always smarter together than we are alone.

2. **It's okay to leave sections blank . . .** Rather than trying to research or debate the "right" answers, put something down quickly, or leave it blank and come back to it later. Some elements, like your unit's mental models, take time to figure out. The canvas is meant to be an organic document that evolves over time. It's okay to say "I don't know" right now.

3. **. . . but not the first two sections.** Remember: If you're adopting a learning-centered transformational approach, your learning designs will be focused less on what you will teach and more on what learners will learn to do in response to instruction—in order to become more expert and independent. We have found that the more expert a teacher, the more she focuses on learners and what they do in response to teaching versus what she does as a teacher. If you skip *envisioning* and *mapping*, you have no chance of consciously *power*-ing the rest of your unit. We advocate flexibility, but starting with E and M is a must.

POWERFUL PLANNING: WE CANNOT DEFY GRAVITY

We are all subject to the laws of gravity, whether we "believe" in gravity or not. In the same way, we are all subject to the principles of EMPOWER as it draws from research on human development, cognition, motivation, optimal experience, development of expertise, and other learning sciences to explain how *all* people learn to become more expert.

Imagine a teacher who does not *envision* his learning outcomes in sufficient enough detail and the resulting aimlessness his learners are likely to feel (see Figure 3.6). After all, if the educator does not know the direction of the unit, how can learners? Similarly, if an educator fails to *map* out the unit into digestible pieces, learners may feel overwhelmed by the depth or breadth of the content; if that same educator chooses not to *prime* or *orient* learners at the beginning of the unit, those learners may feel too uninterested or unmotivated to pursue the energy-intensive act of learning because they may not understand what resources and connections they already possess to deal with the problem at hand, nor understand the purpose and payoff of addressing it. And so on.

■ FIGURE 3.6: EFFECTS OF MISSED STEPS IN EMPOWER

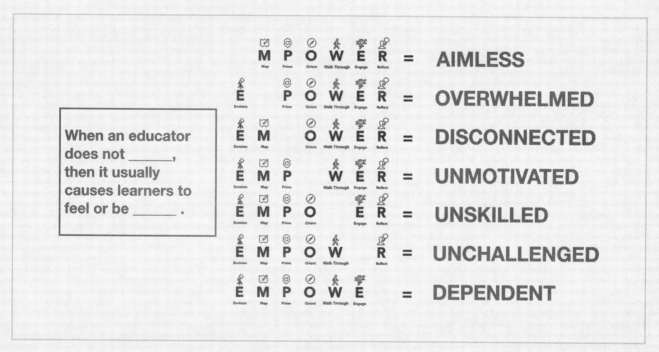

When you *envision*, your teaching will be highly focused and coherent. When you *map* out the steps, you and your students can learn complex strategies together in ways that promote personally and culturally relevant connections, energetic motivation, the development of expert strategies for navigating challenges, and, finally, independence and the capacity to continue improving on your own. In the remaining chapters, we will explain exactly how to enact pedagogical moves aligned to each of these principles, ensuring a successful learning journey for each of your learners.

In psychology, the phrase "name it to tame it" means just that; having the words to express a complex emotion, a disconcerting event, or challenging idea helps you gain a measure of control over it. We hope that having EMPOWER gives you a measure of control over the learning you facilitate and a shared language to discuss it with colleagues.

We cannot defy gravity any more than we can defy the "laws" embodied in a principled paradigm like EMPOWER. In fact, once we started using EMPOWER, we began to notice missed opportunities in even our most successful lessons and units, along with steps we were tempted to skip in the instructional-design process that would have come back to haunt us later.

With the *must-make moves* embedded in our toolkit, we are focused on including essential elements of sound pedagogy in every teaching and learning situation. Next, we will dive deeper into the core design strategies that drive planning, *envisioning* and *mapping*, and determine how to move from initial teaching ideas to clarity and actualization as we create and implement our lessons.

PART 2: ENVISIONING AND MAPPING

ENVISION MAP PRIME ORIENT WALK THROUGH EXTEND/EXPLORE REFLECT

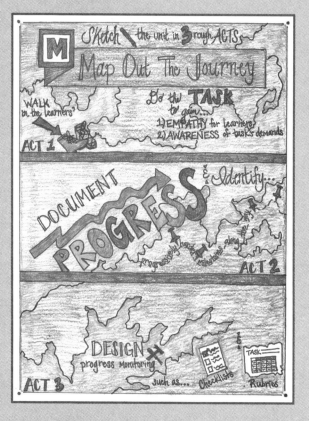

Chapter 4

ENVISIONING THE DESTINATION THROUGH PRINCIPLED PLANNING PROTOCOLS

> **ESSENTIAL QUESTION**
> How does envisioning the destination lead
> to a successful journey?

All teachers who have ever planned day to day know the harrowing feeling of "building the plane while flying it." While we will always love responding to and leading our learners in real time, intentionally choosing future milestones is the first discipline of enacting stellar instruction. Just as the pilot decides where to go before going there and safety checks that his or her plane is fully operational, we, too, will decide on a destination for our students' learning with our feet firmly on the ground and will make sure all the necessary preparations and pieces are in place, so we can plan for the trip accordingly.

In this way, teaching becomes more about thinking like a designer of learning activities rather than like a presenter of information. This is one of the hardest shifts for an educator to make. With limited time, you might want to focus on tomorrow's actual lessons or content rather than on big-picture planning that seems far off. You must fight this urge!

Let's focus on some planning protocols that will help you set meaningful learning goals that you can clearly communicate to your students, colleagues, parents, and other stakeholders.

A MANTRA FOR THIS (AND EVERY) CHAPTER

When you do the work, it works. Trust the process. Once you've done these exercises over and over, this patterned way of thinking will become your new normal. One day, with many repetitions "under your belt," you will be able to complete an EMPOWER sketch in half the time it takes you today and with twice the effectiveness. Then, you will be an instructional powerhouse: a teacher with conscious competence, a mental map for how to teach learners toward real-world expertise, and an expansive toolbox informed by the soundest of principles. Now, let's get started with big-picture planning.

HOW ENVISIONING MOVES HELP
YOU NAVIGATE THE START OF A UNIT

Most educators struggle with goal setting for one of two reasons.

1. **The goals are too broad and not concrete enough.**

2. **The goals are too narrow and not transferable enough.**

The following planning exercises help you walk this tightrope, getting you a "just-right" learning target for any kind of context. No matter how your school or district requests your learning targets, these protocols will help you answer key questions all stakeholders want to know at the outset of any unit:

1. **Where are we going?**

2. **How will we know when we get there?**

3. **How will we know the journey has been a success?**

Once we address those questions ourselves, we then transform the answers into an engaging, accessible final task for learners.

ENVISIONING MOVE 1: GEMS

You've probably seen goals written in this way on a number of lesson plans and whiteboards:

- OKR: Objectives and key results

- SWBAT: Students will be able to

- WALT: We are learning to

- I can . . .

- Learning targets/objectives

- _____ [your school or district example here]

With all the options, it can be hard to sort through the nuances in the vocabulary and choose the appropriate way to express what we're after. To alleviate the confusion, we created . . . another acronym. (Sorry!) Fortunately, it will be the last one you need when it comes to productive goal setting.

CRYSTALLIZE YOUR LEARNING OUTCOMES INTO GEMS

In our work with teachers, we have found successful planning starts with the following:

- **Goal:** Defining some significant new way of thinking or doing that learners cannot do *yet* but will learn to do independently and will use throughout their lives (threshold knowledge); this goal is often a complex process.

- **Evidence:** Capturing the abstract goal in a concrete task (or tasks) that "proves" learners actually achieved the goal; this must be observable and concrete.

- **Measures of success:** Describing the sought-after qualities and characteristics that "strong work" exhibits and then using those traits to measure progress toward mastery.

- **Stakes:** Why this unit and its goals matter *right now*, and why learners should buy in, use it in the future, and so forth.

The primary measure of success in constructing GEMS (Figure 4.1) is *alignment*. In the best examples, GEMS captures the relationship between something abstract (a goal, such as researching a topic); evidence of that abstract goal or process (e.g., a portfolio, report, podcast, performance, or presentation); and what *quality* means when practitioners in this discipline evaluate products in this genre (e.g., qualities such as *informative*, *evidence-based*, *clear*, and *organized* might describe a strong informational text).

■ **FIGURE 4.1: IDEAS FOR YOUR UNIT GOALS: GEMS**

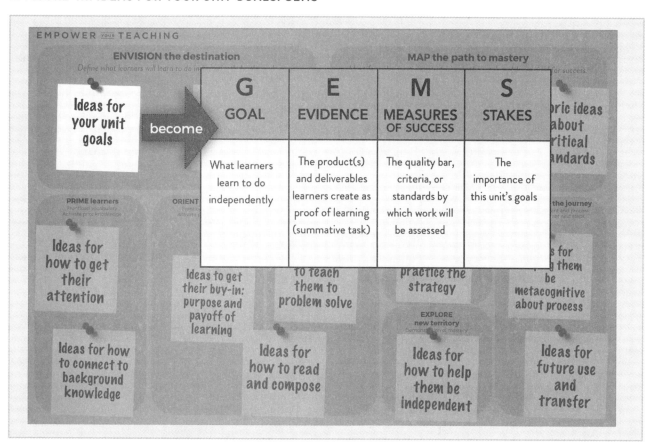

(Continued)

(Continued)

The scaffolded organizer in Figure 4.2, plus your relevant national or local standards and district expectations, should spark your thinking about the first three elements.

■ FIGURE 4.2: GEMS SCAFFOLDED ORGANIZER

G GOAL	E EVIDENCE	M MEASURES OF SUCCESS	S STAKES
❏ Explain/prove/define/ determine causes and effects/sequence ❏ Interpret/evaluate/ describe/rate/judge ❏ Apply/create/solve ❏ Analyze/compare ❏ Empathize/role-play ❏ Self-assess/reflect	❏ **Oral:** conversation, podcast, interview, teaching a lesson, rap song ❏ **Written:** letter, blog, essay, newscast, proposal, story, article, opinion paper, poem ❏ **Visual:** diagram, comic, Thinking Map®, video, model, storyboard, design, advertisement ❏ **Service:** action to assist individuals, groups, or communities	*Create a scale or checklist for the critical standards:* ❏ **For opinions:** persuasive, logical, evidence-based, coherent ❏ **For narratives:** engaging, detail rich, clear, polished ❏ **For informational:** informative, thorough, accurate, balanced ❏ **General criteria:** level of independence, clarity, accuracy, frequency, planning, originality, etc.	❏ Show how the skill is used in the real world ❏ Explore personal uses for the skill/content ❏ Find an audience to share the learning with ❏ Create personal stakes ("carrots") for sticking to the task ❏ Contribute to solving a real-world social problem and be of help to others ❏ Provide a service to the class, school, or larger community

At your average elementary school science fair, you'll find at least one baking soda and vinegar volcano, if not more. These volcanos were prohibited from science fairs at a school Chris worked in because students did not develop any scientific skills or concepts when they built and displayed them. Students knew the outcome ahead of time, which is why they enjoyed them so much, and more often than not the "explosion," and the model that it oozed from, did not mimic real-life volcanic activity.

Let's re-examine the baking-soda-and-vinegar volcano through the GEMS lens to consider how we might make the learning more rigorous and authentic: *What will learners learn to do independently?* (Goal) *What products will "prove" they actually learned what you sought to teach?* (Evidence) *By what standards or qualities will you and your learners collectively assess the products of their learning labor?* (Measures of success) *What is important about this goal?* (Stakes)

The standards (e.g., the Common Core or the Next Generation Science Standards or the versions of these used in your state) can help you to identify goals, evidence, measures, and stakes.

Within a few minutes of playing with a scaffolded GEMS organizer, we managed to capture the science project outcomes clearly and succinctly (see Figure 4.3).

G GOAL	E EVIDENCE	M MEASURES OF SUCCESS	S STAKES
Make sense of the importance of variables in scientific investigations. Test a variety of vinegar brands to identify which one produces the best "explosion" for a volcano.	Lab report: Explain why a particular vinegar might work best by testing for acidity, connecting ingredients to explosive properties, etc. Explain how a vinegar-based explosion is similar to and different from a volcanic one.	❏ Learners closely read and follow directions for a baking soda/vinegar volcano. ❏ Lab report includes an inquiry question and hypothesis, has only one variable, records findings from multiple trials, analyzes results, and reaches a conclusion.	Science is the pursuit of understanding the world and how it works. Learners understand that "good" science controls some factors and tests a limited number of variables. Recording accurate results throughout the process is essential to a successful lab.
Present findings from science experiment	Trifold and model	❏ Informative: *Includes key pieces of information from the lab report. The audience's understanding of explosions, particularly in terms of chemical and physical causes and effects, is enhanced.* ❏ Engaging: *Pictures or illustrations support data.* ❏ Organized: *Information is presented in a logical way.* ❏ Clear and appropriate to audience: *Information can be easily read and understood by peers and science fair attendees.*	Experiments are designed to answer genuine questions or to test the results of another scientist. Writers make decisions based on audience and context. Science and writing are intended for authentic audiences, beyond the classroom teacher. Reading and writing are essential in all disciplines and support the pursuit of goals.

Notice the following features:

1. **Goals are interrelated and interdependent.** Scientific thinking and practices, reading, and writing complement one another. In this example, the learners would engage in the process of reading about the elements of experimental design and then how to conduct a basic baking soda/vinegar volcano experiment—all this before designing their own experiment to extend this understanding. Learners also would need to be taught how to critically evaluate examples, or mentor texts, of the target genre—a science fair trifold for a poster session for explaining an experiment and sharing results (which scientists actually use to communicate findings)—in order to create one. With authentic goals like these, you are often weaving together and addressing multiple standards at once.

In this example, you can see how we have strategically grouped literacy (reading and writing) and content (science) standards.

(Continued)

(Continued)

Structure and Properties of Matter

2-PS1-1. Plan and conduct an investigation to describe and classify different kinds of materials by their observable properties.

Reading for Key Ideas and Details

CCSS.ELA-LITERACY.CCRA.R.1

Read closely to determine what the text says explicitly and to make logical inferences from it; cite specific textual evidence when writing or speaking to support conclusions drawn from the text.

Production and Distribution of Writing

CCSS.ELA-LITERACY.CCRA.W.4

Produce clear and coherent writing in which the development, organization, and style are appropriate to task, purpose, and audience.

In addition to these targeted standards (those we are directly assessing), we are also teaching and revisiting other supporting standards, including science and engineering practices and cross-cutting concepts of the NGSS and speaking and listening standards from the Common Core. Knowledge is a network, not a linear checklist (Perkins, 1986), and good teachers intentionally plan to help learners capitalize on prior knowledge and make connections across disciplines.

A comprehensive example of the standards grouping for this culminating project is available online.

[online resources]

2. **Product ≠ Process.** The mental model we teach learners to master, apply, and transfer is different from the task used as evidence of its completion. "Create an exhibit" is an example of a product; the process is learning how to design an experiment, interpret findings, and think like a scientist. You may need multiple pieces of evidence to verify the learning of complex processes, such as experimental design, research, writing, or conducting scientific inquiry.

3. **Quality matters.** Merely completing the final task is not the same as completing the task with excellence and an eye on quality. Applying measures of success means that learners' work is assessed against critical standards of expertise and held to a high bar. The template shown in Figure 4.4 can help you capture your goal, evidence, and measures-of-success criteria.

ENVISION the destination: Goal • Evidence • Measures of Success

The unit _____
(compelling title of your unit framed as "how to" or question)

teaches learners how to _____
(disciplinary goal that meets correspondence concept (i.e., arguing, storytelling,
conducting scientific inquiry, analyzing historical documents, solving problems))

Learning will be evidenced through _____
(culminating projects and/or summative assessments)

_____

Work products will be judged on criteria such as:

- _____

- _____

- _____   (measures of success
(usually adjectives))

- _____

WHAT'S THE POINT? WHAT'S AT STAKE?

In a good marketing message, a copywriter will often include the "promise" of buying the advertised product and the "peril" of not. Articulating the potential success or loss a customer might experience because of his or her choice can create a sense of urgency within the mind of that customer. We will borrow from this discipline in thinking through the final element of our GEMS, the stakes.

When we think through the stakes, we try to take a step back: *What's the point of this learning? Who would learners be* without *this learning? Who could they be* with *it? What does this learning make possible for learners?*

Said another way, perhaps with more urgency from our learners, *Why do we have to learn this?* This generation of learners will not accept "it's on the test" as justification for learning subject matter. And neither should we. This kind of *stakes* is an example of authoritative informational teaching, not internally persuasive and transformational teaching and learning.

(Continued)

PLC Connection

In a PLC, work through the process of analyzing and deconstructing the standards (or a subset), intentionally grouping them, and envisioning the destination for a lesson or unit via GEMS, so teachers have the time and thinking partners to grapple with this challenging and important task. This should lead to stronger instruction across a grade level and set teachers up for bringing assessments and student work back to a future PLC to reflect upon the intended goals and actual outcomes and how instruction might be revised to more closely align instruction with desired goals.

Here are some prompts to help you fill your *stakes* box:

- How would learners answer, *Why are we learning this?* if asked at the beginning or halfway through the unit? What about at the end?

- What would happen if learners did *not* learn this subject matter and/or strategy? What transformational possibilities exist if they do?

- In what ways will this learning be transferable to learners' current and future lives? What thresholds will be crossed to transform ways of more expert knowing, thinking, and doing?

- What's the *emotional spark* of this learning? What needs can it satisfy?

- How can we justify spending extended time working toward these specific goals given other competing priorities?

- What value will learners perceive in learning this?

These answers should come more or less naturally to you. If you find yourself struggling to answer many of these questions, it might be time to reconsider outcomes for your unit or at least to modify them to address these foundational questions.

POLISHING YOUR GEMS

Here are some common roadblocks to look out for as you think through the GEMS:

The goal does not meet the correspondence concept. This usually happens when a goal is too narrow to be sufficiently authentic—when learners are asked to perform *part* of a process instead of the whole thing. While distinguishing key details from descriptions, asking questions at different levels, and making predictions are all checkpoints along the path toward the destination of interpreting the author's message, they should not serve as the central idea of your unit because those tasks in isolation do not constitute actual expertise. Once readers have generated and asked their own questions, made predictions, and determined the key details that support the main idea about a topic, *then* they can identify a theme or main idea (known as a topic-comment in linguistics); construct a summary; write their review; compare this text to other works; and complete other tasks in which the knowing, doing, and thinking are not divorced from the big picture. This is not to say that our learners do not need principled practice in a skill or facet of the bigger task (like identifying topics and key details). For example, to get skilled at dribbling, basketball players run drills. Similarly, students learning to write descriptively practice with prepared prompts. But just as the players would know the context in which dribbling counts and then *immediately* transfer their learning to a scrimmage and then the game, we must challenge our learners to deploy their descriptive writing skills into creating a setting and then putting this into a fictional story or historical narrative, so they can apply what they learned in its fullest context.

The goal is framed as a discrete application instead of a transferable strategy or skill set. Consider the difference between (1) a learner reading about a career of interest and answering text-dependent questions and (2) a learner writing three-level questions (which mirror expert reading processes; see **Chapter 11**) based on their curiosities, conducting an interview with a person in their chosen profession, and using what they learn to conduct future research. We want our learners to develop mental models and transferable strategies that transcend any one research assignment. By conducting an interview, learners find out how to develop quality questions of different kinds, sequence them in a way that opens up the conversation, and create opportunities for deeper learning and questioning. Ultimately, the mental model for generating questions will guide practice and will position learners to know when, how, and why to conduct personal research that leads to deep conceptual understanding (in this case, about how expertise is developed over time).

The goal does not represent what learners are expected to do independently at the end. Sometimes, we set goals that are bigger than our units; they represent larger long-term goals we have for our learners. At the unit level, the goals you list under "G" represent what learners will do without you by the unit's end. If you know that learners will still require serious assistance for whatever you deem as their final product, consider scaling back what you are teaching and define something learners will truly be empowered to do independently, which is the entire focus of the pedagogy of EMPOWERment. In other words, find a task that is in the learner's zone of proximal development.

The evidence does not measure the goal. Building and labeling a model of a food chain does not prove that learners can explain how energy transfers from one organism to another (a multiple-choice exercise would prove this better, as would asking, "What if there were no plants in our ecosystem?"). A learner could easily build a model based on a picture in a science textbook or off the Internet and copy the labels without an understanding of the ecological network. This type of learning is at a Depth of Knowledge Level 1; it simply requires regurgitation of information.

The tasks we ask learners to do should accurately measure our goals. In this case, we might still have learners create their own ecosystems, perhaps based on different habitats around the world, and then have them write or present about energy transfer in their ecosystem using academic vocabulary and explaining the transfer of energy at each level within the food chain. Learners could be asked how changes in the ecosystem would affect energy transfer and to explain why. This ratchets up the learning to a Depth of Knowledge Level 3 or 4 as learners apply strategic and extended thinking to develop actual understanding and share their knowledge of food chains.

Similarly, completing a worksheet of comprehension questions does not prove learners can closely read, research, identify main ideas, or summarize. As a simple check, ask yourself, "Could learners complete the task without truly accomplishing the goal?" If so, the task is not a true measure of success. Remember: The evidence must substantiate achievement, not just be the last thing learners do.

(Continued)

(Continued)

Measures of success are a list of indicators instead of a band of qualities. *Vanity metrics* are indicators that make someone feel good but don't actually provide insight into overall quality. For example, when buying a car, you might notice one has a shiny coat of paint and a gorgeous interior. These are vanity metrics. But what's going on underneath the hood? Whether the car runs, not whether it has cushy leather seats, is the bottom line and what matters most. Similarly, we must pay attention to more than just the "surface features" when judging learners' work.

In looking at student assessment, vanity metrics include specific numbers of paragraphs (traditionally, three or five) as well as handwriting, neatness, and even conventions when these are not the most pressing qualities of, say, a written story or opinion piece. When we read a real-world editorial in a journal or newspaper, we judge it by its content and style, not by the number of paragraphs it has. Of course, this is not to say that punctuation and spelling are completely unimportant (particularly if those are standards being assessed) but that these metrics are not the most important and not very important at all unless the writing will be shared with a real audience. Teachers' efforts to instill responsibility in their learners are laudable, but taking ten points off for lateness is not an authentic measure of success for an editorial. As teachers, we must differentiate between our behavioral expectations for our learners and the quality of the finished product based on critical standards.

Measures of success should refer to *general* characteristics of quality rather than its specific indicators—as a guideline, think adjectives and adjective phrases. So, instead of requiring that the opinion piece has an introduction, body, and conclusion, think about the *impact* of having those pieces—a written text being *organized* or *structured*. Instead of noting that the opinion piece should include citations from five different sources, think of how you would describe a quality opinion piece—*widely researched* or *evidence-based* or *reflecting multiple perspectives*. Those aren't things you can count. Instead of explaining that there should be an opinion, reasons, and evidence, think about the *impact* of the opinion piece clearly stating the opinion, reasons, and evidence—*convincing to an unreceptive audience*.

Of course, sometimes we need to teach our learners how to create an opinion piece that is *organized* or *structured*, *widely researched* or *evidence-based*, and *convincing*, and we may need to provide more specific guidelines as learners internalize what each of these general characteristics of quality really looks like in an opinion piece. However, we also want to help our learners keep their "eye on the prize": Although we may provide some specific indicators along the way as scaffolds for our learners, we want them to understand the ultimate goals and how these are achieved through the use of specific moves. We also want to gradually remove these scaffolds over time, encouraging our learners to develop their own writing craft and style, as real writers do—and it's important to note that real-world writing rarely follows a rigid template or a specific number of paragraphs or sources. (Though there are must-make genre moves, these can be moved around modularly, used and emphasized in different ways depending on the situation and audience.) Thinking about quality in big-picture terms helps set purposes for the learning and focuses it on what real writers do.

ENVISIONING MOVE 2: GRASP

By now, you have created GEMS that succinctly and successively capture the intended outcomes for your unit. While colleagues, instructional coaches, and supervisors will appreciate your clearly formulated goal(s), your learners may have trouble accessing it. In the next step, you will translate your GEMS into a learner-facing GRASP task.

First, let's examine why this step is important. Consider the differences between the following two columns of tasks:

DOING SCHOOL	DOING LEARNING
Write five paragraphs on a topic to answer a research question presented by the teacher.	Generate and ask your own curious questions and conduct original research to answer these questions; present the findings to an audience.
Name the subject, predicate, and verbs of sentences.	Compose a story using a variety of sentences. Share your stories with your reading buddies. Explain how particular sentences are constructed for meaning and effect.
Complete a lab from the science textbook, following a list of procedures to prove an already understood principle.	Investigate a question of curiosity or a local phenomenon. Create your science experiment to test predictions, and/or conduct research in the community. Interpret and present findings.
Answer problems 1–20 (odds) in the math textbook.	Bring in math problems of interest from the real world related to our inquiry topic, and use models and problem-solving strategies to solve them. Apply the mathematical conclusions to our ongoing understanding of the inquiry topic.
Recall the answers to factual questions to answer the questions at the end of the social studies textbook chapter.	Role-play a current or historical event to explore multiple perspectives on it, engage in a mock election or trial, or create an interactive timeline in order to better understand the sequence and multiple causality of historical events.
Copy notes from the SMART Board, whiteboard, or chalkboard.	Given specific purposes for learning, determine essential information from various stimuli (texts, teachers, etc.) and represent it using mind maps; consider how this will help you to answer a larger question, such as the EQ, or to compose and present to teach others.

What alternative labels could you give to these two lists? What are the major differences between them?

The left column represents **"Doing School,"** or **inauthentic** learning tasks from an informational pedagogy of poverty, while the right column represents **"Doing Learning,"** or **authentic intellectual work** that constitutes transformational learning. Authentic tasks like the ones in the right column promote long-term retention, extension, and use; create opportunities for collaboration within the classroom and with the community beyond the classroom; and are more likely to generate engagement and buy-in from your learners than school-ish kinds of work like traditional tests.

(Continued)

(Continued)

Authentic tasks represent "aims worth aiming for" in school because they approximate the kinds of challenges, problems, and opportunities that learners will face throughout a lifetime: messy, real-world problems that require some kind of technical expertise or strategic thinking and mindful doing to complete. These tasks represent the real work of fields of study, disciplines, professions, and lifelong pursuits. The learning is neither rote nor routine, and has value beyond school (Newmann et al., 2016; Autor & Price, 2013).

Learners who grapple with authentic intellectual tasks have the opportunity to learn something of obvious current and future use, rise to an engaging challenge, and show what they have learned. Provided they experience proper instructional preparation before and during learning, most learners relish these opportunities because everyone is motivated by staking identity through their developing competence (Smith & Wilhelm, 2002, 2006).

Moreover, without authentic tasks, learners will not have the opportunity to practice transferring what they know to new situations. And without the chance to deliberately practice in the classroom, there is little to no chance that they will be able to transfer threshold knowledge to when they are out "in the wild," either. The major litmus test to keep in mind is this: *Does this task have application and transfer value to the world beyond school? Does it* correspond *to real-world expertise and work?*

Whether we imagine lawyers presenting arguments; scientists designing experiments; architects discussing plans in a charette; mathematicians graphically representing findings or statistics to an audience; performers entertaining theatergoers; or journalists interviewing, investigating, and reporting to the public, these real-world tasks are complex, require expert knowledge of concept and strategy, and ultimately create knowledge with value in real-world communities.

The GRASP protocol, drawn from *Understanding by Design* (Wiggins & McTighe, 2005), will help you envision and plan your unit's culminating task. Figure 4.5 shows the components of GRASP.

PLC Connection

Use the GRASP protocol to develop a performance task similar to those your learners will likely experience on their state or national assessments. To create a consistent summative assessment across the grade level, provide time for teachers to brainstorm and craft this assessment in a PLC setting.

■ FIGURE 4.5: THE GRASP PROTOCOL

GOAL	REAL-WORLD ROLE	AUDIENCE	STORY OR SITUATION	PRODUCT OR PERFORMANCE
convince analyze inform explain design test problem-solve provide service of . . .	storyteller historian politician engineer scientist artist graphic designer museum exhibit designer teacher	client/customer fellow learners expert panel community an official pen pal reader	You have been asked to . . . The context/challenge is . . . The issue you must address is . . . The problem is . . . You have an opportunity to . . .	discussion/debate presentation article/essay podcast webpage speech story graphical representations/ public art how-to process descriptions museum exhibit service to class or community

You can convert your GEMS into a GRASP task by simply adding context—a role, situation, and audience (see Figure 4.6).

■ FIGURE 4.6: CONVERTING GEMS TO GRASP

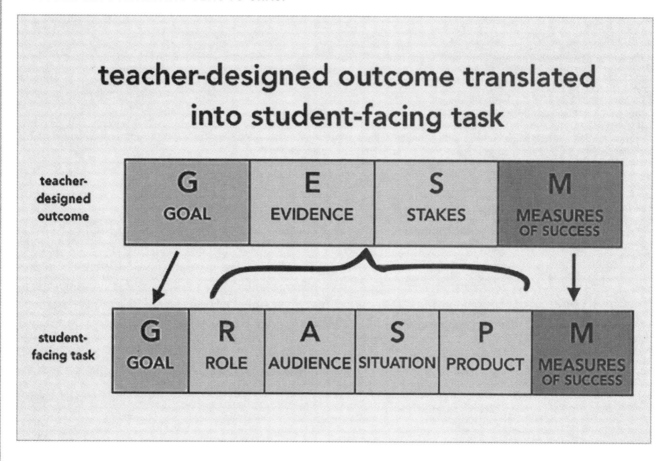

We can represent our scientific inquiry culminating task outlined previously as a GRASP performance task shown in Figure 4.7.

■ FIGURE 4.7: SCIENTIFIC INQUIRY CULMINATING TASK

The students' **goal** is to determine a research question they are curious about and design and conduct an experiment that helps them test their hypothesis about this question. They will present their investigations and findings to the wider community, providing evidence to support their conclusions.

The students' **role** will be a research scientist, presenting at a conference.

The **audience** is students' peers, as well as other students in the school, and parents, teachers, and stakeholders in the school community, ideally professionals that work in the sciences.

The **situation** is as follows: Your class is studying the practices of scientists and responding to the essential question, *How do I know when something is true?* or *What do expert scientists accept as proof?* The students will determine a question that they can investigate as scientists in order to obtain an answer to it and learn how justified conclusions or "truth" are determined.

(Continued)

(Continued)

■ FIGURE 4.7: (CONTINUED)

The **product** will be a presentation at a science fair. First, students will determine an area of interest that they want to investigate and articulate a question about it. Then, they will research science experiments related to the question and about that topic of interest in order to design their own experiment. This lab will test one variable; students will accurately record and write up their findings in a report. Students will then present their key findings in groups at a science fair, so they can visit one another's presentations. Participants and attendees will provide procedural feedback to presenters about their scientific process and final products. Afterward, students will reflect on the feedback and their own process, as well as the evolving conceptual understandings and skills they developed throughout the process. Finally, they will respond to the essential question, *How do I know when something is true?*

Measures of success: The question should be something that cannot be answered with a search engine but must be answered through an original experiment. The research should demonstrate that this experiment does not have a predetermined answer. The experiment itself should be modeled on similar ones that answer a related question, require students to employ the science and engineering practices of the NGSS, and be accompanied by a lab report so it can be replicated by other scientists. The trifold poster presentation should clearly present findings so that a diverse audience can understand the context, experimental process, and findings and test the results. Student reflections should share where they started in the process and trace how they reached their current level of understanding of the scientific content and processes. Responses to the essential question should be supported by evidence from the investigation and reveal how they will apply what was learned in the future.

This type of task outshines the traditional school science fair entry. It provides autonomy and capitalizes on learners' curiosities. It's rigorous, and it's relevant to learners' lives. It corresponds to the actual processes of doing science and to scientific expertise. It even provides additional stakes by asking fellow participants and attendees to provide *everyone* feedback rather than simply judge which project is best. It's important to translate this plan into student-friendly learning targets and to provide success criteria and appropriate scaffolding so learners *grasp* the expectations.

By asking yourself what experts in your subject area actually *know, do,* and *think* and how they *use* the content, you will find yourself on the track toward authenticity.

POWERFUL PLANNING:
GETTING CRYSTAL CLEAR ON YOUR OUTCOMES

The Latin roots of the word *decide* translate to "cut off." In other words, a decision literally "cuts off" other possibilities and allows you to move forward with focus on your chosen path. When you say yes to teaching a specific goal, it means focusing like a laser on that goal. This can be hard because it bucks against the traditional "more, more, more" thinking in school; keep in mind, however, that in any unit learners will remember only a few major concepts or develop a few generative skills at a truly deep and independent level. So where can you focus to have the maximum benefit for the greatest number of your learners? Which important goals will you fully *envision* and apprentice learners into understanding? Remember: Knowledge is a network (Perkins, 1986), so simply by doing one focused thing, many other related goals are naturally met.

Guiding Questions for Envisioning the Destination

- How can I confirm that the unit goal and culminating task (evidence) correspond to performance standards found in disciplines, trades, and other authentic domains?

- Does the evidence selected reflect the *correspondence concept* of real-world expertise and represent a *reliable* way to test learners' new abilities?

- Have I distinguished between the high-impact qualities (often subjective) of strong performance and surface features (often objective)? (For example, for an opinion, focus on persuasiveness, support, and clarity rather than whether the piece "has three details.")

- Have I built sufficient context into the final task for learners?

Chapter 5

MAPPING THE PATH TO MASTERY THROUGH TASK DECONSTRUCTION

> **ESSENTIAL QUESTION**
> How do we design engaging and effective instruction for all learners?

There is a simple way to determine a chef's abilities without tasting a morsel of her food: Watch what happens *before* she cooks.

Before a meal service in any professional kitchen, trained chefs practice an ancient culinary art called *mise en place*. Meaning roughly "putting [everything] in its place," the ritual consists of thinking through and deconstructing all the day's tasks—gathering the tools, prepping and chopping ingredients, visualizing and rehearsing steps of the service, and reasoning through potential trouble spots—*in advance* of the service.

Imagine how chaotic cooking for yourself or your family can be. Multiply that by several more cooks and a few dozen more diners, and you get a typical popular restaurant on any given night of the week. Chefs want to complete tasks ahead of time and to discover issues like being short ingredients or having broken equipment *before* hungry guests' orders pile up. The analytical act of *mise en place* helps chefs anticipate and navigate problems preemptively, preventing them from "getting in the weeds" during a busy service.

Lest we imply otherwise, chefs cannot anticipate *every* issue in the kitchen—troubleshooting along the way comes with cooking—nor can they guarantee a delicious outcome every time—after all, part of being a chef is experimenting. However, there is a big difference between an amateur who follows a recipe and must troubleshoot everything on the spot and an expert who plans ahead and can focus on the real task at hand: creatively cooking the meal. *Mise en place* sets up chefs for success.

Now, let's extend the analogy to your classroom:

- Do you set goals and jump right to lesson planning?
- Do you take the time to process what achieving the goals means for learners and to strategize about all the steps you need to take for learners to achieve the goals?

- Do you react to roadblocks with surprise when they arise? Or can you respond proactively and with perspective because you looked down the road, anticipated challenges, and rehearsed various ways to differentiate and problem-solve?

We know how frustrating it can be to get halfway into a unit before realizing learners are missing a big piece of the puzzle. This is exactly why we intentionally *map the path to mastery.*

MUST-MAKE MAPPING MOVES

In the previous chapter, we captured ideas about our learning outcomes and culminating task(s) and turned them into easy-to-communicate, tangible products: GEMS and GRASP. In this chapter, you'll learn how to perform *"mise en place* for your unit," a careful consideration and analysis of your unit goals to make teaching toward them go as smoothly as possible.

Just as the expert chef breaks down a meal prep before delivering the meal, we break down a learning goal before delivering our instructional sequence of lessons. The process consists of four disciplines related to your end-of-unit tasks, content, and standards (see Figure 5.1).

■ FIGURE 5.1: THE PROCESS OF BREAKING DOWN A LEARNING GOAL

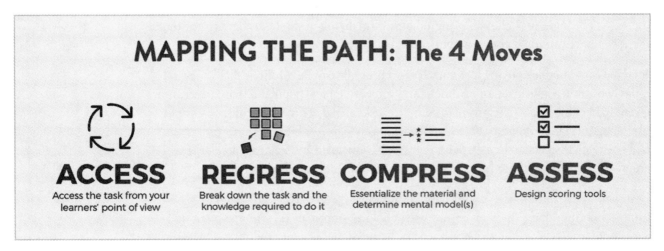

Each move yields specific insights into your unit, its culminating tasks, and how to support students to achieve success with unit goals:

- *Accessing* the task gives you empathy and insight into the unit's cognitive, social, and emotional demands because it requires you to do (ideally) or imaginatively rehearse doing (at the very least) the culminating task on your own and to reflect on the process and all its necessary conceptual, strategic, and reflective elements (knowing, doing, thinking).

- *Regressing* the task helps you break it down into manageable, teachable pieces and to understand the process learners must undertake to complete it.

- *Compressing* means expressing central learning processes or concepts in an easy-to-communicate mental model that is central to the expertise being developed.

- *Assessing* the task refers to developing quality assurance tools (aligned to your measures of success) to help communicate critical standards of success and to manage and convey progress toward the goal.

Though we recommend progressing through the steps in this order, the best order is the one in which all the steps get completed, so skip around if it feels better.

Before we begin, we again offer fair warning that—like the principled protocols of *envisioning* the destination—the disciplines of *mapping* are simple, not easy. At first, they might feel unnatural. Over repeated attempts, you will get better at them; the more repetitions you get under your belt, the easier it will get until it becomes natural for you. This deliberate practice will lead to internalized expertise. Learning *mise en place* is not easy for chefs, either. Once they learn it, though, it changes their practice forever. Expertise involves imaginatively rehearsing the process of task completion. Such is the case with the *mapping* moves. We'll provide navigational tools for finding your way, and the lessons you'll be able to "serve" at the end will be well worth it.

PLC Connection

Complete a task you plan to assign to learners before or during a PLC and discuss it in depth, reflecting collaboratively about the questions listed here. Often, this process produces insights into learner perspectives and potential misconceptions and challenges learners might encounter.

MAPPING MOVE 1: ACCESS TO UNDERSTAND THE TASK'S DEMANDS

Have you ever been surprised to see and hear your learners struggle with a task or concept that you thought would be straightforward when you planned the lesson? This experience speaks to a profoundly difficult aspect of education: comprehending and empathizing with learners' levels of understanding. As educators, we possess levels of disciplinary expertise and content mastery, not to mention years (if not decades) more lived experience that fills out our background knowledge. This is sometimes called the *expert blind spot* or *the curse of knowledge*. When we have this depth of understanding, it makes it harder for us to imagine what life was like before we acquired this expertise. This is, in part, because we have achieved *threshold knowledge*, which has taken us through a gateway to a new way of understanding, doing, and being.

(Continued)

(Continued)

Accessing asks us to acknowledge the blind spots our expertise causes and to assume a "beginner's mind" with respect to navigating and completing our culminating tasks. To achieve this, we advocate the following:

- **Do the task you plan to assign to learners.** Write a short narrative of your own, craft a summary of the reading you will assign, identify the causes and effects of a scientific phenomenon, or research an influential expert. *Whatever you want your learners to do, do it yourself—or at least a miniature version (e.g., write a scene instead of a narrative).* This investment of time and effort will provide great returns for you and your colleagues!

- **Reflect on the process through a learner's lens.** To be metacognitive is to literally "think about our thinking." Reflecting on your composing (e.g., of an opinion, narrative, informational piece), you must ask the following:
  - What is challenging about this type of composing or problem solving?
  - What do you have to know to get started and to navigate this kind of task?
  - What aspects of the task or content are counterintuitive, challenging, or complex?
  - Where might learners stumble? Why?
  - What preconceptions, misconceptions, or evolving conceptions will learners likely have, and how might these support or provide obstacles to achieving expertise?

- **Share what you produce with learners.**
  - Make the most of the time you spend on this process, and share that narrative, summary, explanation, or research with learners when you introduce the task to them. Your example can serve as an invaluable model of how to meet success criteria by providing learners a clear idea of what their target looks and sounds like. You also can share the challenges and your missteps and how you navigated them. This models a growth mindset and lets learners know that the task is challenging but can be navigated through the use of expert strategies. (We sometimes use a think-aloud strategy called "watch the teacher sweat" by completing part of a task in front of students so they can see how we are thinking as we try things out, revise, and navigate challenges [Wilhelm, 2012d].)
  - Let learners be the judge of your work by asking them to grade it, using whatever tool you plan to use with their work. This process provides learners another frame of reference when they tackle the task themselves. Plus, you can hold them to the same high standard they will hold you to!

WARNING: Skipping this step will render the rest of the exercises in this chapter less effective. Remember that, in inquiry as cognitive apprenticeship, teachers are full and collaborative participants in learning and knowledge creation.

MAPPING MOVE 2: REGRESS TO UNDERSTAND THE COMPONENTS OF THE CULMINATING TASK

Regression is the heart of the *mise en place* practice we described at the start of the chapter: breaking a complex task into a sequence of *micro skills*, instructional sequences, and progressions. Regressing tasks and standards often means seeing "between the lines" and extending the line of thought found in national or local standards. The insight you gain during your accessing of the task will prove invaluable here because it will reveal many of the implicit aspects of your chosen learning goals.

When a task is cognitive or literacy based, its component parts tend to fall into eight fundamental categories of thought patterns (Wilhelm, Smith, & Fredricksen, 2012):

1. *Describing*: assigning qualities, traits, and attributes; describing processes

2. *Defining* (including brainstorming): features, characteristics, limits, associations

3. *Classifying*: kinds, groups, sorting, relationships between groups

4. *Comparing*: similarities, differences, commonalities, distinctions

5. *Identifying relationships*: analogies, matching sets, guess the rule

6. *Whole-to-part reasoning*: seeing the structure of things, anatomy, components

7. *Sequencing*: steps, ordering, processes

8. *Seeing causes and/or effects of events*: causality, problem–solution, reasons, motives, impacts, consequences; seeing the reasons for a problem and possibilities for addressing these in a solution

For example, analyzing and performing oral storytelling may require learners to do the following:

-   Identify the audience and their prior background knowledge about the story.

-   Understand the rules of notice for the genre of oral storytelling (Wilhelm & Smith, 2016)—that is, there is a launch line, or hook, to capture the audience's attention at the outset; it's told from memory; and there's a lesson about life near the end.

-   Explain causes and effects of characters' decisions.

-   Describe a character at the beginning, middle, and end of the story.

-   Compare a character at one point in the story to that same character at another point; compare a character to characters in other stories.

(Continued)

(Continued)

- Highlight a character's trouble and how he or she navigates it and with what results.

- Understand how parts of the setting influence the story's development (e.g., by inviting or limiting actions by characters).

- Explain causes, and sometimes effects, of a character's transformations.

- Identify the relationship between the storyteller's choices and the effects on the listener.

Putting that thinking into the genre of oral storytelling might require us to take these steps:

- Compare a variety of storytelling models to identify general success criteria.

- Identify how different parts of a story work together as a whole.

- Understand the genre as a type of text that organizes specific kinds of content in particular ways *to do specific kinds of work and engage in targeted social actions.*

- Compare drafts of stories to the collectively articulated success criteria, and revise the criteria accordingly.

We often marvel at the complexity hidden within tasks when we approach them with this analytical lens. All too often, when learners lack a seemingly obvious skill, we throw up our hands in frustration and move to the next thing. Yet when we take the time to analyze the task and component skills through the lens of our learners, the underlying complex thought processes can become painfully apparent. What also becomes apparent is the assistance and apprenticeship learners will need to master the skill.

As just one quick example, let's consider teaching learners to identify key details while reading. We might ask them to mark key details by underlining them or by putting a star in the margin. But underlining or marking ideas does not provide the scaffolding necessary for learners to learn how to notice and identify key details, much less to interpret how key details work together to express a main idea. This is a complex process that requires learners to first understand the purpose they are working toward with their reading. Then, it requires them to know how authors tip readers off that an idea or move is crucial by recognizing the readers' rules of notice (Wilhelm & Smith, 2016) like direct statements and generalizations, ruptures/surprises, calls to attention like the use of figurative language, or moves that provoke strong reactions and questions. And that's just the start to noticing and interpreting patterns of key details to understand a main idea or theme. Learners also need to identify a topic that is being explored and how the structuring of the key details expresses a comment (main idea) about the topic that can be expressed as a topic-comment (Wilhelm & Smith, 2016). Regressing, like accessing, helps us to identify the complex steps in a task and to identify what learners will need in terms of the assistance we provide through our teaching.

MAPPING MOVE 3: COMPRESS INTO MENTAL MODELS THAT CAPTURE THRESHOLD KNOWLEDGE

Unpacking your expertise and repackaging it for someone else is hard work! How do you get what's inside your head into someone else's? This is essentially what we're doing when we move from *regress* to *compress*. The key is to identify a mental model: a deep and visual understanding of the interrelated aspects of a concept or a map for understanding the process of how to complete a task. Mental models can be understood and expressed through helpful representations, powerful analogies, illustrations, examples, and explanations that make your content comprehensible. Major concepts, tools, and the problem-solving and knowledge-creating processes of a discipline are embedded in these models.

HELPFUL ANALOGIES AND ILLUSTRATIONS

As our beloved mentor George Hillocks used to say, "All learning proceeds from what is currently known to the new." Teaching through analogies leverages this wisdom.

Learners might not know what chloroplasts, which are invisible to the naked eye, do on the surface of a leaf. However, they might already understand the function of solar panels on the roof of a house. If we can create a prompt that asks them to explain how a roof needs solar panels to collect sunlight for the use of the house, it creates a bridge because it's the same way that chloroplasts collect sunlight for the use of the plant. Therefore, chloroplasts represent the "solar panels" of the house.

Looking in and outside of your discipline, what analogies exist for the concept or strategy you wish to teach? What might make a concept easier to grasp for your learners?

VISUAL MAPS

Figure 5.2 shows a visual model of expert reading.

■ FIGURE 5.2: MENTAL MODEL OF EXPERT READING

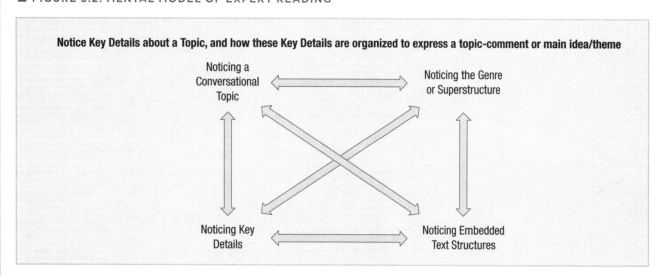

(Continued)

(Continued)

This model of expert reading is the basis of the topic-comment strategy for identifying a main idea and being able to justify it with textual evidence. This identification and justification of main ideas is something that the last several NAEP tests show very few students do. But *they can* do it if they are given the proper assistance and practice using a mental model such as in Figure 5.3 (see Wilhelm & Smith [2016] for an instructional sequence for teaching the topic-comment strategy).

■ **FIGURE 5.3: FLOW CHART OF TOPIC-COMMENT STRATEGY**

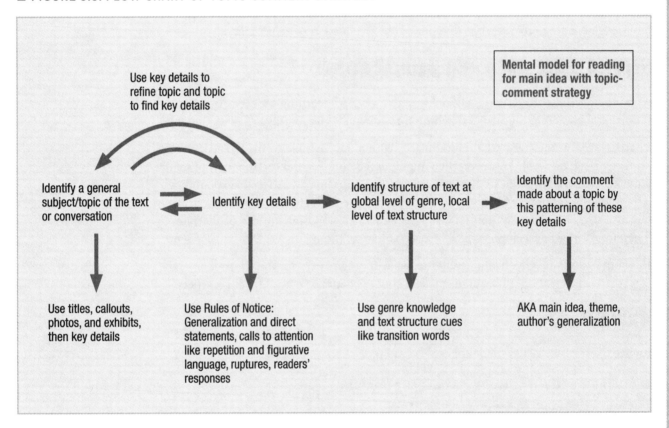

The rules of notice are an instructional support that helps learners identify key details and topics of a text. General rules of notice are *direct statements/generalizations*; *calls to attention* (titles, figurative language, repetition, first paragraphs and introductions, etc.); *ruptures and surprises*; and *reader responses* (Wilhelm & Smith, 2016). For a list of such rules and ideas for how to teach them, see **resources.corwin .com/empower-elementary**.

online resources

Reading or composing a simple opinion piece or argument can be guided with the mental model of CREW (Figure 5.4).

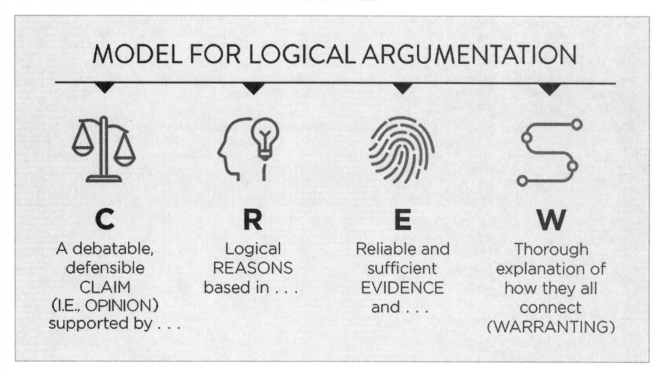

CREW, like all mental models, highlights must-make moves of doing a task. But in CREW, like many mental models, the moves are modular and can be moved around (e.g., a claim can go at the end of a text so that the reader hears the story of your thinking first, then comes to the claim as a conclusion). Moves can also be repeated in different parts of the text.

MNEMONICS AND FRAMEWORKS

Consolidating a process or set of strategies into a mnemonic is another way to create a mental model. For example, we have simplified the tenets of transformative teaching into an easy-to-remember framework in EMPOWER.

Consider the cornerstone skill of narrative writing, a skill set we approach regularly in elementary schools. In *So What's the Story: Teaching Narrative to Understand Ourselves, Others, and the World*, Jim Fredricksen, Jeff Wilhelm, and Michael Smith (2012) use the acronym GSAWS to name the key components of any story: *world of the story, actions, goals,* and *stakes* of the characters involved. When teaching this model to learners for the purpose of composing their own narrative, it's helpful to rearrange the acronym into GSAWS (Figure 5.5) to draw their focus to writing about why characters behave the way they do (goals) and the consequences for success, failure, or something

PLC Connection

Modifying the questions for the GSAWS model creates a map for reflecting on classroom instruction or PD you facilitate. By considering your goals, stakes, struggles, actions, and world, you can deeply analyze your experience, share your feelings, and consider if and how you successfully do or could progress toward meeting your goals.

(Continued)

(Continued)

■FIGURE 5.5: GSAWS MODEL FOR NARRATIVE WRITING AND ANALYSIS

Goals: What is the character after or avoiding? What does she or he require in order to reach this goal?

Struggles: What trouble is the character facing?

Actions: What does the character do to pursue the goal and to overcome the trouble? What does he or she refuse to do, or what is the character unable to do?

World of the character: What does the space that the character occupies feel like? Sound like? Smell like? Taste like? What type of impression does he or she put into the surroundings? How do the surroundings influence him or her, contributing to the trouble or inviting or discouraging certain actions?

Stakes: What are the consequences of failure? Why is the character working toward her or his goals in the first place? Why should readers invest themselves emotionally in the story?

in between (stakes). In his classroom, Adam reimagined this as "SWAG" and asked students: *Does your story idea have SWAG?*

This type of acronym helps learners remember the names for the parts of a narrative. More importantly, the mental model provides a map for instruction to help learners transfer understanding to writing and understanding stories.

A framework can act as a kind of scaffold that expresses the mental map and coaches learners through using it.

GSAWS for CHARACTER

* GOALS of that character

* STRUGGLES—obstacles, challenges to overcome, trouble

* ACTIONS taken by the character to overcome trouble and achieve goals

* WORLD that character inhabits—constraints of that world

* STAKES for the character of overcoming the trouble and achieving goals

Trouble and struggles might involve

- a surprise
- a rupture
- complications
- a change in status quo
- an epiphany
- ambiguity

- a dilemma
- uncertainty
- dashed hopes
- loss
- betrayal
- being overwhelmed

MOMENTS THAT MIGHT CREATE STRUGGLES, TROUBLE, AND DILEMMAS	CHARACTERS WHO MIGHT BE IN THOSE MOMENTS (USE GSAWS)
At a sleepover with friends	
During a sporting event with a coach the character does not like	
At the store with an annoying sibling	
In the car with parents after you received news of a bad grade	A person trying to be cool and impress others
Being asked to sneak into a theater or another event where you are not welcome or are supposed to pay	A student who wants a candy bar, skateboard, or iPhone because . . .
Lies and deceptions	
Accusations—true and false	A student who makes money babysitting
Punishments—fair and unfair	A student who wants to be more healthy because . . .
Encounter with rival or authority	
Answering the phone while playing hooky	
	A parent worried about a child

Source: Adapted from Fredricksen et al. (2012).

The chart (Figure 5.6) is a scaffold that guides learners to get started with GSAWS.

This mental model can also be expressed visually through a flow chart (Figure 5.7).

■ FIGURE 5.7: GSAWS FLOW CHART

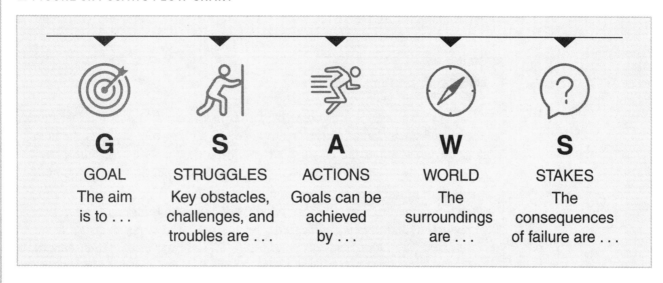

(Continued)

(Continued)

It's important to remember that many mental models, such as CREW and GSAWS, are actually modular. In other words, all the moves are key to the task, but they can be presented in different sequences in order to achieve different effects. Moves can also be repeated and built upon.

TEMPLATES

Another way to mentally model is to *template* a task. Far from simply turning something complex into a simplistic worksheet, to "template" means elucidating a pattern for shaping a piece of work. GSAWS assists with understanding the pieces of a story. The following template can be used to explain how those elements are blended into a story structure. This can be used analytically to summarize stories or to generate them.

Once upon a time, *something happened to someone*, and she decided that she would pursue (a) *goal*. So, with the help of a *guide*, she *devised a plan of action*, and even though she faced *obstacles*, she *kept going* in light of the *stakes of succeeding or failing*. And just as she *hit rock bottom*, she *learned a lesson or got clarity*, and when offered *the goal*, she *made a tough decision*, resulting in *success or failure* and potentially *resolving past issues*. A lesson is expressed through the process and results, including how the character and her understanding were changed.

The template can be designed to build on the GSAWS model by using the words *goal*, *stakes*, and *action*, which are critical to the structure. For example, take the plot of the Pixar classic, *Finding Nemo*, the tenth-highest-grossing animated film of all time and owner of an impressive 99 percent score on the movie review website Rotten Tomatoes:

WARNING: SPOILERS AHEAD!

Once upon a time, *an overprotective father fish named Marlin lost his son, Nemo*, and he decided that he would pursue *finding Nemo*. So, with the help of *Dory*, he *searched the ocean blue*, and even though he faced *sharks, turtles, and being swallowed by a whale*, he *"just kept swimming"* in light of the *prospect of finding his only son*. And just as he *thought Nemo was dead and saw Dory caught in a net*, he learned, *"If you love something, set it free,"* and when offered *Nemo being alive and safe*, he *made the tough decision to let Nemo help free Dory, who was stuck in a net*, resulting in *everyone successfully returning home safely* and *resolving Marlin's overprotective parenting tendencies caused by Nemo's mother being eaten in the first scene*.

Finding Nemo not only won critical accolades from its audience but also received a nomination for Best Original Screenplay despite it fitting the template, beat by beat. The template also explains the hero quest archetype, superhero flicks, romantic comedies, and even *Romeo & Juliet*, with minor tweaking. If your favorite film is a Hollywood classic, there is a 90-plus percent likelihood that it falls into the structure of the previous passage. So what gives? Isn't the popular wisdom to "think outside of the box" when telling a story?

Template mental models address *exactly* this kind of predictable misconception. It is mostly novices who resist "inside-the-box" thinking and rail against confining themselves to a predictable story pattern. As it turns out, the brain *loves* predictable patterns (and so do expert practitioners in any discipline!). When authors try to be clever and stray too far from tried-and-true structures, readers get confused and lose the thread. Effective storytelling becomes less about reinventing the wheel than about leveraging the known elements to maximal effect.

Learners' first exposure to narratives needs scaffolds to create the familiar ebb and flow—the tension and release—of an engaging story. Learners also benefit from "standing on the shoulders" of Pixar, Aristotle, and storytellers who have come before them via a template.

MAPPING MOVE 4: ASSESS TO UNDERSTAND THE DIMENSIONS OF AN EXPERT PERFORMANCE

In drafting your GEMS in the previous chapter, you identified *measures of success*, the traits of exemplary work in the genre or process your learners will master. In the final move of *mapping* the path, you will flesh out each measure of success and articulate different levels of performance in specific detail (see Figure 5.8).

■ FIGURE 5.8: MAPPING THE PATH TO QUALITY TEMPLATE

QUALITY CRITERION	NOVICE	AMATEUR	APPRENTICE	PRO

(Continued)

(Continued)

In order to produce the most real-world rubric you can, we recommend you generate it from real-world models via the following process. We recommend doing this process with colleagues, or even better: with students.

1. Gather and sort a range of learner work in a particular genre or writing form (see Figure 5.9). Don't forget to include what you created in Mapping Move 1: Accessing! Grab a stack of narratives, reports, or presentations from previous years or examples from the Internet.

■ FIGURE 5.9: RANKING MODELS

LEAST EFFECTIVE	SOMEWHAT EFFECTIVE	EFFECTIVE	MOST EFFECTIVE
• Sample A • Sample B • Sample C	• Sample D • Sample E • Sample F	• Sample G • Sample H • Sample I	• Sample J • Sample K • Sample L

2. Ask yourself: What makes the strong ones so strong? What makes the weak ones weak? Name characteristics and qualities of these work samples. (See also "Ranking Models to Articulate Critical Standards" in Chapter 15.) On one color of sticky note, write phrases that characterize the work, such as "cites evidence from multiple sources" or "jumps around from topic to topic." On another color of sticky note, name traits that capture characteristics (e.g., adjectives such as *convincing, logically organized, clear*, etc.).

3. Cluster the sticky notes (or your written ideas) into traits or important dimensions of performance. This is your rudimentary rubric (see Figure 5.10).

4. Repeat this process with learners as you orient them to the learning and continuously refine the rubric, adding in levels of performance, based on real-world examples.

■ FIGURE 5.10: REAL-WORLD RUDIMENTARY RUBRIC

BIOGRAPHY PRESENTATION ABOUT BECOMING AN EXPERT		
INCLUDES IMPORTANT INFORMATION ABOUT THE INDIVIDUAL AND THEIR FIELD OF EXPERTISE	BECOMES THE CHARACTER AND ENTERS INTO HER OR HIS PERSPECTIVE	ENGAGES AUDIENCE WITH BODY LANGUAGE AND VOICE
Shares what makes this individual an expert by sharing major topic-comments, main ideas, and takeaways based on reading and research	Dresses like the character and in ways that suggest the interests, values, commitments, and activities of the character	Makes regular eye contact with audience
Explains the road this character took to achieve expertise using GSAWS	Uses language that the character would use, including revealing and perhaps famous quotes	Uses hand gestures and other nonverbal communication effectively

BIOGRAPHY PRESENTATION ABOUT BECOMING AN EXPERT		
INCLUDES IMPORTANT INFORMATION ABOUT THE INDIVIDUAL AND THEIR FIELD OF EXPERTISE	**BECOMES THE CHARACTER AND ENTERS INTO HER OR HIS PERSPECTIVE**	**ENGAGES AUDIENCE WITH BODY LANGUAGE AND VOICE**
Includes engaging and new information that informs the audience about how the individual achieves expertise and overcomes challenges to get meaningful work done in the world and with what results	Shares perspective and feelings about life history of struggles, actions, stakes, and the world in which they grew and learned	Speaks at a volume that all audience members can hear Speaks at a rate that is easily understood and allows time to comprehend Tone indicates interest in the expert and changes as needed with the content for emphasis and effect

Note: This rudimentary rubric does not yet show benchmark descriptions of levels of performance. Instead, it is focused on important characteristics and qualities for the final product. These qualities could serve as assessment guidelines or be revised into a more complex rubric with levels of performance.

POWERFUL PLANNING: DIGGING DEEP AND DECONSTRUCTING THE LEARNING JOURNEY AHEAD

Each of these mapping exercises represents an acquired expert skill set that you will develop not only throughout your reading of this text but also throughout your career. This chapter represents critical, often overlooked, aspects of instructional design.

If you're feeling overwhelmed, we encourage you to "knock over the first domino": Do the culminating task that you want learners to be able to do. This makes clear that you are a person who values the work you assign, who is still learning, who is reflective, and who is willing to keep getting better. Once you do your task, you will automatically begin the process of task deconstruction. As you're breaking

down your task, you will likely start seeking out the mental models or resources that will anchor your instruction. Once you've done the task and perhaps compared your process with a colleague, you also will have a good sense of how to set up some meaningful milestones or checkpoints. And once you've read a few models from past learners and experts, building a rubric that communicates the characteristics of quality will become easier.

But it all begins with the first step: Do your task, eat your own cooking, and commit yourself to the inquiry, and you will be transformed toward conscious competence and expertise.

Guiding Questions for Mapping the Path to Mastery Through Task Deconstruction

- What have I learned (about the task or how my learners might tackle the task) through doing (or imagining doing) the task myself?

- Have I defined and sequenced the underlying knowledge, skills, thinking, and all the steps required to complete the culminating task successfully?

- Can I articulate a mental model that captures how experts actually understand a required concept or an approach to the assigned task, instead of a "school-ish" formula that reduces complex thinking into rote learning?

- Am I able to flesh out the measures of success into three or more levels of performance in the form of a rubric?

PART 3: PRIMING AND ORIENTING

ENVISION MAP **PRIME** **ORIENT** WALK THROUGH EXTEND/EXPLORE REFLECT

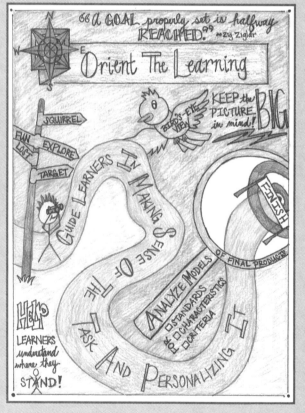

Chapter 6

PRIMING LEARNERS THROUGH A CARING COMMUNITY AND COLLABORATIVE CLASSROOM CULTURE

A Prerequisite for Inquiry as Cognitive Apprenticeship (ICA)

> **ESSENTIAL QUESTION**
> How do we create a strong, supportive, and vibrant learning community?

How many of you have experienced "first day of school" dreams (or should we say nightmares?) in the nights preceding the start of a new school year? The ones where everything goes remarkably wrong, dragons come out of your teacher closet, and the unbelievable happens? One time, Jackie dreamt that all her fourth graders turned into zoo animals of every shape and size and roamed around the classroom creating havoc! Of course, most of the things that occur in our dreams never actually happen in reality but instead are based on our emotions and worries. Good teachers often dream about their learners because the welfare of the class community is at the brink of their consciousness. We teach because we want to do our best for our learners, and we know how important a strong start is with a brand-new group. A prerequisite to doing our best for all learners is to create a strong community through a supportive and collaborative culture that knows how to solve problems and navigate difficulty together.

See *Lesson Plan Canvas* on page 104

The last fifty years of cognitive science have taught us that we are better together (Vygotsky, 1978): Teaching and learning for understanding and application require social assistance and collaboration. We also know that human beings are intensely social and develop through social relationships (Lieberman, 2013). All teachers know the costs for learners—and all human beings—of exclusion and isolation. Inquiry as cognitive apprenticeship (ICA) promotes community—it is how real-world disciplines do their work together, and it is a method for turning classrooms into communities of practice and sites of collaborative meaning and decision making.

What does this mean for us as teachers when we consider *priming* learners for success? It means that we must create a culture of collaboration that supports and rewards reciprocity, risk-taking, and deliberate practice; provides ongoing mutual help; organizes ways to give and receive this support; promotes openness to various ideas; and supports deep learning.

PLANNING FOR PRIMING LEARNERS THROUGH COLLABORATIVE CLASSROOM CULTURE

Let's be honest: A culture of collaboration is crucial yet difficult to achieve. But it can be done, and you can do it. The strategies included in this chapter will help you *prime* learners for the journey by (1) intentionally scaffolding and promoting relationships between everyone in the classroom as learners share their unique stories; (2) developing deeper appreciation, kindness, empathy, and compassion for everyone in the classroom community; and (3) creating an environment of social support that promotes engagement and learning. These strategies also afford learners opportunities to recognize their own relational strengths, acknowledge areas for improvement, set personal goals, and capitalize on the strengths and perspectives of others (see more on reflection and assessment in Chapters 14 and 15). Ultimately, learners experience the power of "together is better" and develop habits of collaboration, as well as strategies for navigating the challenges of working with others.

We all interact on a daily basis in friendships, careers, and community projects, and it is the responsibility of teachers and parents to teach their children how to do so in positive and fruitful ways. A key factor in establishing a democratic, learning-rich, and respectful classroom environment is how we group learners and support them in collaborating. We define *grouping* as the process by which we partner learners in pairs and teams, both on any particular occasion and over time. Sometimes, it is valuable to provide learners autonomy in choosing their own partners and teams, but other times, we assign the groups in ways that afford learners opportunities to interact and learn from diverse partners they may not have chosen. This process works toward social equity and leads to greater camaraderie among individual learners and the class as a whole. This also parallels real-world experiences—learners will collaborate with a wide variety of individuals (some by choice and others by circumstance) who think and act differently than they do in their future education, careers, and life experiences.

Collaborative work provides tremendous opportunities to practice responsibility and accountability to a group and instills both empathy and awareness in learners. This is essential groundwork for a restorative classroom because learners listen to one another's stories and regularly consider how their actions affect members in the community. This work pays dividends down the road in terms of improved behavior, social imagination in seeing and honoring the perspectives of others, and a healthier classroom culture. Although it takes time and deliberate practice, learners in this kind of classroom community engage more deeply, learn more, and appreciate collective decision making and problem solving.

As you do this work, keep in mind that learners will likely struggle initially and then continue to have periodic struggles. This is the time to lean in and persevere through the challenges by providing additional modeling, support, and practice with these skills. With active assistance, learners gradually appreciate the value of collaboration. For example, you will want to establish routines with your learners; create guidelines for collaboration with them; and consider assigning roles, locations, purposes, and tasks for groups. You will also need to monitor the room, sharing feedback with learners and coaching groups to strengthen their collaboration skills.

Each of the strategies in this chapter will help you and your learners build a strong classroom community that serves as the foundation for deep and humanizing learning to occur. They are applicable to all grade levels, and we honor your professional expertise in making these strategies best fit your grade, context, and individual learners. It's also important to note that each of these strategies must be explicitly taught, and—as with any new learning—they must be practiced, revised, and grown into. This means that the first time you try any one of the strategies, it may not go as smoothly as you planned or hoped. Please know this has happened to all of us. Should this occur, we encourage you to take a step back, embrace your growth mindset, celebrate what went well, reflect on what you might do differently, reestablish your expectations, and try, try again. Likely, you will be much more successful the second time and even more so the third time.

Considerations When Designing Activities for Collaborative Classroom Culture

❑ The collaborative activity and method of grouping supports the purpose and goals of the lesson and helps learners understand the potential and satisfaction of interacting and solving problems as a community. (E-M-P-O)

❑ Learners are supported as they practice the skills of collaboration: listening attentively; sharing diverse perspectives; honoring others' ideas, contributions, and strengths; asking good questions; actively participating; being fully present in the work; and believing in the potential of all. (O-W)

❑ Learners have identified the task to be completed by the end of the collaborative activity, have a process for assigning responsibilities and completing the task, and understand how the task will serve and promote the community. (O-W)

❑ Learners focus on helping each other by being supportive, building relationships, and doing the work of communities: learning content, implementing strategies, solving problems, and understanding how to collaborate throughout the process. (W-E)

❑ Over time, learners have the opportunity to work with all other learners in the community, especially those with different personalities, perspectives, and learning styles. (E)

❑ Learners reflect on their experiences in the community, identifying successes and challenges, considering how this learning will serve future collaborations, and setting goals for improved collaboration. (R)

COLLABORATIVE CULTURE MOVE 1: BALANCING THE BOAT

The way groups form and interact with one another is integral to how effectively they collaborate. Due to the social nature of learning, teachers should spend as much time as it takes to create effective groups and to teach learners how to work together. Specifically, learners must understand how to capitalize on their own strengths and those of others.

Balancing the boat is one powerful strategy for creating diverse groupings that stay afloat. To create a diverse and balanced group, it helps to be aware of the wide range of strengths and perspectives of all group members, especially early in the school year. This increases the likelihood that the group will rely on each individual's strengths and will share and challenge new ideas, typically leading to better decisions and results. In addition, this kind of grouping gives learners the opportunity to develop a growth mindset about what could be possible for them to accomplish both individually and as a group. Here's a quick step-by-step overview, followed by a more detailed lesson example:

1. Have learners write about their strengths or complete a strengths and/ or interests survey (a variety of these surveys are available online). When reflecting on their strengths, learners should support their answers with evidence of how they have demonstrated these strengths in the past. The simple question, "What makes you say so?" can help learners dig deeper. In addition to learners' self-reflections, you also may want to use assessment data to help create initial groupings.

2. Have learners complete a Y-chart of what an effective group looks like, sounds like, and feels like. After learners brainstorm, ask them to identify the specific skills necessary to achieve these goals. Then, ask learners to consider their reflections and share who feels she or he has (or is developing) a strength necessary to effective group work. Record a list of names and strengths on the board.

3. Organize learners into balanced groups that represent the diverse population and strengths of the room.

4. As the year goes on and groupings change, you may give your learners the opportunity to select their own groups while reiterating the goal of a diverse group by having groups ask themselves, "How well is our boat balanced?"

Following group creation, the teacher and/or learners assess the balance of the boat by reflecting on the unique qualities or strengths each individual brings to the group. We suggest that initially learners self-assess the balance of the boat. If they struggle to do this independently, consider what steps you might take or recommendations you might offer to support them the next time.

When collaborating in their groups, learners can provide procedural feedback to one another, naming what is going well and the effect this has on the group. Learners can also name productive struggles as well as possibilities for navigating these or alternative ways of proceeding as a group.

Example: Balancing the Boat Activity

Step 1: Frontload the lesson.

Ask learners to reflect on a time they worked in a group. Have them consider what worked well and what was challenging. Ask learners how they would leverage the strengths and address the struggles and challenges they faced if they could go back in time (or if they experience a similar situation in the future). Ask learners how they could replicate or extend the positive experiences. As learners share their experiences, highlight their ideas about attentive listening; sharing diverse perspectives; honoring others' ideas, contributions, and strengths; asking good questions; actively participating; actively inviting others to participate; being fully present in the work; and believing in the potential of all.

Step 2: Introduce the essential question, and explain the purpose of the lesson.

- Explain to learners the importance of learning how to work successfully in groups and how to leverage all the strengths and perspectives of different participants. Frame the lesson with the guiding question, "How do we create the most effective and balanced group?"

- Share with learners that sometimes they will have the opportunity to select who they work with in life and sometimes they won't. Explain that when they have the opportunity to select their own groups, they should not simply choose their friends, but rather, they should consider how to complement the strengths of current group members.

- Tell learners that today we will use a strategy called *balancing the boat* to learn more about one another and form effective groups in our classroom. Explain to learners that the strategy name, *balancing the boat*, emphasizes that we want to have group members with diverse skills so we can balance one another and prevent our boat from capsizing.

Step 3: Have learners name personal strengths.

Ask learners to reflect on their personal skills and strengths that they bring to a group. If helpful, provide a list of strengths for learners to select from, collectively brainstorm a list of strengths as a class, and/or model with a think-aloud about how your strengths benefit a group. Have learners record one or two of their biggest personal strengths to share with the class in today's lesson.

(Continued)

Step 4: Model how learners will introduce themselves and learn more about one another.

- Explain to learners that they will introduce themselves to the class by sharing a strength as opposed to their name.
- Model this first by saying, "Hi, I'm _____" (i.e., "Hi, I'm creative"). "What makes me say so is . . ."
- Learners could also cite an area they want to improve in and, therefore, would like to learn more about from someone else.

Step 5: Have learners introduce themselves and engage in a whole-class discussion about what they learn about one another.

- Allow all learners to introduce themselves in this way and record their names and strengths on a whiteboard, SMART board, or document camera for the whole class to see.
- Once all learners have introduced themselves, discuss the different strengths of learners in the classroom, and honor the diversity of your learners. This is often a great time to highlight cultural resources (such as the ability to speak another language), funds of knowledge based on family backgrounds (such as knowledge of farm or city life), unique experiences, and challenges overcome. Explain how when we work together, we can capitalize on one another's strengths and have others help us in areas where we are not as strong.

Step 6: Create diverse groups by balancing the strengths presented.

- Use learners' strengths to develop categories, and then, group learners; your learners can help create categories as well. Some examples include creative skills ("Hi, I'm good at coming up with new ideas"); knowledge skills ("Hi, I'm a math expert"); effort skills ("Hi, I'm hardworking"); people skills ("Hi, I'm positive"); organization ("I can set goals and help keep people on task"); and so forth.

EXAMPLE CATEGORIES

Creative Skills	Knowledge Skills
<ul><li>Good at coming up with new ideas</li><li>Artistic</li><li>Photographer</li><li>Designer</li><li>Performer</li><li>Successful crafter</li></ul>	<ul><li>A math expert</li><li>A technology user</li><li>Note taker</li><li>Reader</li><li>Writer</li><li>Someone with a good memory</li></ul>

Effort Skills	People Skills
• Hardworking	• Positive
• Ambitious	• Listener
• Self-motivated	• Facilitator
• Persevering	• Encourager
• Willing to try new things	• Problem solver
• Dependable	• Strong feedback provider

- Now, create groupings that represent each of the categories (or as many as possible). You'll want to determine how many learners you want in each group based on the task(s) learners will engage in prior to making your specific grouping decisions. We recommend doing this collaboratively as a class to model how learners might make intentional grouping decisions that balance the boat in the future.

Note: The simplest way to create balanced groups is to take the first learner from each category to form Group 1, the second one from each category to form Group 2, and so on. Of course, you could take this a step further, by looking at the particular character qualities in a group and swapping an individual out one for one with another individual from the same group to establish the best combination of qualities. Substitutions may also be considered based on personalities, needs of the learners, and so forth. However, we encourage you not to overthink the groupings, as learners always have talents they did not express in the activity, and it's hard to tell how groups will really work until you give them the opportunity to collaborate and negotiate with one another. Learners will need these teamwork and negotiation skills as they interact in other groups throughout their lives.

Step 7: Have learners sit with their groups and explore how they will work together.

Introduce the upcoming collaborative lesson and explain what learners will be doing throughout. Have learners share how they believe their strengths might benefit the group in the upcoming lesson. Next, encourage a growth mindset by asking learners to consider an area where they might need support or a goal for improvement. This encourages them to recognize evolving skills (or skills they do not have yet) and to be attentive to and learn from other group members who have already developed these skills. Groups should record these somewhere, so they are cognizant of individuals' goals and their commitment to support one another.

EXTENSION: NAME GAMING/TEAM NAMING

An extension of balancing the boat is to ask learners to give themselves a nickname that identifies a strength. Learners may do this by providing an adjective before

(Continued)

their name, such as "Judicious Jackie" to showcase an ability to solve problems or "Creative Chris" to reflect an ability to think outside the box. This can help learners remember the names of their classmates and acknowledge the strengths each person can contribute to the team. Following the creation of groups, learners also can develop a team name that reveals their collective interests, passions, purposes, or strengths. This requires them to determine commonalities, provides low-threshold practice with the skill of synthesis, and gives them increased ownership and interest in their team.

Checklist for Creating Your Own Balancing the Boat

❑ The teacher assesses his or her learners' collaborative abilities and provides appropriate scaffolding for learners to be successful in balancing the boat. (*Note:* Be sure to remove scaffolds as learners become increasingly independent.) (E-M, W)

❑ Learners are able to recognize and articulate personal strengths and can recognize the strengths of others, as well as how these strengths will contribute to a team's dynamic. (P-O-W)

❑ Learners are able to categorize strengths and develop groups with diverse abilities. (W-E)

❑ After creating groupings, the teacher and/or learners assess the balance of the boat by looking for unique qualities or strengths each individual can bring to the group. (W-E-R)

❑ Learners provide procedural feedback to one another, naming what is going well and the effect this has on the group. Learners can also name productive struggles, as well as possibilities for navigating these or alternative ways of proceeding as a group. (W-E-R)

❑ After balancing the boat and engaging in one or more collaborations, learners reflect on the dynamics so they can gain an understanding of and appreciation for working with diverse learners. (R)

COLLABORATIVE CULTURE MOVE 2: COLLABORATIVE CLASSROOM NORMS

Using guided inquiry through cognitive apprenticeship, learners learn how to help one another do different kinds of work, just like experts apprentice one another to the next step or through a **zone of proximal development** in a community of practice. In the area of collaboration, learners need to (1) know the expectations for positive group behavior, (2) receive feedback about their practice with these expectations, and (3) be supported and held accountable for progressing toward these expectations.

Learners will be most successful when they are involved in the process of naming and creating these norms for classroom collaboration. This process makes learners conscious of the critical standards for collaboration and challenges them to figure out how they will meet these standards. We like to say, "If you can name it, you can claim it." The process of setting norms also gives learners voice in and ownership of the expectations, thus providing motivation to meet the critical standards.

One method of generating classroom norms is to use a Y-chart and have learners brainstorm what a good group looks like, sounds like, and feels like and then create classroom posters detailing the standards for good behavior articulated by learners (Wilhelm, Wilhelm, & Boas, 2009). Learners could do this in a literal fashion, naming specific skills needed for collaboration (looks like: sharing materials; sounds like: responding to others' ideas; feels like: everyone is valued), or they could be asked to create metaphors for each of the three components, as shown in Figure 6.1.

Another method for collaboratively creating norms is to have learners reflect on their participation in teams. It can be beneficial for learners to reflect on both effective

■ FIGURE 6.1: EXAMPLE OF GROUP BRAINSTORM Y-CHART

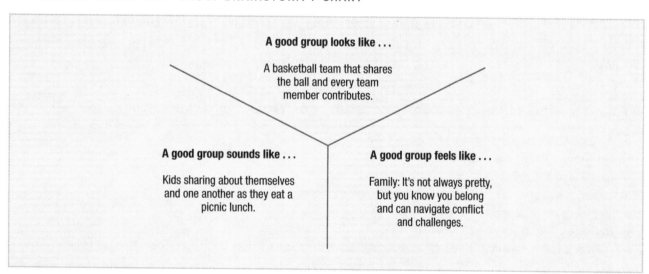

(Continued)

and ineffective teams because we often learn as much or more from the nonexamples as we do from the examples. Following is a step-by-step approach to creating norms this way:

1. Ask learners to reflect on effective and ineffective teams, calling to mind specific examples of teams in which they have participated and naming the characteristics of these teams.

2. After learners reflect on these experiences, have them write the qualities of effective teams on notecards, recording one quality on each card.

3. Ask learners to share out about their experiences and the qualities they noted in table groups. (For younger learners, you might show a cartoon or another video example of an effective or ineffective team and then think together about the qualities of these teams, creating a class anchor chart.) As learners share, the group should look for commonalities and work to create a short list of norms (five or fewer). This often requires learners to synthesize as they create norms that represent the ideas of several group members.

4. Small groups then share out with the class, consider all ideas, and synthesize to form collaborative norms for the whole group.

Following the norm creation process, learners should have an opportunity to brainstorm and rehearse how to meet the norms before there is an expectation to embody them on a daily basis. Specifically, learners should consider the success criteria, "What will it look like, sound like, and feel like when I (and others) meet this norm?" Learners might do this by creating role-play examples and nonexamples of the norms, creating classroom posters of the norms, considering strategies for meeting each norm, or creating memes to display about how to meet the norms (see the meme-making examples in Chapter 9). Having a visual display in the room keeps the norms present and allows learners to hold themselves and one another accountable to them throughout the year (see Figure 6.2).

■ FIGURE 6.2: NORMS FOR CLASSROOM DISCUSSION, MODIFIED FROM JACKIE'S FOURTH-GRADE CLASS

- ❖ Be respectful to others, and listen to what they are saying.
- ❖ Listen to and build on other people's ideas.
- ❖ Offer your own ideas without interrupting or blurting out.
- ❖ It's okay to disagree nicely. Be sure to disagree with ideas, not people.
- ❖ When other people need help, lend them a hand.
- ❖ Ask for help if you need it.
- ❖ Make topics seem interesting. If you don't know enough information about it, be sure to do your homework! You can look for ideas and evidence to support your opinion. Then, you're thinking. Then, you can be sure.
- ❖ Keep talk on-task!

Checklist for Creating Your Own Collaborative Classroom Norms

❏ The teacher envisions what success looks like for a collaborative class community. (E)

❏ The teacher uses knowledge of the learners or polls the class to determine the appropriate amount of scaffolding to provide learners. (M)

❏ Learners activate prior knowledge of effective and ineffective teams to support them in brainstorming possible norms. (P)

❏ Learners understand the purpose behind establishing and maintaining classroom norms and take ownership of the process. (O)

❏ Learners have opportunities to brainstorm possible norms for this context individually, in small groups, and as a whole class. (W)

❏ Through discussion and negotiation, learners agree on the best norms to represent the group and are able to justify these norms. (W-E)

❏ Learners consider success criteria for each norm: "What will this norm look like in action?" "What kinds of ways might I engage to fulfill this norm?" (W)

❏ Learners make a formal/ritual commitment to themselves and to their classmates to honor the norms ("I do solemnly swear . . ." or sign a short contract, etc.). (W)

❏ The norms are clearly displayed in the classroom as a reminder, reference, and accountability measure for learners. (E-R)

❏ Learners have opportunities to review and revise the norms over time. (R)

❏ Learners engage in reflection on how they are doing and share feedback with one another to help better meet the norms. (R)

COLLABORATIVE CULTURE MOVE 3: PEOPLE BINGO

People bingo is a fantastic strategy to use when learners are first getting to know one another. Learners mingle, meet and greet, and find out new information about their classmates. The ultimate goal is to find classmates in the room who fit each of the

(Continued)

(Continued)

categories on a bingo board (see Figure 6.3). The first person to complete the bingo board by filling in each square with a different person's name yells, "Bingo!" This is both a collaborative activity and a friendly competition that encourages learners to meet and learn about as many classmates as possible in a short amount of time. After learners mingle and complete their boards, you can have them share about whom they met and what they learned about their classmates.

■ **FIGURE 6.3: MEET AND GREET: PEOPLE BINGO**

Objectives: Meet some new people. Make connections. Score a "Bingo"!

Directions: Have each person sign his or her name in the appropriate box. Record any information that will help you share about this person later in our discussion. For example, for "Enjoys similar music," record what type of music you enjoy.

Has the same birthday month	Has an interesting pet	You knew before this week	Enjoys similar music	Likes pizza
Plays a sport	Has read the same book	Knows what they want to be when they grow up	Has a unique fear	Was born in a different state
Has traveled outside the country	Enjoys a similar hobby	Ice cream is their favorite dessert	Likes math	Plays a musical instrument
Is an only child (no brothers or sisters)	Can teach you a new skill	Lives in a two-story house	Doesn't like chocolate	Wants to be a scientist
Prefers playing outside to inside	Went to a summer camp	Can speak another language	Has more than three siblings	Has met someone famous

When creating the bingo board, it is important to develop squares that will bring out interesting information and capitalize on the variety of experiences and cultural funds of knowledge in the room. This way, learners are able to gain knowledge about their classmates and the unique skills, interests, and experiences they bring to the larger group. This often helps build community and also helps learners select appropriate groups, gain insights about their peers they may not have otherwise uncovered, and recognize individuals who have experiences to draw from when specific units of study occur later in the year.

VARIATION: LEARNING ABOUT A TOPIC OF INQUIRY

Are you further into the year and already have a strong collaborative culture established? If so, you might use a variation of this activity by placing a range of ideas, categories, or questions related to an inquiry topic of study in each square of the bingo board. Then, you can use this as a frontloading activity to accomplish multiple goals: (1) an opportunity for learners to continue to reinforce the established classroom culture and discover strengths in others, (2) a pre-assessment to see what learners already know and have experienced as related to the inquiry, and (3) a way for learners to activate their background knowledge about the inquiry topic and socially construct new knowledge through interactions with others who have experiences connecting to the inquiry.

An example of this variation is available for download on our companion website, **resources.corwin.com/EMPOWER-elementary**.

Checklist for Creating Your Own People Bingo

❏ The bingo board allows learners to meet and learn unique things about as many of their peers (and perhaps as much about the topic of inquiry) as possible in a short time span. (E-M)

❏ The experiences or questions prompt dialogue about meaningful topics, such as a learner's strengths, challenges, cultural resources, and areas of background knowledge. (P)

❏ Learners understand that the purpose of people bingo is to build community by learning about the individuals within it, and asking follow-up questions as they engage in conversation with their peers in order to dive deeper. (O-W)

❏ Learners monitor and record what they learn and from whom. (*Note:* This is a great way to teach basic citation. Learners may use a sentence stem such as "I learned _____ from _____." In addition to providing credit to the source, this also helps learners know who to go to for more information about a specific topic.) Learners can be asked to cite each other's thinking and experience in future conversations and composing activities. (W)

❏ Following the activity, learners share out about their learning in small-group or whole-group discussion, showcasing what they learned and appreciate about their classmates and how they might use this knowledge or their classmates as learning resources in the future. (W-E-R)

❏ Learners recognize the benefit of using community resources and asking questions of community members and seek out future opportunities to do so. (E-R)

COLLABORATIVE CULTURE MOVE 4: PROCEDURAL FEEDBACK

Another community-building activity that develops a collaborative and inquiry-based culture is procedural feedback (also known as causal or descriptive feedback) (see Johnston, 2011; Wilhelm Douglas, & Fry 2014). Procedural feedback is the kind of quality feedback that actually teaches and informs future action. It is the kind of feedback we all want to give and receive in the real world. It's the type of feedback great teachers give their learners throughout the day when they confer with individuals; interact in small groups; or provide feedback to the entire class about their insights, discussions, or behavior. It's also the type of feedback we want to teach our learners to offer to their peers—and ultimately to themselves. This kind of feedback can be shared verbally or in writing and is helpful during or after almost any learning or performance situation (such as when solving a multistep math problem, engaging in a classroom discussion, or peer reviewing a piece of writing). Learners can also jointly create procedural feedback to an author they are reading or to an expert they view on a YouTube video.

The procedural-feedback protocol focuses on providing meaningful feedback that names the power moves made by a reader, writer, or problem solver; names the meaning or impact of these moves; and then explores potential ways forward. This move starts with the teacher modeling it and increases in effectiveness when it's used peer to peer and when one can use it to monitor and guide one's own activity through feedback to the self. Ideally, learners also have opportunities to share this type of feedback with their teachers in order to improve instruction!

This process has multiple benefits: (1) Learners provide objective or nonjudgmental feedback based on observable data (to peers, authors, and themselves); (2) learners develop a deeper understanding and conscious competence of the moves others and they make as readers, composers, and performers, as well as the reasons they make these moves; and (3) learners express a growth mindset and generate specific ideas about ways forward in a process of continuous improvement. Creating an atmosphere where giving and receiving procedural feedback is the norm also strengthens the community because learners develop empathy for one another; celebrate and help refine each other's work; examine problems; respectfully discuss solutions together; and, ultimately, work to help every member improve, all of which support learners in becoming democratic citizens who make meaningful contributions to our world.

Providing procedural feedback requires two steps to name the cause–effect relationship:

1. Begin with a description of what the reader, composer, performer, or problem solver has done (a move or strategy they used: *The way you . . .*).

2. Describe the effect or impact of that action (attribute the accomplishment to effort, strategy use, or a type of thinking: *had the effect of . . .*).

Be sure to encourage learners to first focus on strengths-based feedback because this allows them to capitalize on these strengths in order to tackle areas of growth.

You'll also want to teach learners how to use procedural *feedforward* to challenge themselves and their peers to move to the next level of understanding or performance. Procedural feedforward focuses on possibilities and potential. In this case, the feedback friend is responsible for providing concrete suggestions or questions for forward movement, as well as the effects these moves might have. All feedback should express a cause-and-effect relationship, but this time, it addresses what could be. Learners develop expertise by naming, emulating, and trying out for themselves the moves of expert readers, composers, problem solvers, and so on.

Using an "I wonder" statement or question to prompt this thinking allows for author's prerogative—the ultimate authority and decision is in the hands of the reader, composer, or problem solver. At the same time, the feedback provides specific possibilities, direction, and potential for the author or problem solver to consider. The author or problem solver is then responsible for accepting, adapting, or rejecting the suggestion and should be able to justify his or her choices. Figure 6.4 provides useful sentence stems young learners can use to deliver procedural feedback and feedforward.

An extension of this strategy can be found in the online resources.

■FIGURE 6.4: PROCEDURAL FEEDBACK SCAFFOLDS

Sentence stems for providing procedural feedback

- The way you . . . led me to . . . because . . .
- The move you made to . . . resulted in . . . /should lead to . . . /exhibited the principle of . . . because . . .
- This quote/excerpt/move . . . made me think/consider/rethink . . . because . . .

Sentence stems for providing procedural feedforward

- I wonder what would happen if . . . (you made this specific move or tried this strategy) because . . . (describe the meaning and effect that you think might accrue from this move, include cause).
- If you did this . . . it might lead to/result in/help the author to . . . because . . .
- What move could you make to . . . (describe desired effect)?

Some examples of procedural feedback

- **When you** reread the previous paragraph and thought aloud about what it meant to you, **it had the effect of** deepening our understanding about a complex section of the text.
- **The way you** used dialogue between the two main characters in your story **helped me to** understand their relationship **because** you showed rather than told me how hard it was for them to agree on anything.
- (Teacher coaching) **The move you made to** invite Emily into the conversation **resulted in** her feeling comfortable to share her idea and encouraged everyone in the group to share. **I wonder what would happen if** you did this same activity in small groups **because** it might allow more learners to actively engage and contribute ideas.

(Continued)

PLC Connection

Feedback focused on procedure, rather than the person, avoids feedback triggers. This increases the likelihood that the feedback will be well received. We recommend that administrators, instructional coaches, and lead teachers model procedural feedback in their interactions with teachers and others in order to encourage teachers to practice procedural feedback with one another to both celebrate successes and consider opportunities in staff meetings, following classroom observations, and so forth. In our own teacher research, we have found that procedural feedback creates a caring sense of teamwork instead of a sense of evaluation and judgment.

(Continued)

Checklist for Creating Your Own Procedural Feedback

❑ The teacher plans for authentic opportunities for learners to practice procedural feedback and determines when learners are ready to share their feedback with peers, perhaps through a simple formative assessment. (E-M)

❑ The teacher models procedural feedback for learners when reviewing expert work (e.g., in a shared reading, in a YouTube video) in student conferences and when responding to student work. (P-O-W)

❑ Learners have access to scaffolds, such as sentence stems, to help them provide quality procedural feedback. (W)

❑ Learners provide procedural feedback and feedforward that is objective/ nonjudgmental and is meant to recognize effort, strategy use, and potential future moves to propel learning to the next level. (W-E)

❑ Learners have multiple opportunities to practice providing procedural feedback over time. (W-E)

❑ Procedural feedback helps both responder and respondent name the moves a real expert makes and explain how these moves work and the meaning and effects of these moves. (W-E-R)

❑ The teacher (and perhaps eventually a peer) provides feedback on the learner's feedback. (E)

❑ Learners eventually provide procedural feedback and feedforward to their own work. (E-R)

❑ Learners have consistent opportunities to reflect on feedback received and given and use reflections to make decisions about future practice. (E-R)

POWERFUL PLANNING:
CREATING A STRONG COMMUNITY OF LEARNERS

By using the methods described in this chapter, we *prime*, *orient*, and apprentice our learners in the necessary skills for creating and growing within a collaborative community. We set the stage for *extending* and *exploring* these skills throughout the year and throughout learners' lives.

We hope this chapter provided a lens to celebrate your current classroom culture, as well as to consider ideas for enhancement. Establishing, growing, and maintaining a strong culture is one of the most important components of any successful learning environment, and we encourage you to experiment with some of these culture-building strategies at the beginning of and throughout the year to create a space where all of your learners will feel included and be successful.

In this increasingly diverse, innovative, and collaborative world, our learners will need skills to work with new people, to discover new ideas and ways of thinking, to solve complex problems, and to adapt to ever-changing needs and environments. These skills do not come naturally. Like any academic skill, we must teach and cultivate collaboration over time and apprentice our learners into developing rewarding and productive personal and professional relationships.

Guiding Questions When Designing Activities to Prime Community

- What is my specific community- and culture-building purpose for this lesson, and how does this strategy help fulfill that purpose? (E-M)

- How will this strategy build and grow the community in my classroom? (E-M)

- How will I build on learners' prior experiences and help them develop and enact a vision for what a strong collaborative community looks like, sounds like, and feels like? (P-O)

- How will I model, mentor, and monitor learners to collaborate successfully and develop reciprocal responsibility and ownership in their collaborations? (W)

- What skills will this strategy assist learners in developing that will help them be more successful in collaborations in the future, and how will I support my learners in naming these skills and transferring them to novel contexts? (W-E)

- How will this strategy model real-world collaboration and assist learners in recognizing moves for establishing a collaborative culture in future schooling, careers, and life situations? (W-E-R)

- How will this strategy promote deep conceptual and procedural learning? (E-R)

- How will the strategy encourage learners to reflect on effective collaboration and the moves they can make to promote it now and in the future? (R)

Lesson: Balancing the Boat

Unit: How do I become an expert?

ENVISION the destination
(Where are learners going, and why?)

GOAL *What kind of thinking is targeted?*	EVIDENCE *What product(s) will serve as proof of learning?*	MEASURES OF SUCCESS *What's the standard and quality-assurance tool?*	STAKES *Why will learners buy in?* *What's the why behind the learning?*
✓ Empathizing ✓ Self-assessing/ reflecting	✓ Constructed (discrete task, long/short response, graphic organizer)	✓ **Checklist**: Assess if product contains essential characteristics/ features.	Use ESSENCE as a guide for buy-in. Your lesson should have one or more of the following: ✓ ES: Emotional spark/salience (i.e., relevance) ✓ SE: Social engagement (i.e., collaboration) ✓ N: Novelty (i.e., new concepts and skills) ✓ CE: Critical/creative exploration opportunities
• Create effective groupings with diverse skills and abilities represented. • Capitalize on the strengths of each individual, and honor all learners in the room.	1. Learner groupings represent the diversity of the classroom. 2. Learners can name personal strengths and strengths in others and use the combination of these strengths to problem-solve and complete assigned tasks. 3. Learners acknowledge and express appreciation of each other's resources and strengths.	☐ Learners share personal strengths and recognize strengths in their peers. ☐ An individual's strengths are used to group learners with diverse abilities. ☐ After creating groupings, the teacher and/or learner assesses how well the boat is balanced by looking for unique qualities each individual can bring to the group.	**ES:** Learners acknowledge personal strengths and strengths in classmates. Learners develop awareness, empathy, and respect for one another by honoring personalities, perspectives, and contributions of group members. **SE:** Learners establish a diverse group who will collaborate and engage in collective problem solving. **N:** Learners will gain insights about and partner with individuals they may not have previously known or experienced. **CE:** Learners will consider diverse perspectives and capitalize on strengths of classmates.

MAP out the path to expertise/mastery
(How would an expert deconstruct and approach this task, step by step?)

TWITTER SUMMARY (3 bullets max)	MENTAL MODELS, PROCESS GUIDES, AND HEURISTICS	A MODEL OF GOOD WORK LOOKS LIKE . . .	DIFFERENTIATION AND LAYERING
Learners recognize strengths in one another to develop a diverse and balanced group that can "stay afloat" and collaboratively tackle challenging and novel tasks by using diverse perspectives, strengths, and *distributed expertise* from all members of the group.	• Model of procedural feedback: Name strengths and moves and their meaning and effects. This honors multiple perspectives and diverse strengths that lead to effective problem solving and synergy. • Ways to map through regression: Before tackling a task, I should consider what types of skills and strengths I need to complete it. An awareness of my own strengths and the strengths of my peers situates me to be deliberate about who I work with; how I honor, access, and leverage the strengths of others; and how each of these will affect the outcome of my efforts. • Leveraging diversity: Problem solving and learning are socially constructed, and a group that has diverse strengths and weaknesses equips me to be more flexible and responsive to a complex situation or task.	Groupings of learners with diverse strengths who support and work well with one another. Learners actively solicit each other's opinions and ideas. Learners acknowledge the contributions of each other and how to make use of these contributions.	• Assuring learners they have valuable strengths to share and helping learners name their strengths, possibly through reflective activities or self-assessments. • Providing a model of a balanced-boat grouping and thinking aloud about its creation and significance. • Guiding the initial balancing-the-boat exercise by categorizing strengths and helping learners develop well-balanced teams. • Using reflective questions to help learners evaluate the effectiveness and diversity of their grouping.

POWER through your lesson
(What is the sequence of initial major must-make instructional moves?)

	PRIME	ORIENT	WALK THROUGH (and check for understanding)	EXTEND AND EXPLORE	REFLECT
Leader	SHARE a story about a time you worked in an effective and diverse group. Explain what you learned from this experience and what you gained by working with others who were different from you. You may highlight such ideas as developing respect for different opinions, learning new ideas from others, and utilizing each other's strengths to be successful. RECORD the benefits of working in effective groups on an anchor chart as you and the learners share stories of previous collaborative experiences.	FRAME today's lesson: SHARE your expectations for collaborative learning, including, but not limited to, these: All learners will, (1) show respect for one another, (2) name and honor the strengths and resources of peers, and (3) actively engage in the learning experience. SHARE with learners that sometimes in this classroom (and in life), they will have the opportunity to select their own partners and teams, while other times, partners and teams will be assigned. EXPLAIN to learners that when they have the opportunity to select their own groups, they should not simply choose their friends, but rather, they should consider the strengths of those around them and who may best complement the current group members. INTRODUCE the strategy of balancing the boat, and explain how this strategy can help learners get to know their peers and establish effective groups with diverse skills who can balance one another and keep the group afloat even in challenging conditions. SUPPORT learners in naming their personal strengths through models and modeling.	EXPLAIN to learners that they will introduce themselves by sharing one of their strengths for the purpose of creating effective groupings. MODEL this first by saying, "Hi, I'm _____" (i.e., "Hi, I'm creative"). ENGAGE in introductions, and record their names and strengths on a whiteboard, SMART board, or document camera for the whole class to see. DISCUSS the different strengths of learners in the classroom, and honor the diversity of your learners. Explain how when we work together, we can capitalize on each other's strengths and have others help us in areas where we are not as strong. CONSIDER the task(s) learners will engage in with these groups, and determine the appropriate number of learners for the group. A good number of group members is usually three to five. CREATE diverse groups by balancing the strengths presented. Begin by naming categories of strengths and then developing groupings that represent each category (or as many of the categories as possible). REGROUP into teams based on the created groups.	DELIBERATE PRACTICE/ ARTICULATE CONSCIOUS AWARENESS: Ask learners to consider when and how they might work to balance the boat in groups in the future. Have learners make a list of times in their life when they have worked in groups in the past as well as when they might work in groups in the future. Then, ask learners to select one of these specific situations and consider the value of having diverse interests, perspectives, and strengths in the group.	Lead a whole-class discussion about this strategy of balancing the boat. Ask learners how they felt about using this strategy to form their groups today and how they might use this strategy to inform their grouping decisions in the future. Ask learners, "What will you look for in future group partners? Why?" Conclude the lesson by sharing with learners that they will be working in these groups for some activities but not all activities over the next couple weeks. Encourage learners to consider the strengths different group members bring to the group during these activities.
Learner	REFLECT on a time you worked in a group. This could be a positive or a negative experience because we can learn a great deal through both examples and non-examples. Consider what worked well and what was challenging. NOTICE: As peers share their experiences, look for commonalities and answer the question, "What can we gain from working in diverse groups?"	CHECK FOR UNDERSTANDING: REPHRASE the goal of the balancing-the-boat strategy. REFLECT on the guiding question, "How do we create an effective and balanced group?" CONSIDER what skills and strengths you can bring to the group, and record one or two of your biggest personal strengths to share with the class in today's lesson.	GUIDED PRACTICE: Consider the upcoming collaborative lesson, and discuss how your personal strengths might benefit the group in this particular activity, and also consider an area where you might need help or support. DIFFERENTIATE: Monitor the room as learners engage in discussion and provide support via prompting and questioning as necessary. RECORD these ideas in a designated area, so all learners are aware of and can benefit from this knowledge.		HOMEWORK EXTENSION: Have learners complete a self-assessment after they engage in a collaborative activity with their group to evaluate how well their group worked together, as well as the roles each person played in the group. Learners may use this assessment to set goals for how they will work with their group in the future. Learners may set individual and group goals.

online resources 🔎 For a blank version of this canvas and additional moves at each level, see the more articulated lesson plan online: **resources.corwin.com/EMPOWER-elementary**

Chapter 7

PRIMING AND ORIENTING LEARNERS THROUGH ESSENTIAL QUESTIONS

> **ESSENTIAL QUESTION**
> What types of questions effectively frame and promote learning?

In elementary school, Chris tried to fill his time with games of touch football, capturing grasshoppers, and reading books about World War II prison escapes. Whenever school interrupted those activities, he responded to teachers with the refrain, "Why do we need to learn about this?" As a teacher, Chris anticipated the same question being posed to him, and he wanted to have a response at the ready. This response took the form of an essential question that engages learners, establishes a clear purpose for a unit of instruction, and helps learners apply and transfer what they learn right now to their own lives and to their future lives beyond school.

See
Lesson Plan Canvas
on page 124

It's powerful to frame instruction through the lens of open-ended questions because the implicit purpose of any challenge is to formulate a potential answer or solution. Essential questions invite learners to explore the concepts and tools experts use in their fields and extend their own thinking, rather than assume someone else's opinions or thoughts. Looking at the world through the questioning lens opens learners up to new ideas and perspectives; cultivates social imagination; builds empathy; and allows all of us (at whatever age) to determine what is most internally persuasive, compelling, and useful—and to know why.

PLANNING FOR ORIENTING LEARNERS THROUGH ESSENTIAL QUESTIONS

How do essential questions differ from any other type of question in a unit of study? First and foremost, they are interesting to a diverse audience because they should engage everyone in the class, including the teacher. While your learners may be similar in age, they need something generative to *prime* and activate their existing background knowledge, interests, and perspectives.

A way to test whether or not an essential question meets the priming threshold is the *8–80 rule*. Pose your essential question to someone who is eight years old, or thereabouts, and then pose it to an eighty year old, or somewhere in that neighborhood, and for good measure, pose it to someone between those age groups. If all of these parties find the question worth considering, your essential question has passed the first litmus test. Take, for example, potential essential questions in our throughline unit: *How do I become an expert?* and *What do experts do?* Both an eight year old and an eighty year old possess and are probably pursuing expertise in *something* and will bring to the table insights about either question.

The next criterion is the *search engine test*. In addition to being of interest to a wide variety of people, the essential question should be something experts ponder. If experts care about it today, this ensures there is an already existing body of knowledge you can rely upon as touchstones in your instructional *map*. Run your essential question through a search engine, such as Google, and look for two patterns in your results:

1. **Relevance:** Experts are trying to answer this question right now, or they have done so in the recent past.

2. **Authentic inquiry:** There is not a single, clear, correct answer that can be found quickly online. Inquiry is not about finding information but, instead, requires seeing patterns, creating knowledge, and staking positions about debatable issues.

Finally, the essential question provides the purpose for content-driven tasks. Important ideas and skills with a clear answer are framed as **guiding questions**, which fall under the overarching umbrella of the essential question and can be considered subquestions of the essential question. Sometimes, guiding and essential questions are used interchangeably because they're so closely related. We differentiate them because an essential question *primes* the interest of learners via its generative nature; guiding questions *orient* the learner to the things he or she needs to learn, both conceptually and strategically, to address the essential question.

One way to think about the relationship between essential and guiding questions is as the hub and spokes of a bicycle wheel (see Figure 7.1). The essential question is the hub of the wheel: Everything is connected to it, and it provides the focus and purpose that move learners through the unit. The guiding questions are the spokes that connect to the hub: There are many of them, they are narrower in nature, they have a distinct start and end, and they support the essential question. For example, an essential question in math could be "How do I know which mathematical operation to use?" The guiding questions might be "What's the most efficient way to add integers? What's the least efficient way to subtract integers? What are mathematical models to represent addition and subtraction?" Guiding questions often require *walk-throughs* because they represent new, more expert understandings that are necessary to address the essential question.

The bicycle wheel metaphor illustrates another important criterion of essential questions: The answers change and evolve as you learn more about the topic, *priming* the evolving interests of your learners throughout the unit. As learners answer each guiding question and deepen their knowledge about a subject, their perspective on the essential question will likely change—or, if nothing else, their justification for keeping their position the same will grow stronger. This generative quality of essential questions abets the *reflection* process when we draw the attention of our learners to how their answers evolve over time. These changes in understanding are evidence of learning. In fact, if understandings do not fundamentally change (e.g., by being revised or deepened, or becoming more justified and structured), then our teaching is not transformational.

■ FIGURE 7.1: VISUAL OF ESSENTIAL/GUIDING QUESTION HUB AND SPOKES

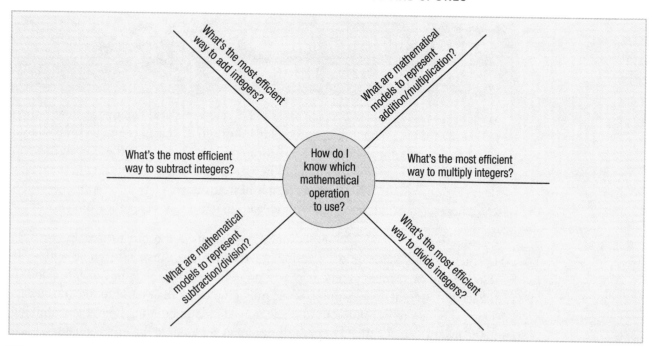

Considerations for Designing Essential Questions

❑ The essential question aligns with the purposes and goals of the unit. (E)

❑ The essential question provides both focus and latitude for the learning that will occur. The essential question engages learners, and it will require them to develop new capacities that reflect real world expertise. (M)

❑ Learners buy into the essential question, the primary focus of the learning, seeing it as connected to them and their concerns, and see the purpose for and future applications of this learning. (P-O)

❑ Pursuing the essential question will help apprentice learners into greater expertise with conceptual and strategic threshold learning goals. (P-O-W)

❑ The essential question motivates learners to navigate the resources, assigned tasks, and culminating project and helps learners form connections with prior knowledge and new knowledge. (P-O-W-E)

(Continued)

(Continued)

❑ Learners appreciate how essential questions frame and drive learning and learn how to begin asking their own. (W-E)

❑ Learners have multiple opportunities to reflect on the essential question and to explore how their learning and ideas changed, confirmed, or grew over time. (E-R)

ESSENTIAL QUESTION MOVE 1: ESSENTIAL QUESTION TRACKING

We have all been guilty of crafting an essential question, writing it on the board when we launch the unit, and failing to regularly return to it. Teachers and learners should revisit the essential question every day throughout the course of the unit in order to connect their new learning with prior knowledge, to focus learning, and to track how their learning grows. This routine establishes curricular coherence—when learners know how today builds on yesterday and leads to tomorrow, deeper learning occurs.

One method for tracking essential questions is concentric circles (see Figure 7.2). Learners record the essential question in the smallest, innermost circle and write responses in each subsequent circle over time. For example, learners may respond in the second circle at the beginning of the unit, employing their background knowledge. Then, they can reflect in the third circle, rereading and building upon their thinking in the first two circles after a week of study or a major focus of the unit concludes. Each time learners do this, they have an opportunity to name their changes in understanding and to *extend* their learning because each response connects their thinking from lesson-level guiding questions to the big picture, the essential question for the whole unit.

■ FIGURE 7.2: EQ TRACKING WITH CONCENTRIC CIRCLES

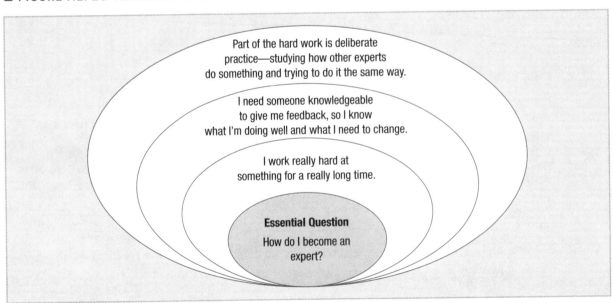

After another designated time frame, learners respond in the fourth circle, and their varied responses over time underscore how there is not one simple answer to complicated questions. The circles grow larger as learners' knowledge expands. Of course, limitless numbers of circles can be added. At the conclusion of the unit, learners read all of their responses, looking for trends and recording observations about how and why their thinking shifted over time. Additionally, learners should consider what experiences and ideas changed or reinforced understanding. When learners review the evolution of their responses, this *reflection* develops an awareness of the impact of new ideas and experiences on their thinking.

Checklist for Creating Your Own EQ Tracking

❑ The teacher carefully crafts a quality essential question for the unit of instruction and intentionally plans how it will be introduced to learners. (E-M)

❑ Learners engage with the essential question over time in a variety of ways, including, but not limited to, reading, writing/composing, discussions, problem solving, and interactive activities such as drama. (P-O-W)

❑ Learners' responses to the essential question grow over time as they integrate new evolving understandings and make connections to the world beyond school. (W-E-R)

❑ Learners reflect on their previous thinking each time they revisit the essential question tracking sheet/visual, and they use this to look forward and to inform thinking about their culminating project. (O-W-E-R)

ESSENTIAL QUESTION MOVE 2: TWENTY QUESTIONS

Essential questions can be deceptive: Their brevity might lead one to believe that they're easy to write. We wish that were the case. The remaining strategies in this chapter scaffold the creation of quality essential questions.

In this second strategy, called *twenty questions*, we advocate for generating essential questions by identifying a multitude of possibilities and writing many drafts. It's always

(Continued)

easier to "braindump" questions on paper than to try to craft a perfect essential question right off the bat. After composing multiple drafts of potential essential questions, combine, revise, and polish the results into an overarching question or two that motivates and engages all learners.

The strategy itself is relatively simple, and we have outlined it in a few basic steps:

1. On a blank piece of paper, write the numbers 1 to 20, and aim to compose this many questions. Another approach is to set a timer for five to ten minutes and write as many question drafts as possible during this time frame. Before you start the timer, write a central standard or focus for the unit at the top of the page to keep you grounded as you brainstorm.

2. As you write, turn off your internal editor and compose with the understanding that a few of the questions will be dreadful and some will be mediocre but also with the conviction that some will be decent and, if you're lucky, a few will be strong. (If this doesn't happen, though, know you aren't alone.)

3. Next, identify the most promising questions from your list. Remember that questions should be student-facing, immediately engaging to learners, and require the development of more expert ways of knowing, doing, and thinking.

4. Now, revise these questions into one or two that best align with your instructional goals. You can do this by selecting one and focusing on word choice or by putting together the pieces of several questions to create a solid one—or maybe even a truly awe-inspiring one!

Example: Essential Question Brainstorming

Questions for a science unit when the content focus is on the solar system and outer space:

1. How big is the solar system?
2. Where is Earth in relation to everything else in space?
3. Is there life on other planets?
4. Why do the other planets, galaxies, or multiverses matter to us?
5. What would happen if Earth was the only planet in the solar system?
6. How did we discover the planets in our solar system?
7. How are we exploring space?
8. Have we found all the planets in our solar system? And how do we know?
9. <u>Should we explore the other planets in our solar system?</u>

10. Is it possible to explore the other planets in our solar system?

11. What do we know about the other planets in our solar system?

12. What's the order of the planets from the sun?

13. How big is Earth in relation to the other planets in the solar system?

14. What does it take to become an astronaut?

15. Why do people become astronauts?

16. Should we continue to have a space program in the United States? Do all countries have a space program?

17. Why have humans always been so interested in space?

18. What if the government stopped supporting space exploration?

19. How will learning about the planets and stars help me in everyday life?

20. How are stars born? How do they die?

We underlined the most promising questions because they are interesting to students, require expertise to address, and move beyond information to deep transformational understandings: 9, 16, 17, and 19. Once you're comfortable with this process, share your thinking aloud with learners, to highlight the qualities you're looking for in an essential question. Typically, we craft essential questions for learners early in the school year; however, we quickly induct them into the process of composing them. Another option is to ask learners to vote for the questions they believe are the most promising and to explain why they think so. This apprentices them into the process of creating their own. Invite learners into the revision process as you refine the question you will use for a unit. Involving learners early on and throughout the unit is helpful because it increases their investment in the questions and models an authentic writing process.

Example: Essential Question Refinement

After several revisions and some feedback, we came up with the following potential essential questions for our study of space based on our twenty-questions brainstorming process:

- How does space exploration influence life on Earth?

- To what extent should the United States support space exploration?

- What should be our purpose and responsibility in space exploration?

- What are the limitations of human space exploration?

Note: These will likely be refined or changed year after year as we consider the overall goals of our unit of study, our diverse learners and their needs, and the feedback we receive from our learners. Also, various guiding questions will be added to help learners develop the conceptual and strategic knowledge that is needed to address the essential question.

(Continued)

(Continued)

Because it would take too much time to respond to all of these questions, we select one from that list that best aligns with our content objectives and the type of reading, writing, math, and science that we want learners to do in this particular unit. Other questions might become guiding questions (e.g., the third and fourth questions could easily serve as guiding questions for the second one). Several of our draft questions were nonexamples because they were closed-ended, too open-ended, or just not interesting. For example, questions such as 1, 12, and 13 would not lead to engagement, deep learning, and high-road transfer.

Some of the original drafts needed only minor revisions, but these revisions had noticeable impacts. Take the question, "To what extent should the United States support space exploration?" The original draft started partway through that sentence with, "Should the United States . . . ?" Phrased that way, it elicits a "yes" or "no" response. Adding "To what extent . . ." positions learners alongside members of Congress and NASA staff who grapple with this issue every year as it requires careful thought and justification.

Checklist for Creating Your Own Twenty Questions

☐ The teacher rapidly generates a plethora of potential essential questions, making sure not to censor the list during this generation process. (E-M)

☐ Invite colleagues and/or learners to brainstorm questions with the teacher because this often leads to divergent thinking and more ideas from which to draw. (P-O)

☐ Learners share feedback on the essential questions before, during, and after instruction and provide reasons for their evaluations that reflect the purposes of framing inquiry with an essential question in order to move from learning information to learning for expertise and transformation. (W-E-R)

ESSENTIAL QUESTION MOVE 3: INVOLVING LEARNERS IN THE EQ PROCESS

Twenty questions is an open-ended strategy. Following are more structured ways to compose essential questions that include learners in the process. First, model the process of posing questions for learners, as it will apprentice them to create their own. The think-aloud strategies in Chapter 10 illustrate how to leverage that modeling. Afterward, learners try to draft their own essential question for the unit or a guiding question for a personalized or small-group inquiry. The following strategies involve learners in generating essential questions.

THINK LIKE A JOURNALIST

Using a journalist's five Ws and one H questions—*Who? What? Where? When? Why?* and *How?*—provides the groundwork to generate many questions that examine a topic from multiple sides. Revise the initial questions into essential questions using the lenses that follow.

Mathematics can be a challenging area for drafting essential questions because there's a clear right-or-wrong answer to textbook questions. In this example, we'll focus on determining the volume of various shapes and use the questions *Who? What? Where? When? Why?* and *How?*

Example: Essential Questions for Math Volume Unit

Essential Question Brainstorm:

- **Who** discovered how to determine volume?
- Who needs to measure volume as part of their job?
- Who doesn't need to measure volume?
- **What** is volume?
- What are ways to measure volume?
- What is the meaning of *volume*?
- What are the differences between liquid and solid volume?
- **Where** did the concept of volume come from?
- Where is volume important?
- **When** is volume important?
- When will I use volume in my everyday life?
- **Why** do we need to determine volume?
- Why do we use so many different units to measure volume?
- **How** much space do we need?
- How do you determine volume?
- How do we compare volume in different units?
- How can we use knowledge of volume to solve problems or get work done?

Most of these questions do not fit the criteria we shared earlier in the chapter, but the scaffold provides a starting point. Improve these drafts with the following lenses for revision.

(Continued)

(Continued)

QUALITY AND COMPARISON

Using the preceding list of questions about volume, we can add words that address quality and comparison, such as *best, worst, greatest, least, most, easiest, hardest, influential, effective,* and *ineffective.* Here are some revisions to that initial list with quality or comparison in mind:

- What's the best/worst way to determine volume?

- What's the hardest shape for which to determine volume?

- When is volume the most important measurement?

- What's the best way to improve consumer awareness about volume?

Adding a qualifier makes some of those more informational questions like "What's the formula for volume?" more debatable by reframing as "What's the most efficient way to determine volume?" Adding a qualifier also narrows overly open-ended questions. "Where do we use volume measurements?" becomes "Where is determining volume most important, and why?" and "Who invented how to determine volume?" becomes "Who was the most influential mathematician in finding volume?" Qualifiers inject an element of debate to make the learning even more engaging.

IMPACT

Another type of question that relies on "How?" as a starter are those related to impact, which connects a basic question to a more meaningful or important outcome in the world beyond school. Writing questions with this lens in mind specifically addresses "How will I use this in the real world?"

- How does volume affect how we conduct business?

- How does volume influence our decisions?

- How does the unit of measurement affect our perception of volume?

- Why is determining volume important to issues of fairness?

As you can see, considering something like impact forces the reader to consider larger issues of significance, ethics, influence, cause and effect, problem–solution, and the like. These types of connections can be useful in a self-contained elementary classroom because they support a multidisciplinary approach.

APPLICATION

Application questions are similar to those about impact because they consider the use and significance of learning. The key distinction is that application questions suggest learners take action in some way. Such questions provide useful tie-ins to field trips, social action, and service-learning projects. Take these examples:

- What's the best way to teach the concept of volume?

- How should volume be labeled on various products, and why?

- What are the costs and benefits of switching the United States to the metric system?

In order to respond to these types of questions, learners need to know about more than the skill or concept itself. This type of outside connection foregrounds a purpose for learning the skill in the first place.

ETHICS

These questions are similar to application questions; the major difference is that these types of applications have a moral or ethical element to them, such as the following:

- How much should people know about volume and measurement before they purchase a house or other product/service?

- How might switching to a universal measurement affect issues of fairness?

- What, if any, responsibility do restaurants have to inform customers about the volume of their food and drink?

Questions of an ethical or moral nature will likely spark deep engagement and even controversy in your classroom. While you want to be cautious, it's critical for learners to learn how to disagree. Ethical questions, or anything controversial, provide an opportunity for parent and community involvement because people from various sides can share their opinions, listen, and disagree in a civil manner.

ANALOGIES

"How?" questions can lead to formulating analogies, which are a way to connect one field or idea to another. Consider, for example, the following:

- How is volume like descriptive language?

- How is Archimedes's discovery of volume like the invention of Velcro?

- How are formulas for volume like a cookbook?

These analogies connect science and literacy with mathematics, which could build on the prior knowledge of learners, lead them to make cross-curricular connections,

(Continued)

and prepare them for other inquiries taking place at the same time or later in the school year. Constructing analogies also encourages learners to move beyond the informational focus of some questions and makes them transformational by requiring deep learning, judgment, and justification.

WHAT IF . . . ?

Especially in math, an area where answers seem so clear-cut, revising questions to include "What if?" makes them more meaningful. This step requires reconsideration of something learners may take for granted, such as formulas.

- What if humans knew the exact volume of what they consumed each day?

- How would we determine and communicate volume if there were no standard units?

Sometimes these revised questions veer away from the original five Ws and one H list, but this broadens our scope and draws attention to the impact and value of the topic of study. What ifs also encourage learners to think creatively about a situation. This lens is helpful for promoting multiple responses and creativity.

COMMUNITY CONNECTION

Many of these lenses connect the topic of study to the outside world. One way to make a subject more relevant to learners is to connect it with the local community. This can be especially helpful when designing guiding questions that support the unit's essential question. Like the other lenses, this approach promotes multiple responses and transfers beyond the classroom. The following are examples from our community:

- How does the volume of water in the snowpack and river flows affect quality of life in Boise?

- In what ways would listing volume in metric and standard units aid citizen scientists, tourists, immigrants, and refugees in Boise?

- In what ways would teaching metric volume better prepare learners for a global workforce?

Checklist for Involving Learners in the EQ Process

- ❑ The teacher considers the unit as a whole, as well as its specific components and major goals, when crafting possible essential questions. (E-M)

- ❑ The teacher and learners generate and then revise initial question drafts through a new lens, such as ethics, application, and so on. (P-O-W)

□ The teacher and learners apply critical standards (perhaps by using a checklist for quality essential questions) to their questions to inform revisions; essential questions should be open-ended; be debatable; require threshold knowledge to address; and be personally compelling, socially significant, and so forth. (W-E-R)

□ Following the unit, the teacher and learners reflect on the essential question and "the work" it did for learners in the unit; they record these thoughts to inform future iterations of the essential question and unit. (E-R)

ESSENTIAL QUESTION MOVE 4: QUESTIONING CIRCLE

The *questioning circle* (Christenbury & Kelly, 1983) highlights the different resources learners need to draw on in order to respond to an essential question: the text/data, personal experience, and world/disciplinary knowledge. The questioning circle highlights connections between a text, a reader, and the world at large by asking learners to reflect on the text or material being studied, their personal lived experience, their knowledge about the world, and the connections between each and all of these. (See Figure 7.3.)

- **Self (Reader/Learner):** Questions about the personal experience and thinking of the reader, which only she or he can answer. These types of questions elicit background knowledge, interests, and attitudes. Because they are not text dependent, ask these questions before reading as a formative assessment. After reading, return to these questions to highlight how the text affected the thinking or attitudes of the reader.

- **Text (Data):** These types of questions focus on the meaning of the material. They are a means to check for comprehension and encourage learners to make inferences about key sections of the text.

- **World:** These are questions about the wider context, disciplinary knowledge, the life of the author, and related events in the world. They add meaning to the material by situating it in a meaningful context of use and among related themes and ideas. Ask these at any point during the reading because the text could relate to them in so many different ways.

- **Self/Text:** These questions require understanding of the text/data, combined with the reader's experience. There could be more than one justified response because of the focus on the transaction between the text and the reader. These questions encourage readers to articulate how the text connects to their experience.

(Continued)

(Continued)

■ FIGURE 7.3: QUESTIONING CIRCLE GRAPHIC ORGANIZER

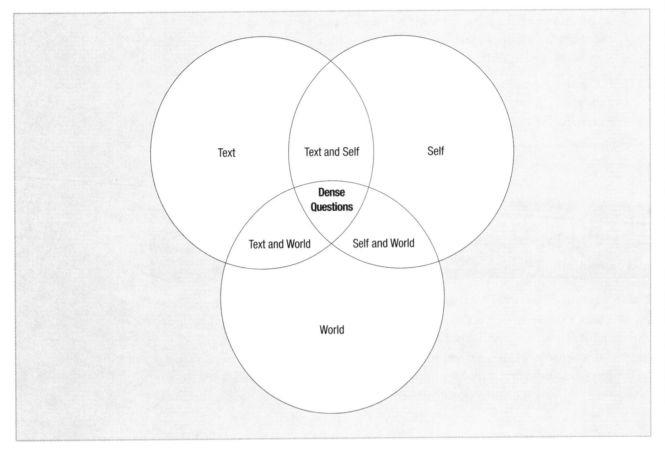

Source: Christenbury and Kelly (1983).

- **Self/World:** These questions orient the learner to a central issue, idea, or theme at play in the world that relates to the inquiry. They activate background knowledge and interest in ideas related to the text.

- **Text/World:** Like self/text questions, these can have more than one answer because the text can connect to more than one event or idea. Text/world questions make the text more meaningful by creating a context for understanding and applying understanding. Identifying connections between the main text and other texts and ideas, issues, and events in the world makes this type of question essential for generalizations about a theme or main idea.

- **Dense/Essential Question:** One of the strengths of this strategy is how it places the essential question at the center of the questioning process. Ask it at any time in the process—early on to activate schema, during the middle to highlight how a text speaks to an issue, and at the end as part of a summative assessment. This question demonstrates that answering an inquiry question and achieving deep understanding require combining personal experience, world knowledge, and the text or data under consideration.

One of the best features of this strategy is the flexibility for sequencing questions. A lesson could start with any section of the questioning circle: the text, learner, or world. Play to the strengths of your learners, and start with questions they can answer confidently. Leverage those responses to build background knowledge they will need to answer subsequent questions (see Figure 7.4). Another strength is that this strategy foregrounds the various kinds and combinations of knowledge that any learner needs to bring to bear to make meaning of a text or data set and to expertly pursue an inquiry.

■ FIGURE 7.4: QUESTIONING CIRCLE FOR "THE STAR-SPANGLED BANNER"

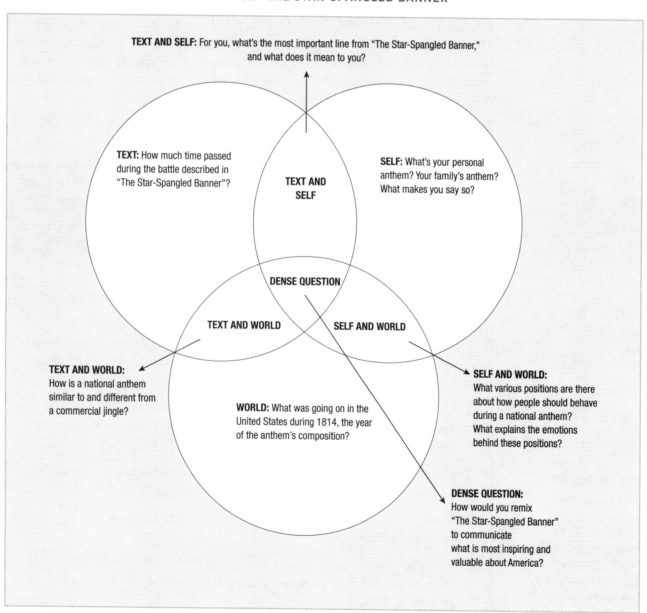

(Continued)

(Continued)

The example graphic organizer represents how and where different types of questions intersect. Posting this in the classroom communicates to learners at a glance the balance of questions they are asked and the connections they are encouraged to make. It also makes it easy to communicate learning targets by showing learners what knowledge resources they will focus on for a particular lesson and exactly how it connects with the essential question.

If you want to narrow the instructional focus, introduce one circle or question type at a time. For example, start with self questions because all learners should be able to respond to these, regardless of reading level. Afterward, teach about text questions. Explicitly teaching these two types prepares learners for self/text questions with simple question types. Familiarity with question types is essential because it communicates to learners what they need to do to formulate an answer. This is another example of apprenticeship into the moves that expert readers make. In order for learners to reach this level of expertise, they need to learn how and when to ask certain types of questions and use the various resources available to them, which always include resources from one's own experience, from the material under study, and from the context of the discipline and world where knowledge is developed and used.

Checklist for Creating Your Own Questioning Circle

- ❑ The teacher carefully crafts and sequences questions to build understanding of the inquiry topic, paying special attention to the entry points most beneficial for his or her learners. (E-M)

- ❑ The questioning circle primes and orients learners to the topics, texts/data, and tasks in the unit and prepares them for increasingly complex questions. (P-O)

- ❑ Questions not involving the text generate engagement through personal connection and establish a larger purpose, context, and applications for learning. (P-O)

- ❑ Questions involving the text require learners to provide evidence from the material to justify the answer or extend the meaning of the text. (W-E)

- ❑ Learners use answers from initial questions to access and address the more complex questions asked later. (W-E)

- ❑ The teachers and learners generate new questions over time and craft and/ or revise the essential question based on the questions asked throughout the process. (E-R)

PLC Connection

Work in leadership or grade-level teams to generate EQs for professional development initiatives, school improvement, or policy making and for common units using ideas from this chapter.

POWERFUL PLANNING: ESSENTIAL QUESTIONS FOR DEEP UNDERSTANDING AND DEMOCRATIC DISCUSSIONS

The strategies in this chapter provide you and your learners with the support to compose essential questions. Mastering this skill (and should we say art?) makes you the captain of your instructional ship, able to involve your learners in *mapping* their own focus and the course to reach it.

Essential questions establish where you want to "drop anchor" for a particular unit of study and the extent to which you want to *explore* and *extend* learning in that area. Using the first strategy in this chapter, essential question tracking, learners can *map* their own progress, and you (and your learners) can assess the degree to which they have explored new territory based on their ability to craft longer and more sophisticated responses throughout the unit. Altogether, this makes for a more purposeful and authentic learning experience because you're *priming* and *orienting* the class for all the adventures ahead. You know your learner population much better than the authors of the best curriculum guides, and learners know their own interests better than anyone. Thus, you and your learners should have the final say on the essential question that guides their learning, as well as on continually updating and revising it.

Give yourself permission to write a "pretty good" essential question or two for your unit. Only after you try one out will you understand its strengths, shortcomings, and future possibilities. Think of any essential question as a prototype that you have permission to revise and improve based on user feedback. Taking the risk to compose original essential questions is worth the effort because it gives you and your learners control over purpose and content, and it leads to high-level engagement. This process is also an apprenticeship into expertise since experts in all fields and expert readers of the newspaper or any other text always frame what they read in terms of big conversational topics and debates worthy of learning about and participating in. This focuses their reading and response and makes the process more purposeful and usable.

Ultimately, considering essential questions is a critical skill for participation in a democracy, one of our ultimate goals of education. The essential question requires learners to consider different viewpoints; teaches them to ask thoughtful questions; and simulates the skills learners will need to know and be able to do in the workplace, in personal relationships, and as citizens. All too often, questions in school have one correct answer. However, as we all know, most of the big disciplinary questions and many of life's questions are not that simple. It's invaluable for learners to practice thinking through challenging, real-world questions in a safe environment, prior to encountering these kinds of questions throughout their lives.

Guiding Questions for Generating or Improving Essential Questions

- What is my central topic of inquiry, and what level of focus should my essential question have to meet the scope of this topic and my instructional goals for developing threshold knowledge? (E-M)

- How will my learners be involved in the creation or revision of the essential question and guiding questions? (M-P-O-W)

- Which strategy will be most effective in helping me and my learners craft the essential question for this unit? (M-P-O-W)

- How will I model, mentor, and monitor learners to participate in the essential question creation and revision process? (P-O-W)

- What questioning skills do I want to help my learners develop, how will I teach these skills, and how will I help them to explore these skills in authentic contexts? (W-E)

- What opportunities will I structure for myself and learners to reflect on the essential question, revisions to it, and the knowledge that develops from pursuing it? (E-R)

Lesson: Essential Question

Unit: How do I become an expert?

ENVISION the destination
(Where are learners going, and why?)

GOAL *What kind of thinking is targeted?*	EVIDENCE *What product(s) will serve as proof of learning?*	MEASURES OF SUCCESS *What's the standard and quality-assurance tool?*	STAKES *Why will learners buy in?* *What's the why behind the learning?*
✓ Explanation/ reasoning ✓ Application of skill/strategy ✓ Self-assessing/ reflecting	✓ Constructed (discrete task, long/short response, graphic organizer)	✓ **Simple:** √–, √, √+ on discrete facts/skills	Use ESSENCE as a guide for buy-in. Your lesson should have one or more of the following: ✓ ES: Emotional spark/salience (i.e., relevance) ✓ SE: Social engagement (i.e., collaboration) ✓ N: Novelty (i.e., new concepts and skills) ✓ CE: Critical/creative exploration opportunities
Engage learners' interest in the unit by exploring the overarching essential question for the unit. Intentionally integrate reflection and discussion about the essential question throughout the unit to build on initial thinking and reflect on the learning that has occurred. Ask learners to monitor and record major changes and deepenings of their understanding regarding the essential question.	1. Learners can name and are conscious of the essential question throughout the unit. 2. Learners have multiple opportunities to build on their learning about the EQ through writing, speaking, and listening. 3. Learners record major changes and additions to their learning and reflect on what changed or deepened their learning.	√– = Learner completes only some of the concentric circles and/or his or her responses lack depth. √ = Learner completes all concentric circles with two or three sentences of thoughtful reflection. √+ = Learner completes all concentric circles with two or three sentences of thoughtful reflection and reflects on how his or her learning has grown throughout the unit.	ES: The essential question is interesting and relevant to the learner. Learners are able to respond to the question based on their experiences. SE: Learners discuss their responses to the essential question in partners, in small groups, or as a whole class. N: Learners build on prior understandings as they interact with new ideas throughout the unit. CE: Learners integrate new learning from the unit to answer the essential question in following reflections.

MAP out the path to expertise/mastery
(How would an expert deconstruct and approach this task, step by step?)

TWITTER SUMMARY (3 bullets max)	MENTAL MODELS, PROCESS GUIDES, HEURISTICS	A MODEL OF GOOD WORK LOOKS LIKE . . .	DIFFERENTIATION AND LAYERING
Learners explore the essential question and track their learning over time using a concentric circles graphic organizer.	Evolving understandings build on prior understanding—even if that prior understanding was incorrect. Expert understanding requires thinking about thinking: metacognition through reflection on personal learning and growth and how they have occurred and become internally persuasive.	Each section is filled out with a new understanding that develops from a previous one or that represents a justified change in one's thinking.	Create concentric circles with the essential question already printed in the centermost circle. Allow learners to talk out their ideas before writing in response to the EQ. Model reflecting on your learning and growth via a think-aloud before and during the unit, recording insights in the concentric circles. Work with learners one on one or in small groups to help them reflect on their learning and notice patterns and growth between the circles. Use sentence stems that encourage reflection or connections.

POWER through your lesson
(What is the sequence of initial major must-make instructional moves?)

	PRIME	ORIENT	WALK THROUGH (and check for understanding)	EXTEND AND EXPLORE	REFLECT
Leader	SHARE the essential question for the unit, "How do I become an expert?" ASK learners to define the term *expert* and record learners' thinking on an anchor chart.	FRAME today's lesson: EXPLAIN that learners will consider the essential question for the first time today and revisit it throughout the unit. INTRODUCE the concentric circles graphic organizer learners will use to track their thinking and opinions over time. PROMPT learners to record the EQ in the centermost circle of the graphic organizer.	PROMPT learners to respond to the EQ with their current thinking in the second-largest circle. PROMPT learners to read over their reflections and highlight one to three most valuable points to remember and share.	DELIBERATE PRACTICE/ ARTICULATE CONSCIOUS AWARENESS: As learners read, write, speak, and listen, respond to the EQ in the concentric circles. Encourage them to consider and discuss how the new learning connects with their personal experiences and how the essential question and evolving understandings apply to the real world.	Every time learners revisit the essential question, they should reread what they wrote the previous time, reflect on their new learning, and refine and revise their thinking and reflect on how their understanding was changed. At the conclusion of the unit, ask learners to reflect on and discuss their growth from the initial to the final reflection. OPTIONAL SELF-ASSESSMENT: Have learners self-assess their opinionaire using the $\sqrt{-}$, $\sqrt{}$, $\sqrt{+}$ system explained previously.

(Continued)

POWER through your lesson
(What is the sequence of initial major must-make instructional moves?)

	PRIME	ORIENT	WALK THROUGH (and check for understanding)	EXTEND AND EXPLORE	REFLECT
Leader				Ultimately, the goal of learners reflecting on this unit's question, "How do I become an expert?" is for learners to identify the moves real experts make to develop and hone expertise and seek to emulate these moves as they are apprenticed into increasing expertise.	
Learner	DEFINE the term *expert* by considering experts they know in the real world and/or looking up the term in the dictionary. REFLECT on the essential question by asking any clarifying questions.	RECORD the essential question in the center-most circle. DISCUSS with partners how and why they will use this concentric circle graphic organizer today and in the future to record their changes in understanding, how these happened, and how these changes lead toward increased competence and even expertise.	GUIDED PRACTICE: After responding in writing and highlighting the most valuable points, engage in small-group discussions and add to their writing. DIFFERENTIATE: Allow learners who are more hesitant to share to work with partners first and/or share an idea from a partner using the sentence frame, "My partner _____ [name] said _____." DEBRIEF: Ask one member from each group to share an idea aloud. Keep a class concentric circles anchor chart to record and reflect on the class's evolving thinking.		HOMEWORK EXTENSION: Have learners create a physical product, such as a flow chart, storyboard, or other visual, to trace their learning about the essential question and what texts, activities, or moves changed their understandings.

Chapter 8

PRIMING AND ORIENTING LEARNERS THROUGH FRONTLOADING

> ### ESSENTIAL QUESTION
> How do we ignite and sustain the spark for deep learning?

Jackie is an avid game player—and maybe just a little competitive, too. She and her friends enjoy standing game nights where they try to save the world through Pandemic Legacy, a cooperative episodic game with an overarching story arc in which play changes based on the success or failure of your decisions in previous games. In short, the game is always different, and the decisions made in one game forever change future games. Talk about a lot being at stake!

See *Lesson Plan Canvas* on page 140

When preparing to play this new game, just like any other new learning, it was essential to get *primed* and *oriented*. The group first read the directions, which came in the form of a multipage manual. Not only was there a great deal to remember, but everything seemed both important and unfamiliar. Have you ever had this experience? Perhaps when you learned about a new teaching practice or read through a new curriculum? What did you do to help digest and process this new information? Jackie and her friends relied on the following: (1) their previous knowledge of similar cooperative games, (2) their interest in learning how to play this new game and an intrinsic motivation to be successful, (3) an understanding of the purpose and goals of the new game, (4) a mental model of the processes to meet the goals, and (5) a deep belief in one another. Learners often feel overwhelmed by the complexity of new learning challenges, but when teachers activate prior knowledge, interest, and motivation; set clear purposes and payoffs; and, most importantly, believe deeply in the potential of their learners, they open the door to learner success.

Any successful unit of instruction must begin with *priming* and *orienting* learners. In the previous chapter, we discussed how to prime and orient learners through essential questions, and in this chapter, we explore how frontloading further prepares learners for success with new learning. (It's also worth noting that these practices can be done in reverse order; frontloading can be used to elicit learners' connections to the inquiry topic, which teachers and learners can leverage to articulate essential questions.) No matter the topic, cognitive science tells us that to move learners from their current understanding to deeper and more robust expert levels of understanding, teachers must meet learners where they are and then provide scaffolding and support to move them forward.

Teachers provide support prior to learning through *priming*—by activating learners' prior knowledge, interests, and personal connections to the new learning. Teachers also *orient* learners to the learning by considering the purposes and personal as well as social payoffs of the learning. This practice of priming and orienting has many names, such as prelearning, anticipatory sets, or activating prior knowledge. Here, we'll refer to it as **frontloading** (Wilhelm, Baker, & Dube-Hackett, 2001) because it's where we activate prior interests and experience, and preload knowledge, skills, and vocabulary that are necessary resources for learners as they engage in the new learning challenge(s).

PLANNING FOR PRIMING AND ORIENTING LEARNERS THROUGH FRONTLOADING

When determining what and how to frontload, first think about the sparks that have led you to various inquiries. What stimuli, needs, challenges and problems, readings, experiences, and discussions have made you want to inquire into a new topic or dive even deeper into a known one? Likely, the same kinds of things that motivate you will also motivate your learners. Identifying these catalysts prepares you to create similar experiences for your learners.

The question is always how much to frontload. We want to provide enough frontloading to activate our learners' prior knowledge and interests that relate to the inquiry, so they have resources to bring to the learning. As George Hillocks told us, the only resources you have to teach someone something new is what they already know and care about. This is the foundation of all new learning. At the same time, we want to give only "just enough" so that learners are prepared for success and develop their own need to know.

The duration of frontloading activities depends on the extent that you need to put learners in a mental space to develop new understandings, provide the necessary resources for proceeding, promote vocabulary acquisition, and create a heightened sense of interest and engagement. Frontloading activities also serve as formative assessments and a template to measure growth against throughout a unit of study.

Remember that frontloading is something you do at the beginning of a unit *and* when new and significant challenges are introduced within the unit. Similar to a KWLH (what you know, what you want to know, what you learned, and how you learned it) strategy, all frontloading can be returned to at various points in the unit to gauge progress and for more *priming, orienting,* and *reflecting* on the learning and on how understanding has changed. As you *map* out your unit plan and checkpoints, consider when, how, and why you might revisit the frontloading activities you engage learners in at the beginning of the unit.

As you employ the frontloading strategies you will find in the remainder of this chapter, consider how they will work for you and your learners given the goals of your unit (e.g., some of the strategies here focus on thinking and problem solving while others focus on writing or discussion). We also encourage you to remember the following: (1) All of these strategies are generally effective across grade levels and disciplines, although you will need to tweak them to best fit your content, context, and individual learners, and (2) frontloading strategies are usually brief and fairly simple and, therefore, may be one of the first strategies you try from this book. As you experiment, consider this checklist of success criteria.

Considerations for Designing and Implementing Successful Frontloading Activities

❏ The teacher intentionally designs and sequences the frontloading activities to support the larger goals of the unit and to prepare learners for success in meeting these goals. (E-M)

❏ The frontloading activity activates and builds learners' prior knowledge regarding the unit topic. (P-O)

❏ The frontloading activity motivates learners to engage with the topic of inquiry by helping them make personal connections and see the purposes; payoffs; and personal, disciplinary, and cultural relevance of the learning. (P-O)

❏ The frontloading activity helps learners establish personally compelling purposes and applications for their learning and encourages them to work toward these purposes. (PO)

❏ The frontloading activity helps learners clarify what they are coming to know and begin to monitor their learning progress. (W-E-R)

❏ The teacher designs and implements opportunities throughout the unit for learners to return to the frontloading activities to extend and reflect on what they have learned, often in preparation for completing the culminating project. (E-M, W-E-R)

FRONTLOADING MOVE 1: OPINIONAIRE

Opinionaires are a type of survey that require learners to activate prior knowledge, use this knowledge to form opinions and provide evidence for these opinions, share their opinions and evidence through discussion, and build knowledge as they hear the perspectives of their peers. Opinionaires have the strongest impact and greatest relevance when they relate to an essential question from the unit because they allow learners

(Continued)

(Continued)

to consider the inquiry question and reflect on its significance from different angles. Here is a brief explanation of the opinionaire response process:

1. Learners respond to the opinionaire statements using the appropriate coding (true/false, agree/disagree, etc.); see our throughline unit example in Figure 8.1. While responding to these statements, learners should record some of the thinking that leads them to their opinions.

2. Learners then move into discussion in partners, in small groups, or perhaps eventually as a whole class. Often, the discussion leads them to explore other perspectives, deepening or revising their own thinking. As learners examine and argue about the topic(s), they recognize that inquiry is about exploring genuine curiosities about the people and world around them. This requires learners to engage in higher-level thinking and use evidence-based reasoning as demanded by all next-generation standards.

3. Although opinionaires are typically a frontloading strategy, learners should revisit them at one or more points during the unit, particularly after they explore new ideas. Learners can also practice perspective taking by retaking the opinionaire through the lens of a major character, historical figure, expert, or author.

■ FIGURE 8.1: MINDSET OPINIONAIRE WITH WHERE DO I STAND? DISCUSSION FOR THROUGHLINE UNIT ON EXPERTISE

Directions: Next to each statement, write whether you strongly agree (SA), agree (A), disagree (D), or strongly disagree (SD). Then provide some evidence or justification to support your opinion.

OPINION	STATEMENT	JUSTIFICATION (WHAT MAKES YOU SAY SO?)
	Some people are born smarter than others.	
	Effort, practice, and not giving up can make me more successful at anything.	
	The most intelligent people are the most successful people.	
	My capacity will grow when I embrace challenges and learn from feedback and criticism.	
	Only so many people can be successful. There are always winners and losers.	
	When I get feedback from others, my intelligence and capacity grow.	

online resources ⟋ This figure is available for download at **http://resources.corwin.com/EMPOWER-elementary**

PLC Connection

Frontload staff discussions about important issues (like assessment) using an opinionaire for faculty to share their initial thinking and to gain a quick formative assessment. Follow this with a deeper dive into the different types of assessment and the benefits and challenges of each, allowing faculty to explore research and socially construct new knowledge about the types of assessment. At the conclusion of the learning, have faculty return to their opinionaire and reconsider the statements and how their thinking evolved.

CREATING AN OPINIONAIRE

When creating an opinionaire, brainstorm or search for a list of statements about your topic that are both interesting and controversial. One way to think of these statements is to consider two very different perspectives about a topic and write statements that represent each opinion. Another option is to search for quotes about the topic and revise them into statements. It is important that the statements are firm, and it's often helpful to include absolutes, such as *always* or *never*, to make them more controversial and discussion worthy. You want the statements to be debatable, meaning that it is likely some learners will agree while others will adamantly disagree. This requires learners to take and defend a clear stance.

Checklist for Creating Your Own Opinionaire

☐ The opinionaire includes a manageable number (six to twelve) of learner-friendly statements reflecting different perspectives. (*Note:* Begin with an even smaller number for younger learners or in initial practice opportunities.) (E-M)

☐ The opinionaire includes clear directions and a continuum for learners to respond to each statement (e.g., strongly agree, agree, disagree, and strongly disagree). (P-O)

☐ The opinionaire statements elicit prior knowledge, curiosity, and interesting and relevant personal connections related to the essential question and/or topic of inquiry. (P-O)

☐ Learners have opportunities to develop, share, and justify their thinking through writing or speaking and listening. (W-E)

☐ Learners initially respond independently to the opinionaire statements and then move to small-group and later to larger-group sharing to debate and defend their thinking. (*Note:* This honors individual thinking and processing time and engages all learners in sharing and in deep thinking about the statements.) (W-E)

☐ The opinionaire is relevant over time and provides opportunities for learners to revisit statements throughout the unit to analyze thinking after new learning has occurred and/or to consider how various authors and characters might respond to the statements. (E-R)

FRONTLOADING MOVE 2: WHERE DO I STAND?

"Where do I stand?" is a frontloading and discussion technique that has multiple benefits. It provides an opportunity for sharing perspectives with mixed partnerships as well as a chance for learners to get more oxygen and glucose to their brains (essential components of brain functioning, according to neuroscience). This strategy can follow an opinionaire or ranking statements/scenarios (see Frontloading Move 4) to get learners discussing and defending their opinions. However, this strategy can also stand alone, allowing learners to respond to a reading or a visual stimulus, such as a political cartoon, or to a single meaty question or controversial statement worthy of deep discussion or debate.

In "Where do I stand?" different areas of the room represent different statements or opinions, and learners move to the area that best represents their perspective. They then defend their stance with evidence. Using our example mindset opinionaire, we use the four corners of the room for learners to take a stand. Each corner is labeled one of the four opinions: "strongly agree," "agree," "disagree," and "strongly disagree." After making their claim, learners should be able to answer the question *What makes you say so?* to ensure that they have evidence and reasons to support their position. It's also important to give learners time to discuss their position with peers who agree with them before summarizing their opinion and argument for the whole class. Naming the purpose and goals behind this activity may be helpful as well. For example, one goal may be to argue a particular point of view and persuade others to believe it. An equally important goal is to teach learners to have an open mind and listen to different perspectives, reporting on how others' thoughts changed or challenged their thinking.

As learners listen to the other arguments and perspectives, they can choose to move to different corners of the room that represent their evolving beliefs. You'll want to encourage learners to choose a specific corner initially; however, it is not uncommon for one or more learners to end up in the middle of the room or between two corners. It's also not uncommon to have learners change their minds as they receive new information and ideas from their peers. When this occurs, be sure to note which learners have made a shift, and ask these learners to share with the class why and how their thinking changed. A note of caution, however: For some learners, the opportunity to move around the room is too great, and they may choose to move multiple times with limited rationale. By making it an expectation that you will ask learners who relocate to provide a rationale for their movement, you eliminate unintentional movement and help to ensure the strategy remains structured and supportive of learning.

This strategy requires learners to engage in a variety of important and complex moves that speakers and collaborators use in the real world. First, it encourages learners to deeply consider important issues and ideas, stake and justify a position, practice sharing their opinions with evidence, summarize their own and others' thinking, and listen to and address the opinions presented by their peers.

Example:
Mathematical Thinking: Number Sense

Label each corner of the classroom with a different letter: A, B, C, D.

Here are four numbers. Decide which one does not belong with the rest, walk to the corresponding corner, and come up with an explanation for why that number is different from the other three.

A: 9

B: 16

C: 25

D: 43

Explanation: As you can see, there are a variety of ways to respond to this question: A doesn't belong because it's the only single-digit number, B doesn't belong because it's the only even number, C is the only number divisible by 5, and D is prime. This is an excellent way to gauge the level of complexity that learners can think and share about a topic, practice academic vocabulary, and safely take academic risks.

THREE CORNERS

A simple variation is to modify the number of corners and options presented. For example, if used in math, you may create a triangle of three vertices with the labels "never true," "sometimes true," and "always true" and have learners respond to mathematical statements with these claims and evidence to support them. This serves as a great formative assessment and allows the teacher to gain insights about a learner's misconceptions in order to anticipate potential challenges and provide the appropriate scaffolding.

ON THE LINE/FOLD THE LINE

Another variation of this strategy is to have learners stand on a physical continuum from "strongly agree" on one side of the room to "strongly disagree" on the opposite side of the room. This requires learners to assess the extent to which they agree or disagree. They will talk to several people to determine where to place themselves on the line. Then, you can fold the line in half, pairing learners with opposing viewpoints and allowing them to discuss their opinions and evidence to try to convince their partner of a different perspective. A scaffold you may provide is to give each learner one minute to share his or her perspective and then allot a minute for discussion. After learners finish, it is important to give them the opportunity to reposition themselves on the original line. When you do this, observe learners who made dramatic shifts along the line, and ask them to share who and what changed their perspective.

(Continued)

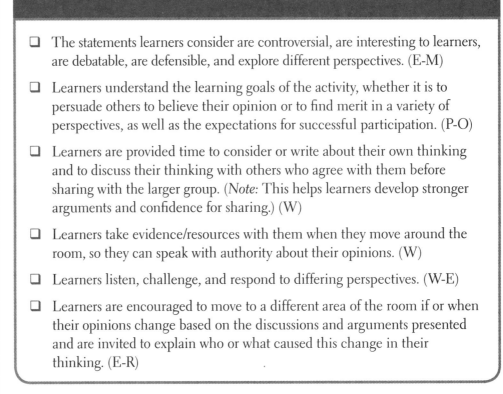

(Continued)

Checklist for Creating Your Own Where Do I Stand? Activity

❑ The statements learners consider are controversial, are interesting to learners, are debatable, are defensible, and explore different perspectives. (E-M)

❑ Learners understand the learning goals of the activity, whether it is to persuade others to believe their opinion or to find merit in a variety of perspectives, as well as the expectations for successful participation. (P-O)

❑ Learners are provided time to consider or write about their own thinking and to discuss their thinking with others who agree with them before sharing with the larger group. (*Note:* This helps learners develop stronger arguments and confidence for sharing.) (W)

❑ Learners take evidence/resources with them when they move around the room, so they can speak with authority about their opinions. (W)

❑ Learners listen, challenge, and respond to differing perspectives. (W-E)

❑ Learners are encouraged to move to a different area of the room if or when their opinions change based on the discussions and arguments presented and are invited to explain who or what caused this change in their thinking. (E-R)

FRONTLOADING MOVE 3: SEE-THINK-WONDER

See–think–wonder is a relatively simple yet powerful strategy that can be used as a frontload for almost any topic and unit of instruction. It mirrors the process of inquiry by asking learners to identify and observe data (*What?* What are the indisputable facts?), to make inferences (*So what?* What do the facts and connections between them mean?), and then to ask questions and consider applications (*Now what?* How might I apply what I am learning? What might I inquire about next?). This process mirrors the process of expert reading that proceeds from literal decoding (see—name what is literally there) to the inferencing (think—figure forth from what is there and how details are connected), to evaluating, extending, and applying what has been learned (wonder). For this strategy, we select visually striking and interesting images related to the topic of inquiry. As learners look at these images, they consider the following questions: *What do you see? What does it make you think? What do you wonder?* As they answer these questions, they record their ideas in a three-column note-catcher. In this way, learners activate prior knowledge, make connections, and name what they know and want to know about the topic of inquiry. (*Note:* The stimulus may be a visual, or it may be an object, video clip, audio recording, and so forth. In the case where it's aural instead of visual, simply change the word *see* to *hear*, or ask learners to record basic observations of the stimulus.) See Figure 8.2 for an example from Jackie's class.

■ FIGURE 8.2: SEE-THINK-WONDER EXAMPLE

In this see–think–wonder, learners are positioned as scientists as they notice and name characteristics of living beings in order to define the term *reptile* and classify vertebrates.

Guiding Question: What is a reptile?

Images courtesy of Pixabay.com/PublicDomainPictures

 SEE	 THINK	 WONDER
• I see four different animal images. (Katy) • All of the animals are on land. (Ben) • Each animal is the same color as its surroundings. (Evelyn) • The snake has scales, but the turtle has a shell. (Patrick) • All of the animals have legs except the snake. (Scott)	• I think these animals are cold-blooded. (Jason) • These animals are good at camouflage. (Carissa) • All of these animals seem to have a way to protect themselves. (Jenny) • I think the second picture is a tortoise because turtles are usually found in the water. (Todd)	• Is the third picture an alligator or a crocodile? What's the difference? (Chris) • Can some or all of these animals swim? (Marty) • What are all the things these animals have in common? (Amanda) • Do these animals lay eggs or have live babies? (Page) • Why have these animals developed these similar traits? (Jeff)

Follow the initial writing in this activity with a conversation that may occur in partners, in small groups, or as a whole class. Small groups can make anchor charts to share their thinking, or the teacher can record learners' ideas on a whiteboard, anchor chart, or projected presentation during a whole-class discussion. Listen to all ideas shared by learners, even if the conclusions they draw are still evolving. This doesn't

(Continued)

(Continued)

mean you cannot or won't address misconceptions (either at this time or in the future) but simply that you honor where they are at and use it as a formative assessment of learners' understandings and a guide for moving forward: Throughout the discussion, look for ways to help learners tie this conversation to the essential question. Later in the unit, have learners refer back to the notes or anchor charts they created to revise, refine, or add on to their original thinking.

STICKY NOTES

You may choose to have learners engage in the see–think–wonder as a class by having them write their *see, think,* and *wonder* ideas on colored sticky notes and post them on the whiteboard or on an anchor chart for the group to review. In this case, it can be helpful to designate one color for each column to differentiate between what learners see, think, and wonder. We recommend keeping learners' sticky-note ideas so you can return to them later in the unit, reflecting on how the class's learning has developed over time.

Checklist for Creating Your Own See–Think–Wonder Activity

❑ The stimulus is accessible and relates to important themes, events, ideas, or questions learners will discuss, read, and write about later in the unit. (E-M)

❑ The stimulus activates and builds background knowledge about the topic of inquiry, is compelling to the learners, and creates purpose for the learning. (P-O)

❑ Learners engage in thinking and inferring about the stimulus, leading to generative questions and applications, positioning them for deeper critical thinking about the topic of inquiry. (W)

❑ In the follow-up discussion, the teacher honors all learners' ideas, building upon them to explore new territory and help learners connect the known with the unknown. (W-E)

❑ Learners consider what they learned through the discussion and/or return to the stimulus later in the unit to celebrate their new understandings. (W-E-R)

FRONTLOADING MOVE 4:
RANKING STATEMENTS OR SCENARIOS

Ranking statements or scenarios is a great way to encourage close reading and supporting opinions with evidence and reasoning. It's also a powerful way to spark discussion and debate. Further, it often prompts learners to form or revise their thinking about the essential question, and it allows the teacher to introduce important topics or ideas they will explore throughout the inquiry.

In this strategy, we provide learners with three or more different statements or scenarios about a topic and have them rank them in some kind of order. The simplest method is to have learners rank them from best to worst or most to least (see Figure 8.3). Encourage learners to record notes on the statements, highlighting or annotating the scenarios as they read to provide evidence and reasoning for their ranking.

Following this ranking, learners can discuss their thinking in small groups with the goal of listening to different points of view and working toward a consensus. (If this cannot be achieved, all group members should at least understand and be able to explain the perspectives of those who are outliers.) The goal is not to "win everyone to your side" but, rather, to provide reasonable opinions supported by evidence, consider a variety of perspectives, and try to come to the best group consensus possible.

PLC Connection

We've included two ranking scenario models to use in PLCs, both of which ask teachers to rank units of instruction to answer the question, "What makes a quality unit?" on the companion website, **resources. corwin.com/EMPOWER-elementary**.

■ FIGURE 8.3: "SMART" RANKING EXAMPLE

Guiding Question: What does it mean to be smart?

Directions: Rank the following statements from 1 to 8. Use a "1" for the most important sign of being smart and an "8" for the least important sign of being smart.

____ Doing well in school

____ Making a lot of money

____ Being a hard worker

____ Practicing in the way that experts do things

____ Getting along with people

____ Being good at problem solving

____ Being quick to respond

____ Being able to create (or add) something new to how people think about or do things.

(Continued)

(Continued)

PLC Connection

Any topic for PLCs or professional development can be usefully primed and oriented with the activities from this chapter or other frontloading moves.

Checklist for Creating Your Own Ranking Statements or Scenarios Activity

❑ The ranking includes multiple statements or scenarios that are plausible, are challenging to learners, and represent different perspectives on the topic of inquiry. (*Note:* There should be *no* clear answer about the best or worst statement or scenario.) (E-M)

❑ Statements or scenarios are relatively short, allowing learners to read and rank them in fifteen minutes or less. (E-M)

❑ Statements or scenarios are based on real-life ideas, stories, and experiences and are related to key situations, themes, questions, and ideas from the topic of inquiry. (P-O)

❑ The teacher explains the expectations for the ranking activity and may even model how to annotate or defend a response with evidence and reasoning prior to asking learners to participate in the ranking. (P-O)

❑ Learners take notes and/or annotate the statements or scenarios in order to provide evidence for how they ranked them. (W)

❑ Learners have opportunities to engage in discussion, writing, or extended thinking following the initial ranking activity. (W-E)

❑ Learners discuss their rankings and revise their thinking based on the varying perspectives shared. (E-R)

POWERFUL PLANNING: FRONTLOADING TO BUILD THRESHOLD KNOWLEDGE

Each of the featured frontloading strategies generates interest, activates and builds background knowledge, helps learners make connections, and engages learners in real-world thinking and transfer. All of this sets the foundation for success, building the **threshold knowledge** required by the inquiry. In addition, frontloading strategies serve as a formative assessment so the teacher can be flexible and responsive to his or her individual learners' needs. In short, frontloading has a great deal of benefits, which is why we must intentionally plan for it.

As you work to create your own frontloading activities, consider which ones will have the most impact for the learners in your classroom, as well as which ones will accomplish your learning goals. We also encourage you to consider when and how you might return to these activities so learners can justify prior understandings, add to or revise their thinking, or completely change their opinions as they develop deeper understanding around the topic(s) at hand.

It's easy to overlook frontloading, given everything teachers must do in a day. As a result, we recommend *mapping* out when and how you will return to your frontloads during the design phase of your unit, making it easier to ensure this beneficial reflective opportunity occurs for your learners during the actual instruction.

Guiding Questions for Designing Frontloading Activities

- What makes this frontloading activity the right "move" for this unit or particular moment? (E-M)

- At what strategic points in the unit should I revisit the frontloading activity and reflect on how student thinking has evolved? (E-M)

- What is the most meaningful way to hook my learners and encourage them to activate background knowledge that prepares them for success with future learning? (E-M-P-O)

- How does the strategy help learners set individual and social purposes for learning? (O)

- How will I teach my learners to engage in this activity? What scaffolding and supports will lead to success? (W)

- What opportunities will I build into the unit for learners to return to the activity to reflect on their initial understandings, and how and why these have changed and grown over time? (E-R)

- When and how will I reflect on this strategy and the degree to which it met my purpose and my learners' needs? (R)

Lesson: Opinionaire and Where Do I Stand?

Unit: How do I become an expert?

ENVISION the destination *(Where are learners going, and why?)*			
GOAL *What kind of thinking is targeted?*	**EVIDENCE** *What product(s) will serve as proof of learning?*	**MEASURES OF SUCCESS** *What's the standard and quality-assurance tool?*	**STAKES** *Why will learners buy in? What's the why behind the learning?*
✓ Explanation/ reasoning ✓ Perspective taking ✓ Self-assessing/ reflecting	✓ Selected response (MC, T/F) ✓ Performance assessment: microargument justifying one's claims/responses on the opinionaire	✓ **Simple:** √−, √, √+ on discrete facts/skills	Use ESSENCE as a guide for buy-in. Your lesson should have one or more of the following: ✓ ES: Emotional spark/salience (i.e., relevance) ✓ SE: Social engagement (i.e., collaboration) ✓ N: Novelty (i.e., new concepts and skills) ✓ CE: Critical/creative exploration opportunities
Activate schema and interest by engaging learners in responding to controversial statements and then explaining and defending these opinions about a topic using evidence and reasoning.	1. Learners consider the essential question and related content by reading and responding to statements with their opinions. Opinionaires may be true/false or ask learners to respond with a degree of agreement (SA: strongly agree, A: agree, D: disagree, or SD: strongly disagree). 2. After this quick response, learners may respond in more detail by providing evidence and reasoning to support one of their opinions before discussing the statements with others.	√− = Learner responds to only some of the statements using the appropriate coding (T/F, etc.) and/or is unable to defend his or her opinions. √ = Learner responds to all statements using the appropriate coding (T/F, etc.) and is able to defend some of his or her opinions. √+ = Learner responds to all statements using the appropriate coding (T/F, etc.) and is able to defend all of his or her opinions with evidence and some kind of reasoning—the application of a rule, value, or principle to the evidence.	**ES:** Learners apply background knowledge and life experiences to form, state, and defend their opinions. Young learners, especially, enjoy sharing their opinions on a most anything. **SE:** Learners share their opinions with peers. Through this discussion, they build on each other's ideas, consider new perspectives, and assimilate new knowledge into their schema. **N:** Learners often encounter new ideas and perspectives through the opinionaire and follow-up discussion. **CE:** Learners consider other perspectives and integrate new learning into their schema.

MAP out the path to expertise/mastery
(How would an expert deconstruct and approach this task, step by step?)

TWITTER SUMMARY (3 bullets max)	MENTAL MODELS, PROCESS GUIDES, HEURISTICS	A MODEL OF GOOD WORK LOOKS LIKE . . .	DIFFERENTIATION AND LAYERING
Learners can state and defend their opinions about a topic using evidence and some reasoning.	• Basic argumentation: generating claims and supporting them with evidence and reasoning.	See the example on page 130.	Opinionaire statements should be developmentally appropriate. Forewarn learners that they may have limited or no knowledge about some of the statements and simply encourage them to do their best. Explanation of specific vocabulary in the opinionaire statements. Opportunities to work with peers who responded similarly to develop evidence for their opinions before defending them to the larger group. Models and modeling as needed.

POWER through your lesson
(What is the sequence of initial major must-make instructional moves?)

	PRIME	ORIENT	WALK THROUGH (and check for understanding)	EXTEND AND EXPLORE	REFLECT
Leader	REMIND learners of the essential question for the unit, "How do I become an expert?" and encourage them to consider how the statements they think and talk about relate to the overall essential question. REVIEW the terms *opinion* (for younger learners) or *claim* (for older learners) and *evidence* and REMIND learners to support their opinions or claims with evidence. For older learners, explain that evidence must be reasoned about through the application of a value, principle, or rule, to connect it to the claim.	FRAME today's lesson: EXPLAIN that today learners will use an opinionaire to explore what they think about intelligence and success. FOREWARN learners that they may have limited knowledge or experience related to each statement, and note that we will continue to think and learn about these ideas throughout the unit. EXPLAIN to learners that they should read the statements and mark their opinion next to each statement: "Write SA if you strongly agree, A if you agree, D if you disagree, and SD if you strongly disagree."	ENGAGE learners by having them complete the opinionaire, responding to each of the statements using the appropriate coding. EXPLAIN to learners that they will now select one statement that they most strongly agree or disagree with and write an explanation of their thinking at the bottom of the page, supporting their opinion with evidence from their experience (and an explanation of how it supports the claim). CHECK FOR UNDERSTANDING: Monitor the room to ensure all learners are successful in selecting and responding to one of the statements. MODEL how to support one of the opinionaire statements with evidence in discussion.	DELIBERATE PRACTICE/ARTICULATE CONSCIOUS AWARENESS: Learners reflect on their learning by considering how the discussion has moved their thinking forward and on the importance of supporting opinions with evidence (and reasoning that explains how the evidence supports the claim). Learners may choose to modify their responses to some statements and also will focus on their writing at the end of the opinionaire. Prompt learners to write in response to this question, "Now that you have discussed these statements with your classmates, how has your thinking about this statement changed? What caused this change in your thinking?"	To conclude the lesson, ask learners to complete the following exit ticket: "Why is it important to support your opinion with evidence? (and support evidence with reasoning?) How does evidence (and explanations of it) from others impact your willingness to listen to their opinions?" OPTIONAL SELF-ASSESSMENT: Have learners self-assess their opinionaire responses using the √, √, √+ system explained previously.

(Continued)

(Continued)

	POWER through your lesson (What is the sequence of initial major must-make instructional moves?)				
	PRIME	**ORIENT**	**WALK THROUGH (and check for understanding)**	**EXTEND AND EXPLORE**	**REFLECT**
Learner	REFLECT on the essential question by discussing your current thinking about it with peers. DEFINE OPINION, CLAIM, AND EVIDENCE (and *reasoning*, as appropriate) and practice with a partner stating an opinion (about anything) and supporting it with evidence and an explanation of how the evidence connects to the claim.	CHECK FOR UNDERSTANDING: *Rephrase* the purpose and directions for the opinionaire activity with a partner.	GUIDED PRACTICE: Learners work in partnerships to discuss their responses to each statement. Learners should discuss *all* statements, even if they agree with one another, making sure they can support their thinking with evidence from their lives. DIFFERENTIATE: Monitor the room as learners engage in discussion, and prompt learners to provide evidence for their thinking if it is lacking. Support struggling learners by asking questions about or providing examples of evidence they may use to support their opinions. *Optional enrichment activity:* USE Where do I stand? to engage the class in whole-group discussion about the most debatable statements. (Determine the top two or three most debatable statements through informal observations or by taking a poll.) Provide learners the opportunity to discuss with near peers (those who think similarly) before sharing their opinions with the whole group. DEBRIEF: Learners reflect on and possibly change their opinions about specific statements based on the discussion. Learners are specifically encouraged to discuss how and why their opinions have changed.	Ask learners to consider what would alter or confirm some of their strong opinions. Have learners think about a specific situation where they will share an opinion in the future and what evidence they will use to support this opinion and encourage others to agree with their line of thinking.	EXTENSION: At various times throughout the unit, ask learners to return to the opinionaire and reconsider their responses to the statements, and add or revise their evidence and reasoning. You may also ask learners to revisit these statements with a new lens, perhaps the lens of a character they are reading about, the author of a text, or another person they know (e.g., a parent or sibling).

PART 4: WALKING THROUGH, EXTENDING, AND EXPLORING

ENVISION MAP PRIME ORIENT WALK THROUGH EXTEND/EXPLORE REFLECT

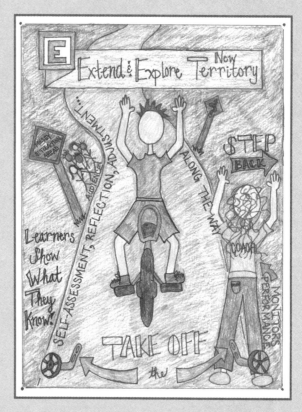

Chapter 9

WALKING LEARNERS THROUGH WITH VISUALIZATION STRATEGIES

> **ESSENTIAL QUESTION**
> How do we support learning by making thinking and learning visible?

The saying "A picture is worth a thousand words" reminds us of the incredible power of visuals to develop, represent, and communicate meaning. Stop for a moment and consider how often you create visuals in your daily life: to develop thinking, get a handle on complex ideas, make plans, keep track of important information, think through an idea that hasn't fully formed yet, represent an idea in a new form, communicate or extend your thinking, or just for fun. This visual thinking may take the form of pictures and flow charts in a journal you use to capture ideas, a simple to-do list that you cross off to visually celebrate completed tasks, a sketch you make on your notes during a presentation, an outline of major ideas, a graphic organizer, or myriad other forms. As teachers of teachers, we cannot tell you how many times we discard our technology or more traditional forms of writing in favor of sticky notes or a chance to sketch out ideas on paper.

Jeff's research demonstrates that expert reading is intensely visual (Wilhelm, 1995, 2012c, 2014), and Ericsson and Pool (2016) explain how expert mental models of understanding are really visual representations, models, or maps for task navigation and problem solving. Recognizing how much we (and other experts) develop and demonstrate learning through visuals reminds us of how important visuals are to apprenticing learners into different ways of knowing, creating, and representing meaning.

Using visuals and visualization strategies is also a democratic move that works for inductive and restorative practice because it helps all learners achieve greater access to and capacity for learning. Visuals are an alternative mode of representation that provide concrete ways for diverse learners to experience data and make meaning. This is why visuals play a big role in Universal Design for Learning (UDL), a framework teachers use to design instruction that best meets the needs of *all* learners. Consider all the ways visuals aid meaning making:

- A visual accompanying a text is often what captures the attention of an audience, priming and orienting them in ways that elevate both engagement and comprehension.

See *Lesson Plan Canvas* on page 161

- Creating and responding to visuals is a concrete and active form of learning that supports all learners, including those who experience learning challenges.

- Visuals support learners who are learning English as a new language and other learners with limited academic vocabulary in ways that make meaning immediately accessible and that help them cultivate new capacities of learning, knowing, doing, and thinking.

- Visuals allow many learners to access and use their strengths or preferred learning style (multiple intelligences) to address and improve in less developed areas (Wilhelm, 2012c).

- Learners who enjoy reading visual texts typically also embrace developing and expressing their learning in a visual way. Allowing learners to share their thinking visually can lead directly to their communicating more effectively in other modes (see Wilhelm, 2012c).

- Visuals are a powerful method of representation that support knowledge development. Using different kinds of multimodal texts—such as newspaper articles, films, YouTube videos, magazines, cartoons, music videos, posters, graphic novels, and more—provides learners with immediate access to ideas and allows them to directly experience data; see different sides of issues; take in information in diverse ways; engage with short, meaningful texts; and sometimes see things more vibrantly and in color. Comprehending these visual and multimodal texts requires readers to make the same highly sophisticated moves they need for any other text: comprehending, predicting, inferring, and synthesizing information. In fact, we've found that nearly any concept, strategy, or genre we want to teach can be taught through a painting, cartoon, or other visual (see Wilhelm & Smith, 2016).

Using a variety of strategies in your classroom capitalizes on different learners' interests and strengths and leads to deeper understanding. Visualization becomes a springboard for more abstract forms of comprehension and expression.

PLANNING FOR WALKING LEARNERS THROUGH WITH VISUALIZATION STRATEGIES

As we explained in our introductory description of EMPOWER, *walk-through* is the central move of apprenticeship. Without a robust walk-through there is no teaching for transformation nor for changed ways of knowing, doing, thinking, understanding, or being. Therefore, we seek to engage our learners daily in moving toward the work and understanding of real experts through modeling, mentoring, and monitoring. Experts in all fields use visuals to support their intake of information, to develop understanding, and to represent and communicate ideas. Consider, for example, architects who create blueprints, engineers who build models, and storyboard artists who visualize stories for books or films. A *walk-through* with visual strategies can be a gateway for learners to new ways of understanding.

The visualization strategies in this chapter require and support learners to productively struggle through their zones of proximal development (ZPDs) and eventually achieve new zones of actual development (ZADs) (Vygotsky, 1978). Each strategy invites, encourages, supports, apprentices, and rewards learners as they move forward to take risks and to deliberately practice knowing, thinking, and doing (3-D teaching and learning!) in ways that advance expertise. (*Note well that using visual assignments that do not assist learners to develop a new strategy or capacity are not a form of apprenticeship.*) Teachers and learners should find the strategies in this chapter enjoyable and engaging—after all, reading and creating meaning through visuals is fun (sometimes hard fun, but always fun)! Consider how you might plan to use some of these visualization strategies in your own units of instruction to meet specific learning goals, keeping in mind the following success criteria.

Considerations for Designing an Effective Visualization Strategy

❑ The visualization strategy provides a creative approach for accessing, "seeing," exploring, examining, developing, or expressing, thus stimulating different parts of the brain than traditional instruction. (E-M-P-O)

❑ The visualization strategy must help the user to learn something that she or he cannot yet fully do on her or his own. This new knowing, doing, or thinking should match learning goals for the unit or lesson. (E-M)

❑ The visualization strategy works to move learners toward independence in understanding an important concept or performance strategy as they develop, represent, and share their evolving understanding of complex texts or tasks. (W-E)

❑ The visualization strategy engages learners in deep processing, knowing, doing, thinking, and making that corresponds with that of experts and the correspondence continuum (and is not simply providing a creative outlet). (W-E)

❑ The visualization strategy has guidelines and critical success standards that learners use to direct their creative process and evaluate the quality of their product. (E-R)

❑ The visualization strategy provides a chance for learners to reflect on and name their learning. Learners also rehearse for high-road transfer as they name opportunities for future use of the strategy, as well as for newly achieved conceptual or strategic learning. (R)

VISUALIZATION MOVE 1: PICTURING THEMES WITH THE TOPIC-COMMENT STRATEGY

Here, learners are asked to identify and convey a theme or main idea from a reading or an experience via an image. The steps are as follows:

Step 1: Learners must first acquire new knowledge through some form of input: reading, listening, viewing, or engaging in a direct experience.

Step 2: Next, learners identify what's most important, filtering through the new learning to identify key details, determine a central topic or subject (something all the key details pertain to), and then identify patterns of key details about the topic. (See Chapter 5 for an introduction of the topic-comment strategy, pages 74–76). Please note that any text, however simple, has multiple possible topics. The important thing is for learners to identify a central topic that all the key details relate to.

Step 3: Then, learners determine the comment made about the topic by the arrangement of the key details. This will be an overarching idea or theme. Learners create a visual image that captures the topic-comment. Learners then write out a statement of the topic-comment (the main idea or theme). Learners may also select a meaningful quotation to accompany and support the visualized theme. (Note that some learners may choose to write their statement or select the quote prior to creating the visual. Provide differentiation and multiple entry points for learning by allowing learners to approach the visual in whatever way makes the most sense to them.)

Step 4: After learners create their visual, they share their creation with peers to demonstrate their understanding of the studied text or experience. This activity provides deliberate practice with identifying and representing key details, topics, textual patterning, and main ideas, which are always comments about a topic. It also provides deliberate practice with speaking and listening as learners teach one another through the sharing of their thinking about the text's topic-comment and how their visual captures how the text worked to express that meaning (and perhaps other effects as well). Peers then provide procedural feedback that allows the composer of the visual to reflect and consider possibilities for revision. Figure 9.1 shows an example.

■ FIGURE 9.1: PICTURING THEMES FOR THE MATHEMATICAL PRACTICE STANDARDS

Student caption:

General topic: Persevering in solving problems.

Key details: Look for a way to start. Monitor progress, and change strategies when there's a challenge. Ask if things make sense and are going well. Put in effort over time.

Topic-comment: Persevering in solving math problems requires figuring out how to get started and what tools and strategies to use when things get hard.

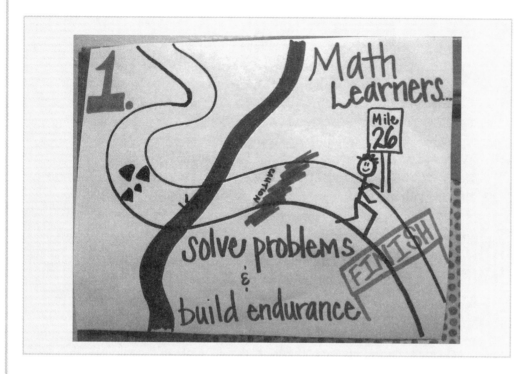

online resources ▸ For an extended mental map of the topic-comment strategy and a printable planning chart for identifying the main idea to use with picturing themes, see the companion website. Also, the secondary-level *Planning Powerful Instruction* book contains a powerful sister strategy called *picture mapping*.

Checklist for Creating Your Own Picturing Themes

❑ The teacher selects a complex and interesting text or experience that pertains to the classroom inquiry and asks learners to translate the work into a visual or multimodal form for the purpose of developing new conceptual and strategic knowledge. (E-M)

❑ The teacher primes learners' interest by asking them to make connections between the text or task and what they already know. (P)

❑ Learners explore models of picturing themes, analyzing the words and visuals chosen and noting "the work" the composer did. (*Note:* Specifically, we want learners to notice how the images portray and make a comment on a real-world topic.) (P-O)

(Continued)

PLC Connection

We recommend using the same *picturing themes* lesson shown in this chapter's canvas (as well as the jigsaw found in the Chapter 12 canvas) to help teachers explore and make sense of the complex Mathematical Practice Standards (or any other complex educational idea or process). This is a perfect example of when teachers should do the task first before asking their students to do so. By engaging in these tasks, the teachers will develop a deeper understanding of the standards and how to help students internalize the standards for themselves. Teachers can likewise be asked to read an article on an educational issue the school or department is addressing, using the topic-comment strategy to picture the theme.

(Continued)

❏ The teacher thinks aloud to model the process of identifying key details, a topic (a general subject all the details comment on), the structure or pattern of the details, and then the overarching idea or theme expressed by the structuring of those details. The teacher then creates the picturing themes visual to capture this topic-comment (main idea or theme). (*Note:* With narrative texts, it can be helpful to analyze the main character and how he or she changes over the course of the text in order to determine the theme. With informational texts, it's important to analyze what is the most important audience takeaway or implied social action to determine the overall essence.) (W)

❏ Learners are supported via strategies (such as rules of notice), questioning, and coaching as they identify key details, a potential central topic, the organization of the key details, and then the theme expressed by that structuring of details. They are supported to create a visual that captures the heart of the matter: a topic-comment (main idea or theme) and how this was expressed through the patterns of key details about the topic. (W-E)

❏ Learners are encouraged to make intertextual and real-world connections between their creation and other learners' picturing themes, as well as with other texts, experiences, and real-world applications. This ensures they learn widely about the inquiry topic. (W-E-R)

❏ During the share out, learners articulate and justify their thinking process, explaining how they identified the topic-comment (main idea or theme) and why they chose the visual(s) and words to represent their learning. (R)

VISUALIZATION MOVE 2: SKETCHNOTING

Have you ever seen a video where a narrator uses a pencil to sketch and make notes on a whiteboard, showing connections, sequencing ideas, or indicating how one idea builds on another? If so, you've seen sketchnoting in action!

Sketchnoting, or visual note-taking, provides an opportunity for dual-coding and processing (Paivio, 1986), which means that understanding is deepened by using and honoring both verbal and nonverbal processing. In sketchnoting, learners can tell the "story" of their learning from any text or experiences by using sketches or visual displays of data to accompany and enhance written notes or an oral presentation. Sketchnotes likewise can capture the major takeaway (topic-comment) from any text, experience, or sequence of learning activities. This strategy helps learners determine what's important by identifying the general subject (topic) and capturing the key details about the topic; representing relationships, patterns, or processes within the text (such as showing the relationship between characters or representing how something is

150

done); and composing a meaningful visual that helps them make sense of their learning or communicate it to others.

Sketchnoting can work in a variety of ways and for different purposes and should be unique to the individual and her or his preferences for understanding and representing what has been learned. Some learners might rely more on visual sketches, while learners who have a linguistic preference might sketch less and write more. Further, visuals may be used strategically to connect, separate, and emphasize the most important ideas. Location, size, color, and fonts are all used to help make these distinctions.

In addition to providing an alternative form to typical note-taking (which, in itself, is beneficial), sketchnoting can be helpful for learners with visual preferences as it allows them to exercise choice in their learning and make meaning in a way that makes sense to them. Likewise, those who are not yet as comfortable with visualization strategies can be helped to grow in this area. Learners enjoy sharing their sketchnotes to learn from one another and gain new perspectives on both the content and the strategy. A learner's sketchnotes also provide a record of learning and a valuable resource to use in the future for review, reflection, and continued growth. For more information on sketchnoting and some brilliant examples, we encourage you to check out Tanny McGregor's (2018) *Ink and Ideas: Sketchnotes for Engagement, Comprehension, and Thinking.*

Prior to using this strategy, you might show a video about sketchnoting and/or model it in front of your class. As you sketchnote, you can name the moves you make while reading, such as these:

- Identifying key details (and perhaps how you use rules of notice to identify them [Wilhelm & Smith, 2016])

- Identifying a topic by figuring out what all the key details pertain to and creating a visual of it (Note well that any text has multiple topics. Any topic that all the key details pertain to will yield a justifiable topic-comment or main idea.)

- Determining the pattern of these details and how you will visually represent this pattern using text, images, icons, arrows, and other ways to indicate structural relationships

- Identifying a potential topic-comment (main idea or theme) expressed by this pattern of details about the topic

- Experimenting with different fonts, sizes, colors, icons, symbols, and locations of words and pictures to determine what is the most powerful way to capture and express various ideas

After learners try their hand at sketchnoting, it is important to have them reflect on the use of this strategy. You might ask them how they felt about the sketchnoting process, how it differed from traditional note-taking, how they used visual tools to create meaning and effect, and how they see themselves using this strategy in the future.

(Continued)

PLC Connection

Whether or not you're familiar with sketchnoting, we encourage you to check out RSA Animate's *Drive: The Surprising Truth About What Motivates Us* at bit.ly/2PTSZ5k. This video uses sketchnoting to explain the human needs for purpose (the reason we are here and how we might impact the world); mastery (the opportunity to grow and become better at something significant); and autonomy (the ability to make meaningful choices, develop independence, and direct our lives) shared in Daniel Pink's popular book *Drive*. Following the video, consider the power of sketchnoting, but also take time to discuss how well and in what ways your classroom, school, and district promote and might enhance opportunities for members to develop purpose, mastery, and autonomy, which are major goals of all cognitive apprenticeship and guided-inquiry approaches.

(Continued)

ADDITIONAL SCAFFOLDING

For younger learners, it's helpful to chunk a text or activity into manageable sections. We recommend the following:

- As learners read or view a text as a class or in small groups, have them highlight and identify the key details of each section of the text.

- Have learners create visuals for each of the sections of the text on notecards.

- Encourage learners to consider structure by organizing the notecards, considering how the key details and the different sections of text relate and build on each other and then showing the connections between ideas using additional symbols, words, or images.

■ FIGURE 9.2: EXAMPLE SKETCHNOTES OF THE EMPOWER MODEL

We've used sketchnotes throughout the book as section introductions to illustrate elements of the EMPOWER model and how they work.

Checklist for Creating Your Own Sketchnote Activity

❑ The teacher considers how and when sketchnoting might be used to understand, review, or reflect on a complex text or task. (E-M)

❑ The teacher explores and maps the process of sketchnoting (doing it herself or himself first) in order to name the steps and highlight what learners could do. This prepares her or him to model the process for learners in the lesson. (M)

❑ The teacher considers the types of materials learners will need: types of paper, pencils, colored pens or pencils, crayons, and/or technological tools. (M)

❑ Before creating their own sketchnotes, learners view and analyze models of sketchnotes and identify purposes, critical elements, moves, and techniques. (P-O)

❑ Learners identify the key details from the learning and visually represent these, showing connections between them. (W)

❑ Learners explain how they identify key details, topics, and patterns in the text and how those things work together to express main ideas. (*Note:* As learners do this, they develop threshold knowledge of the topic-comment strategy, which works to express main ideas from any text, data set, or learning experience.) (*Note:* Encourage the use of sketchnoting when learners are learning important concepts that will be used or built upon later.) (W-E)

❑ Learners determine an approach to sketchnoting and use the key details, topics, patterns, and main ideas to visually represent and make meaning of complex concepts, processes, or stories. (W)

❑ Learners reflect on their sketchnotes and the choices they made to achieve certain meanings and effects. They also refer to their sketchnotes as a resource for future discussions or assignments. (E-R)

VISUALIZATION MOVE 3: MEME MAKING

Memes are extremely popular these days. We often see them used to communicate ideas and emotions in e-mail, texts, and more. Meme making is an opportunity to combine popular cultural images with individual creativity. On its most basic level, a meme is an image paired with a humorous saying, sometimes a pun. A meme makes the reader consider, "What story is being told or what comment or idea is being expressed by this meme? Why did the author select this particular image and combine it with these particular words?"

When we consider the strategy of meme making, we must first consider the demands a meme places on a reader. Memes are often simple but not simplistic, including an image and very few words. This means that composers must be

(Continued)

(Continued)

intentional about the details they include, so the reader has enough information to determine the meaning. Ultimately, this requires the reader to make an inference about the underlying meaning by connecting the dots between the few key details provided. Composers and readers also must connect to the original inspiration for a meme. This use of world knowledge and combining it with textual information is necessary to all expert reading (see Chapter 11 on questioning). It requires only a basic level of inferencing to "get" a meme without knowing its origin; you just use the context clues. However, knowing the origin or cultural reference will greatly deepen meaning and enjoyment. It also requires a deeper level of understanding in order to repurpose an existing meme or create an original one readers will understand and enjoy. Thus, meme reading and meme making are enhanced by understanding references to world knowledge in the form of cultural stories, pop culture, and iconic images.

When teaching learners to create memes, we must first provide multiple models. As we define and explain the purpose of a meme, learners practice reading them and reflect on their process. They can consider the genre requirements of a meme (what elements does a meme have to have, and what social purposes does a meme work for?), creating a checklist of the characteristics they should use in their own meme compositions. (We call these "gotta do's" and "wanna do's"—genres have elements that are absolutely required, but they also have elements that could be used but don't have to be.)

In one fifth-grade class, after reading multiple memes, the learners came up with this definition of the meme as a genre: A *picture or figures that are a reference (an allusion) to popular culture, along with a short text. The picture and words work together to create a comment that critiques or makes fun of something like a social norm or suggests a social action in the world. The meme invites a comparison from the meme character's experience or situation and situations in which the meme reader finds herself . . . it's usually funny, like a joke, by jolting you into seeing something in a new way.* (For more on how to help learners understand genre, see Wilhelm & Smith, 2016.)

We think these fifth graders have a workable definition. Therefore, memes can be used to remix ideas, to capture any self-to-text or self-to-experience connection, to express a main idea or takeaway for any text or experience, and to put a personal comment or spin on any idea. They can also be used to parody ideas or to promote particular ways of thinking or doing things. Memes require and reward seeing connections; making inferences; and identifying implied generalizations, evaluations, and applications. Memes provide deliberate practice for these expert strategies of expert reading and the process of inquiry.

After determining the genre requirements, learners should have the opportunity to consider multiple models of memes, assessing how well these memes meet the definition and checklist they have created and determining what elements they want to emulate in their own compositions. Following this review (and possibly ranking) of models, think aloud as you create and reflect on your own meme. Mentor learners in creating their own meme by providing support in the form of questioning and coaching. Digital meme generators, such as imgflip.com/memegenerator, can be used for meme creation, but their use should be monitored closely because they include popular images that are not always appropriate for young children. Another option is makeameme.org/memegenerator, where you can upload your own image for the meme. Knowyourmeme.com provides a lengthy and detailed origin of any meme you can imagine. This is a useful teaching tool to investigate the origin and evolution of a particular meme. We referenced it to verify the syntax for the "Sharpen All the Pencils" meme (Figure 9.3), which is known generally as "X all the Y." Following the composing of memes, encourage learners to self-reflect on their meme by considering how readers may interpret the details (both words and images) and the main idea expressed by their meme. Will readers recognize the reference to popular culture? Does the meme meet the genre requirements articulated in the checklist?

As with all of the visualization strategies in this chapter, once learners have had the opportunity to experiment with meme making, they should share their creations with an authentic audience and solicit feedback about how well their meme communicated the intended message. Feedback should help learners reflect on how well their memes conveyed an intended message and what revisions they might make to convey their message more clearly. Learners may want to revise their memes based on the feedback of their peers.

One great way to practice this is to use memes to display your classroom rules. Current cartoon characters would be a good way to do this, as most learners have a common understanding of these characters and their personalities. An even better idea would be to include learners in the creation of the classroom rules and then ask them to work collaboratively to create memes for each rule. You can display the memes in your classroom so you and your learners can refer to them throughout the year.

PLC Connection
Take time to collaboratively create norms for specific processes like PLC meetings or analyzing student work together with your team, grade level, or staff (see Chapter 6). This creates community and buy-in from all members. Then, members can work together to negotiate wording as they synthesize their ideas into three to five norms that can be turned into memes.

■ FIGURE 9.3: CLASS RULES MEME

Image source: Allie Brosh, Hyperbole and a Half (http://hyperboleandahalf.blogspot.com/2010/06/this-is-why-ill-never-be-adult.html).

(Continued)

(Continued)

Checklist for Creating Your Own Memes Activity

❏ The teacher considers where in the learning process meme making might be used by learners to capture, interpret, comment on, and share their learning. The teacher plans for such experiences to meet threshold knowledge goals in the context of the larger unit. Meme making and meme reading typically require seeing connections, inferencing, critiquing, evaluating, and/or applying. (E-M)

❏ The learners consider their experience with memes, including when and where they have encountered them, the purposes served, and so forth. (P)

❏ The teacher provides examples of memes that are culturally and developmentally appropriate for learners and invites a discussion about what makes a meme a meme (promoting genre knowledge that is required whenever one reads or composes a meme) and what makes these particular memes significant, meaningful, and/or humorous. (*Note:* This helps learners deepen their understanding of what a meme is, "the work" memes can do, and how they get this work done.) (P-O)

❏ The teacher models how to make a meme to make a point or comment about a particular topic or idea, thinking aloud as he or she does so. (W)

❏ Learners have access to and use a variety of materials to create their memes in an analog or digital format. (W)

❏ The learner uses a complementary image and caption to convey a culturally and developmentally appropriate message about a text, experience, norm, or aspect of the topic of inquiry. (W)

❏ Learners have the opportunity to share their memes with peers to see if they have clearly communicated a culturally significant message. (E-R)

❏ Learners share their memes with a wider audience and reflect on how they are received and understood; learners also consider how they may use memes to communicate messages or work for transformed understandings and social actions in the future. (R)

VISUALIZATION MOVE 4: TABLEAU(X)

A tableau (singular) is one picture, photo, or still scene used to convey an event, moment in time, scene, concept, process, or part of a process. Tableaux (plural) are a *series* of connected images or scenes that helps learners identify and showcase a series of events, a process, the pattern or structure of a text, thought patterns such as cause-and-effect or problem-and-solution relationships, or various aspects of a concept. For example, learners may use tableaux to tell the story of a marathon: They may start with a picture of when the starter pistol fires, followed by a picture of a runner and some fans cheering on the sidelines, then a picture of the runner struggling, and finally a picture of the runner crossing the finish line. They might even provide a picture of the backstory (why the runner took up the challenge or how she or he trained) and figure forth to the poststory (what happens as a result of meeting the challenge). These pictures could be drawings or actual photographs that represent the process.

Tableaux can also combine elements of visualization and drama when learners create still "pictures" or "statues" with their bodies (see Wilhelm, 2012a). Using the previous example, one learner may be the runner, another the starter, another a challenge, while two other learners serve as the finish line, and another learner stands ready to place a medal around the runner's neck.

Still another variation of tableau is *tableau vivant*, in which a still picture or statue comes to life as learners are "tapped" and begin to move or talk about their experience or the meaning of their position in the tableau. In tableau vivant, learners may be allowed to use props, but often, they can create all elements—animate and inanimate—with their bodies. To add an additional element of fun and challenge, you may encourage groups of learners to guess what the other groups are "acting out" in their motionless representations. Those involved in the tableau can be tapped awake to speak or be interviewed (examples of these kinds of tableaux can be found on the DVD of Wilhelm, 2012a).

Here is a *walk-through* for creating tableaux to represent a narrative, which can easily be modified for informational texts.

Step 1: Choose the text or text segment that you wish to depict and visually share with your audience—typically peers in the classroom, though the audience could be more extensive.

Step 2: Consider why the audience will be interested in the text or excerpt you have read (or experience you want to relate) and what they will need to learn from the story you tell. (If learners are engaged in the same inquiry but different texts are being read in a jigsaw, there will be a need for all to learn about what others have read or experienced.)

Step 3: Identify the important scenes and details your audience will need to know. Consider the journalist's five Ws and one H (Who? What? Where? When? Why? and How?). Keep in mind that authors use rules of notice to "signal" readers to

(Continued)

(Continued)

notice particular details and scenes: the first and last scenes, ones that are surprising, ones that signal a climax or change in direction, ones that offer new and important information, ones that are different in some way, ones that are described in great detail, and the like.

Step 4: Brainstorm how to present these scenes visually in a way that will communicate all of the important details to the audience. This requires learners to determine what is important and to synthesize their learning. (*Extension challenge*: Use as few details or scenes as possible to communicate the whole story or meaning of a text.)

Step 5: Create visual depictions of the scenes. (*Note*: It can be helpful for learners to sketch out their ideas during the drafting stage.)

Step 6: Make notes on the back of drawings about what you need to point out to the audience about each scene when you orally present them. For example, you might include a topic word or a one-sentence summary of the scene, explain how this scene connects to the prior or following scene, point out key details and explain how these details are important, or express a major theme or takeaway through the topic-comment strategy. When you are done with an individual tableau, you should be sure that your audience will have completely understood and "seen" that whole section of the text. Likewise, the audience should understand the connections between the different tableaux that are presented.

Step 7: Afterward, review the tableaux for cohesiveness.

Step 8: Rehearse your presentation as a group, making sure everyone is involved.

Step 9: Present it!

Step 10: Get feedback, and reflect on how well you did and what you could do to improve your presentation.

PLC Connection

Any of the visualization strategies found in this chapter can be used in PLCs or professional development as a way to help staff process complex information, such as the takeaways from a professional article or exploring the process of adopting a new curriculum or implementing a new grading policy. Participating in these strategies also helps teachers gain insight and empathy for their students who are learning to use visualization strategies.

■ FIGURE 9.4: TABLEAU EXAMPLE FOR *THE SOLDIER WHO WOULDN'T TELL*

Tableau from a sequence of tableaux for *The Soldier Who Wouldn't Tell:* The Union general prosecuting Sam Davis for spying begs Sam to reveal the person who gave him the Union military maps. This would save Sam from hanging. When Sam refuses, the general expresses his admiration for Sam and shakes his hand.

Checklist for Creating Your Own Tableau(x) Activity

❑ The teacher identifies opportunities within the unit plan for learners to use the tableau(x) strategy to summarize a section of text, review or propose a process, or deepen their knowledge about the topic of inquiry. The teacher determines how to teach learners to create their own tableau(x) to meet the instructional goals. (E-M)

❑ The teacher creates interest among learners for using visual or dramatic tableaux by connecting to the uses of visuals to learn, understand, and communicate and by helping learners anticipate the joy of play and experimentation. (P-O)

❑ The teacher models how to create a tableau or shows models of tableaux to engage learners and help them define what success looks like. (P-O)

❑ Learners identify key events, scenes, or other details from a text, data set, or learning episode and use these to convey the major ideas, represent the scenes or situations, showcase a theme, and/or show text structure or patterns of meaning. (W)

❑ Learners use as few details or scenes as possible and appropriate transitions between them to communicate the whole story and/or most significant meanings of a text. (W)

❑ Learners have the opportunity to watch and engage with other groups during the tableau(x) presentations, providing procedural feedback or interviewing the composers about their compositional choices. (W-E-R)

❑ Learners reflect on their tableau(x) scene(s) and their experience composing them, often explaining the tableau(x) and their compositional choices and considering the meaning and effect of other options. (R)

(See Wilhelm, 2012a, for more on dramatic tableaux and 2012c for visual tableaux, including many extensions and variations).

POWERFUL PLANNING: VISUALIZING FOR DEEPER UNDERSTANDING, DIVERGENT THINKING . . . AND FUN

Visualization supports the navigation and comprehension of complex texts, concepts, and processes. Visualization also supports the creation of mental models and maps (and can be used to express mental maps through flow charts and the like) and engages learners with varied modes of representation and expression by providing opportunities for deep and divergent thinking. Visualization engages learners in work that promotes understanding, retention, and creativity.

The visualization strategies featured here assist learners to more deeply explore and understand; develop creative ways of thinking and problem solving; organize and represent their thinking in meaningful ways; and, most importantly, make sense of the world. Effective teaching is all about modeling, mentoring, and monitoring learners to independence in the classroom and ultimately in their lives beyond school. Visualization is a powerful and concrete way to model, mentor, and monitor. Visualization strategies and visuals also count big time in the world beyond school. It's important to provide multiple opportunities for learners to engage in these sorts of activities to make their thinking visible. Learners will grow in their abilities and become increasingly independent with practice, feedback, and opportunities to revise.

Guiding Questions When Designing Visual Activities

- What is my purpose for using this particular visualization strategy? What work will this visualization strategy do to develop deeper comprehension, explore new conceptual and strategic understanding, or assist learners to further develop their own expert meaning-making processes? (E-M)

- When might I give learners choice of which visualization strategy they use or ways to extend and modify a strategy? (E-M)

- What materials and tools will learners need to support the visualization activity? What additional materials and tools might learners want? (M)

- How will learners be helped to identify prior experiences with the power of visuals to engage and promote understanding? (P)

- How will I motivate my learners to engage in this visualization strategy and help them see the benefit of using visuals to deepen and communicate their understanding? (P-O)

- How will I model, mentor, and monitor learners with this visualization strategy to ensure they can mirror and articulate the moves and problem-solving processes of experts more independently? (W)

- How does the visual strategy promote an expert way of reading, composing, or problem solving and assist learners to do something difficult and new that leads to enhanced expertise and understanding? How does the strategy help learners understand an expert mental model or map for making meaning? (E)

- What opportunities will I give my learners to reflect on what they have learned and how they might use this learning in the future, including reflecting on the power of visualization in general and specific visualization strategies in particular? (R)

Lesson: Picturing Themes

Unit: How do I become an expert?*

ENVISION the destination			
(Where are learners going, and why?)			
GOAL *What kind of thinking is targeted?*	**EVIDENCE** *What product(s) will serve as proof of learning?*	**MEASURES OF SUCCESS** *What's the standard and quality-assurance tool?*	**STAKES** *Why will learners buy in?* *What's the why behind the learning?*
✓ Interpretation ✓ Self-assessing/ reflecting	✓ Performance assessment: open-ended essay/writing; products (i.e., RAFT); concept map	✓ **Checklist**: Assess if product contains essential characteristics/ features.	Use ESSENCE as a guide for buy-in. Your lesson should have one or more of the following: ✓ ES: Emotional spark/salience (i.e., relevance) ✓ SE: Social engagement (i.e., collaboration) ✓ N: Novelty (i.e., new concepts and skills) ✓ CE: Critical/creative exploration opportunities
Capture the essence of a text, data, or experience by illustrating and naming "the big idea": a main idea or theme that can be expressed as a topic-comment. Identify key details, a topic of the text, and the patterning of key details about a topic. Use these in service of articulating the main idea or theme, also known as a topic-comment. Convey the meaning behind the picturing themes image to peers, using simple argumentation to highlight evidence, and explain how that evidence (the patterning of key details) contributes to expressing a main idea about a central topic.	1. Learners determine the overarching theme of a text by noticing key details, patterns of key details, and a topic. 2. Learners create an image, accompanied by a meaningful quote and explanation of its significance to the theme. 3. Learners then explain how their image and quote capture the topic-comment (theme/main idea) expressed by the patterning of key details about the topic.	Picturing themes checklist: ❑ The visual captures the heart of the matter, a main idea or theme that can be expressed as a topic-comment. ❑ The visual includes visual images that are complemented by a meaningful quote to represent and support the theme. ❑ Learners share their visual and quote. They articulate their thinking about how this composition works to express the theme, explaining how their composition captures the topic-comment (theme/main idea) expressed by the patterning of key details about the topic.	**ES:** Learners express their learning through an alternate modality. Visuals are often used in everyday life to enhance written or spoken expression. **SE:** Learners may work in partners or groups to create their visuals. Sharing of visuals is also a critical component. **N:** Learners could express their learning about the theme in this way for the first time. The topic-comment strategy may be new to them. **CE:** Learners apply their learning by using picturing themes in their independent reading and listening.

(Continued)

*Please note: This lesson is a complement to the Jigsaw lesson canvas in Chapter 12.

MAP out the path to expertise/mastery
(How would an expert deconstruct and approach this task, step by step?)

TWITTER SUMMARY (3 bullets max)	MENTAL MODELS, PROCESS GUIDES, HEURISTICS	A MODEL OF GOOD WORK LOOKS LIKE . . .	DIFFERENTIATION AND LAYERING
Expert readers identify overarching themes and convey them in meaningful ways to others.	• Recognizing key details, the pattern of details, and a topic (general subject) are necessary for readers to extract a main idea or theme from any text (i.e., a topic-comment).	See example in Figure 9.1.	Levels of assistance: Learners may need practice and scaffolding with identifying key details, patterns of details, and topics so that they can identify a main idea/theme. The teacher provides models and modeling as needed. The teacher provides scaffolds and prompts such as the rules of notice or labeled examples of picturing theme images. Learners may engage and work with different kinds of groups. The teacher and peers offer continual procedural feedback.

POWER through your lesson
(What is the sequence of initial major must-make instructional moves?)

	PRIME	ORIENT	WALK THROUGH (and check for understanding)	EXTEND AND EXPLORE	REFLECT
Leader	REVIEW the term *theme* and the process of recognizing key details, patterns of details, and topics in a text to identify the theme. Review that a theme is a kind of main idea that can be expressed as a topic-comment. PROMPT learners to practice with a simpler text. Begin close to home by having learners use themselves as the topic and their lives as the central text, analyzing details and changes in their life experience to determine a theme that represents who they are, *or* select and read aloud a children's book (select one about mathematics such as *Math Curse* for a twofer), thinking aloud and using the topic and patterns of key details to identify the main idea or overall theme while reading.	FRAME today's lesson: REVIEW the guiding question for this lesson, "What do expert mathematicians do?" REMIND learners that we will be using the Mathematical Practice Standards to help us answer this guiding question. REMIND learners to capitalize on the work they have done in the preceding jigsaw lessons (see "Jigsaw Lesson Plan in Chapter 12"). EXPLAIN: "Creating visuals of each of the Mathematical Practice Standards will make the practices of expert mathematicians concrete for all of us. We want to internalize these same practices so that we can become more expert mathematicians!"	SHOW models of picturing themes visuals, and have learners discuss what they notice about these visuals. CHECK FOR UNDERSTANDING: Ask learners, "How did you know to notice these particular details in the visuals?" EXPLAIN the expectations for the product by sharing what each visual should include and the checklist by which you will assess the visuals. *Optional scaffold if needed:* MODEL the process of creating a picturing themes image by thinking aloud about one of the Mathematical Practice Standards. Share your inner dialogue as you identify the key details within the passage, identify a central topic, analyze the patterns of key details and how they express the theme, and create a visual complemented by a quote to represent this theme. CHECK FOR UNDERSTANDING: Have learners explain the process for identifying the theme as a topic-comment.	DELIBERATE PRACTICE/ ARTICULATE CONSCIOUS AWARENESS: Learners reflect on the process and choices they made in identifying the main idea or theme, choosing their quote, and creating their visual. As learners share their visuals with peers, they articulate this process and explain how their mathematical practice looks in both a math class and in their lives. Peers provide procedural feedback to one another, and learners have time to revise.	LEADERS MODEL REFLECTION ON THE STRATEGY: Leaders model assessing a visual representation against the picturing themes checklist to ensure expectations are met. Leaders use the roundtable strategy to involve learners in evaluating the example. The learners can engage in rating the example compared to the models they examined at the beginning of the lesson, asking, "How close is the model to expertise? What next steps could be taken?"

POWER through your lesson
(What is the sequence of initial major must-make instructional moves?)

	PRIME	ORIENT	WALK THROUGH (and check for understanding)	EXTEND AND EXPLORE	REFLECT
Leader				Once all visuals have been completed, they are posted in the classroom, and learners brainstorm real-world applications of each of the Mathematical Practice Standards in small groups or as a class. Learners write these applications on sticky notes and post them on the appropriate posters. Encourage learners to continue doing this for the next several days, and provide opportunities for learners to reflect on and name the practices they use daily in math class. Learners can likewise be prompted to consider other uses for using the picturing themes technique in school and in life. They can look for how variations of picturing themes are used in picture books, visual displays, advertisements, etc.	
Learner	ANALYZE a simple text to identify key details and patterns to determine the theme of the text in partners, then small groups, and then as a whole class. TRANSFER the theme into visuals (known as transmediation, a proof positive of understanding) by creating a visual that gets at the heart of the matter to express a main idea or theme. REFLECT on what was challenging and helpful in this experience.	REFLECT on the guiding question, and keep this question in mind throughout today's lesson. REVIEW the jigsaw placemats (see Chapter 12) from yesterday's lesson to identify the key details, topic, and overarching theme of the selected Mathematical Practice Standard.	GUIDED PRACTICE: Learners work in partnerships or triads to review their assigned Mathematical Practice Standard and to create a picturing themes visual to represent a topic-comment/main idea behind this math practice. DIFFERENTIATE: Learners are assisted by the teacher through questioning and coaching. Successful peers can also assist. DEBRIEF: Learners reflect on their assigned Mathematical Practice Standard and how they use this practice in their own lives.		LEARNERS REFLECT ON THE STRATEGY: Learners can further reflect on the strategy by discussing how it helped them develop and represent their thinking and how they may use it in the future in their independent reading and learning. LEARNERS ALSO REFLECT ON TOPIC-COMMENT: "How can you use the topic-comment strategy to find a main idea or theme about any text?" LEARNERS REFLECT ON THE CONTENT: Learners reflect on what they have learned and set a goal for the future via this writing prompt: "Which of these mathematical practices do you use most often in your life? Which mathematical practice is a strength of yours? Which mathematical practice do you want to improve on in the future?" HOMEWORK EXTENSION: Learners are asked to practice this strategy with a text of their choice (such as a book, cartoon, or movie).

Chapter 10

WALKING LEARNERS THROUGH WITH THINK-ALOUD STRATEGIES

> **ESSENTIAL QUESTION**
> How can we make expert processes of reading, composing, and problem solving accessible, visible, and available to learners?

Popular tourist destinations worldwide, regardless of culture and geography, share a common feature: area residents offer their knowledge to visitors as guides. Sometimes, their expertise is streamed into earbuds, spelled out in signage, or provided personally by a tour guide. All of these forms of guidance help novices navigate, interpret, and learn about the terrain.

See *Lesson Plan Canvas* on page 181

For many learners, the critical reading and writing processes that occur in school are as unfamiliar to them as Machu Picchu or Pompeii is to a tourist. A teacher's role is to guide learners through the process of understanding complex concepts and processes, and one of the best ways we can do so is by **thinking aloud**—the explicit modeling of using expert strategies by verbally or visually sharing our thought processes while we engage in our work. The think-aloud conducts a *walk-through* for learners of an author, reader, or problem solver's moves to help them understand how the meaning-making process works (e.g., how to notice key details and text features, how to interpret and explain the meanings and effects of various text structures, or how to generate a claim from evidence).

Think-alouds are a *must-make move* of inquiry for cognitive apprenticeship (ICA) because they make otherwise invisible strategies and mental models of expert reading, composing, or problem solving visible to learners (Wilhelm, 2012d). Most of the think-aloud strategies in this chapter support reading comprehension because it's a focus area for elementary learners that transcends disciplines and can be adapted to the particular demands of different text types, but think-alouds can be used to model how to navigate any difficult concept or problem-solving process. Think-alouds are effective for learners who are learning to read as well (e.g., when teachers model which phonological rules to consider when decoding a word or share how context clues are used to support comprehension). Once you get comfortable using a think-aloud in one content area, try it in others; learners can always benefit from more examples of expertise in action, whether it's setting up a science experiment and analyzing data or figuring out the costs and benefits of various ways to solve a mathematical problem. Thinking aloud means taking off the top of your head and letting learners see what you are doing as you read, compose, and problem-solve in expert ways that they can adopt.

PLANNING FOR WALKING LEARNERS THROUGH WITH THINK-ALOUD STRATEGIES

When you *map* out a think-aloud focused on reading comprehension, be sure to select a text that is within the zone of proximal development (ZPD)—something learners can access with support and scaffolding that they cannot yet do on their own. Limit the length of text by using something like a children's book, a poem, or an excerpt of a longer text so that the think-aloud will be tightly focused and engaging. Be sure that the excerpt requires and rewards using the concepts and/or strategy that you are teaching.

An accessible and engaging text should *prime* the learners' interest in the task and topic and offer challenges to their current level of understanding so that they can move to the next level. Before a think-aloud, a teacher plans or *maps* out what moves she or he wants to model for learners, much like a tour guide would draw up an itinerary before a trip. When teachers think aloud, learners can see the moves and success criteria necessary for the new learning and experience a *walk-through* to a new level of expert practice.

Learners vary in their expertise at reading, writing, and problem solving and need different levels of support from think-alouds. Some learners may benefit from additional *walk-throughs* in small groups, more teacher modeling, or practice with less complex or more visual texts (see the section on access and differentiation in Chapter 2). Alternately, using think-alouds with more complex texts for learners who are advancing quickly provides a great way to *extend* and *explore*. As you read each of the following strategies, consider how to adapt them to your context and the needs of your learners, using various forms of differentiation.

Returning to the metaphor of the tour, anyone in the class could potentially become the guide. Early in the process of learning a skill, the teacher is the only one familiar with the territory, so she or he serves as the class tour guide. As learners deliberately practice, *extend*, and *explore* skills and strategies through thinking aloud, they can then play the role of tour guide for younger learners and for their less expert peers. The capacity to do a think-aloud of one's own for a complex text or task reflects conscious competence and proof of learning. Helping learners develop think-aloud skills can be scaffolded by asking them to start by verbalizing their thinking processes while engaging in basic procedural activities they are already experts in, such as participating in playground games. Another approach would be to record learners completing a task or performance and then ask them to think-aloud retrospectively about what they were doing and thinking as they went through the task.

Allow learners to choose topics, texts, and focal strategies for their own think-alouds; this leads to increased relevance, engagement, and ownership in their learning. Think-alouds led by learners can occur in pairs, small groups, or larger groups, and they provide a grand opportunity for learners to *extend* and *reflect* when they receive feedback from peers and teachers alike. This feedback is critical in helping them to hone their skills, develop a common academic language, and reflect on and practice their thinking.

After a trip, travelers love to share pictures, stories, and highlights with friends and other potential tourists. In so doing, the storyteller distills the most salient and memorable parts of the journey. Likewise, when learners think aloud after a task to review their process (called a process analysis) or when a think-aloud is followed by a discussion about crux moves and how to apply them in different contexts, it serves as a tool for extension and reflection.

Considerations When Designing and Conducting a Think-Aloud

❑ The think-aloud focuses on a particularly challenging or meaningful section of text, a complex process, or a problem that is at the learners' instructional level or ZPD; it is a challenge that learners can navigate *with the help of the think-aloud* but cannot *yet* navigate alone. (E-M-P-O)

❑ The teacher (or classroom expert) models how to use specific strategies, how to read a specific kind of text, or how to solve a particular kind of problem. The think-aloud is task- or text-specific and is focused on goals necessary for successfully completing that text or task. (W)

❑ The think-aloud is conducted in chunks, allowing for processing time between each one. Teachers and learners use writing and/or discussion to encourage learners to record and reflect on the moves being made. (W-E)

❑ The think-aloud names and makes visible the moves that expert readers, composers, and problem solvers make in order for learners to become conscious of these strategies and then transfer these moves to their own practice. (W-E)

❑ The think-aloud is used by teachers and learners as formative assessment data, providing a snapshot of where learners are on the path toward expertise, and to determine how strategies might be extended and used next. (R)

THINK-ALOUD MOVE 1: CUED THINK-ALOUD

In a *cued think-aloud*, the cue, or prompt, brings learners' attention to a specific tip-off that a particular strategy may be useful. For example, in a cued think-aloud about predictions, a teacher might articulate why she or he chooses to make a prediction at the conclusion of a chapter that ends on a cliff-hanger, as opposed to in the middle of

(Continued)

(Continued)

a description of the African savanna. Cued think-alouds prompt the reader to think about **when** the strategy is required and **why** it is used, as well as how to use it. These are some of the most crucial components for learners to *walk through* on the path to expert reading.

Cued think-alouds can be applied to virtually any focal strategy or skill, but in elementary schools, they're frequently used with the general reading strategies that readers use *every time* they successfully read any kind of text:

- Activate background and set purpose for reading

- Summarize: bring meaning forward through the text

- See connections: intratextual (patterns within the text—details inside the text to other details inside that text—necessary for making inferences) and intertextual (patterns across texts: text-to-text, text-to-self, text-to-world)

- Make inferences based on these patterns or by figuring forth from meaningful details

- Ask questions: factual, interpretive, critical/applicative

- Monitor understanding and self-correct

- Make predictions

- Visualize story worlds and create visual mental models of new concepts and processes

In the following cued think-aloud example using the book *Fish in a Tree* by Lynda Mullaly Hunt (2017), we model how to see connections and make meaning of them. Because the book is set in a school, learners should have some prior knowledge. A major theme in the book is employing a growth mindset to overcome learning differences, a theme that connects well with other texts in our throughline unit. Ideally, learners would have their own copy of the text in front of them and follow along while the teacher reads aloud and pauses intermittently, or cues learners, to think aloud about the different types of connections they are making. Depending on the needs of learners, those places where the teacher stops and thinks could be referenced or marked in some way so learners know when to stop.

PLC Connection

Use a cued think-aloud while grouping standards for a unit, selecting a balance of content and literacy standards to support the goals of an instructional unit. Model how to select targeted standards (those standards that will be a central focus of the unit and will be assessed to mastery) and supporting standards (those standards that will supplement the targeted standards, be reinforced from previous instruction, or frontload future instruction), as well as how to deconstruct the standards into student-friendly learning goals. Likewise, a think-aloud or group think-aloud could be used while teachers read a research article or another short article about a topic related to current professional development.

Example: Cued Think-Aloud

Cued Think-Aloud Lesson of *Fish in a Tree* by Lynda Mullaly Hunt

Focal Strategy: Making Connections

TEXT	TEACHER
It's always there. Like the ground underneath my feet.	
"Well, Ally? Are you going to write or aren't you?" Mrs. Hall asks.[1] If my teacher were mean it would be easier.	1. Questions in a text are always something to notice because they are a call to attention. When the author or character phrases a question like this in the text as a challenge or command, it makes me wonder what I would do if I was in that character's shoes. Now, I want to compare how the teacher in the story handles this. This is a text-self connection.
"C'mon," she says. "I know you can do it." "What if I told you that I was going to climb a tree using only my teeth? Would you say I could *do it* then?"	
Oliver laughs, throwing himself on his desk like it's a fumbled football. Shay groans. "Ally, why can't you just act normal for once?"[2]	2. This reminds me of when I see football players dive for the ball on TV. I like how the author uses a simile to describe this action. Similes are a call to attention. Shay's comment also reveals Ally's character. If she never acts normal, I can figure out something about her.
Near her, Albert, a bulky kid who's worn the same thing every day—a dark T-shirt that reads *Flint*—sits up straight. Like he's waiting for a firecracker to go off.	
Mrs Hall sighs. "C'mon, now. I'm only asking for one page describing yourself."	
I can't think of anything worse than having to describe myself. I'd rather write about something more positive. Like throwing up at your own birthday party.[3]	3. Ally's refusal to even try shows she might have a fixed mindset, like we read about the other day. The throwing up kind of shocks me and that makes me notice it. This is a reader's rule of notice and a text-self connection. I wonder why she is so over the top about this, so absolutely against it. It's a call to attention when behavior is over the top.
"It's important," she says. "It's so your new teacher can get to know you."	
I know that, and it's exactly why I don't want to do it. Teachers are like the machines that take quarters for bouncy balls. You know what you're going to get. Yet, you don't know, too.[4]	4. As a teacher, I disagree with what the student thinks, at least as applied to myself, because I feel like I am willing to mix things up and surprise students. Points of disagreement are always something to notice. This is called a reader's rule of notice, and it's also a text-self connection.
"And," she says, "all that doodling of yours, Ally. If you weren't drawing all the time, your work might be done.[5] Please put it away."	5. This is like Ramon from the story *Ish* because he spent all his time drawing, too. I wonder what her reason is for doodling. It might just be that she likes to draw, or it might be that she's trying to avoid something else. When you make a connection to another detail in the text or even a different text, that is something to notice. This one is a text–text connection.

If this is the first time learners see the process of making connections, ask for general observations about how connections are identified. If learners are more familiar with the process, they can name and track the types of connections they make: details within a text, from the text to personal experience, from the text to other texts, or from the text to the world in general. Connection making can be scaffolded through the use of sentence frames or recurring phrases used in the think-aloud, such as "This reminds me of . . . ," "I know . . . ," "*x* is like . . . because . . . ," and so on, so learners can begin making these moves themselves.

(Continued)

(Continued)

EXTENSION: FREE-RESPONSE THINK-ALOUD

Free-response think-alouds are useful to get a formative assessment, to extend and explore expertise, or at the end of a unit to see how learners are using various strategies. It is less focused as a teaching tool because in a *free-response think-aloud*, there are no specific moves in the text or reading strategy that are cued. Teachers or learners freely articulate their thought processes, unedited, as they read a text. They share anything they are thinking, feeling, noticing, questioning, doing, or connecting to while reading. They also may summarize and illustrate why and how they notice details and features of the text and how they interpret these. This demonstrates the cognitively complex process of expert reading, as the reader fluidly uses a variety of comprehension strategies, orchestrating them all to make meaning. Free-response think-alouds can also support instruction in other skills, such as annotation (thinking and responding on paper) as a part of the close-reading process. At the elementary level, this can be especially helpful, because annotation is likely a new skill to your learners. Hearing and seeing a *walk-through* about how and why you annotate helps learners develop their own habit of annotation, a skill they will need throughout their lives.

Example: Analyzing a Math Word Problem

Here we use a free-response think-aloud to model how an expert mathematician analyzes a word problem. In addition to demonstrating how to flexibly move between the general reading strategies and task- or text-specific strategies, free-response think-alouds are also useful to model specific kinds of problem solving because they break a complex text into manageable chunks. In this example, the free response also models for learners how to make connections with similar problems, notice key words and information, and ask specific kinds of questions. This makes free-response think-alouds an excellent tool to help learners access and understand the Mathematical Practice Standards.

TEXT	THOUGHTS
Jackie and Chris want to throw a party for both of their classes, but they are unsure about how much it will cost.	This reminds me of my class party!
There are 28 learners in Jackie's class and 27 learners in Chris's class. Every learner will bring one guest to the party.	In other problems, *cost* is a very important word. It would be hard to throw a party without knowing how much it cost.
They plan on giving everyone two tacos and a bottle of soda. They can buy a box of 10 tacos for $8 and a 12-pack of sodas for $6.	I'm going to take note of these numbers because I'll need to know how much to buy based on the numbers of people. The more people who attend, the more expensive it will be.
How much would it cost for them to provide every learner, the teacher, and one guest per learner two tacos and a soda?	As the host, it's important to know how much food and drink to buy. I noticed there are numbers related to money here, so I will note them on my paper.
	One challenge is that the tacos and sodas come in boxes and packs, so I can't buy exactly the number I want. A model will help me visualize what I need to do in this situation. I'm going to draw a bar model for the number of taco boxes I need to buy in order for everyone to have two tacos.

Checklist for Creating Your Own Cued Think-Aloud

❑ Before modeling the cued think-aloud, the teacher identifies the focal strategy and then reads and flags or annotates the text, rehearsing what she or he will say during the model think-aloud to highlight the use of the strategy and how she or he knows when and why to use it. (E-M)

❑ The teacher chooses a short but rich text, data set, or problem that requires the focal strategy. (M)

❑ The teacher models the focal strategy by thinking aloud, connecting what's being done back to learners' experience and forward to what they need to do when thinking aloud on their own. (P-O)

❑ The teacher distinguishes between a read-aloud and a think-aloud, which reveals what is going on strategically in the reader or problem solver's head. (O-W)

❑ Learners are given cues (e.g., underlined words and phrases) about what to notice and scaffolds, such as sentence stems, that help them use, think, and talk about the focal strategy. (O-W)

❑ Learners have their own copy of the text so they can follow along with the teacher, and they have been given a task or deliverable to focus on while observing and again when they take over the thinking aloud. (W)

❑ Learners can speak their think-aloud into a recording device or aloud to a peer but more typically write it, putting the text or problem on the left side of a sheet and recording what they notice and do next to the details that prompted these thoughts and actions. Sticky notes, a notebook page set next to a page of reading, and other devices also work for think-aloud annotation. (W)

❑ Learners are provided multiple opportunities to practice using the skill or strategy with the teacher, their peers, and eventually on their own. (W-E)

❑ A debrief discussion or reflection occurs, where learners articulate the moves made and how these moves worked to create meaning or solve problems; learners then work to construct a mental model of the process of task completion. (R)

THINK-ALOUD MOVE 2: FIX-UP STRATEGIES

One of the most significant differences between accomplished and struggling readers (or problem-solvers of any kind) is that accomplished readers notice when something doesn't make sense and have strategies for "fixing" it. Cued think-alouds about *fix-up strategies* can prepare learners for those struggles before they dive into challenging texts or tasks. This sequence of instruction provides learners a set of self-monitoring and correction skills they can use while reading any text and spares them from frustration and a sense that their "toolbox is empty."

Fix-up strategies presuppose that even expert readers may often struggle with complex text, but they have ways to productively navigate the struggle. *Priming* learners to the importance of this skill makes the process of struggle and correction visible and affirms that it is part of expert reading. The mistakes and missteps of experts are an overlooked and widely underrepresented part of the learning process (which is why our throughline unit focuses on cultivating a growth mindset and considering the process of productive struggle to become an expert).

Here are some prompts a teacher could use during a fix-up strategies think-aloud:

- I'm unsure about . . . so I will . . .
- What did the author just try to share? I think I need to . . .
- Maybe I should think more about . . .
- At first, I thought . . . Now, I need to figure out . . .
- What I thought before made sense. Now, it doesn't make sense because . . .
- One thing I could do to help me understand right now would be to . . .
- Since I didn't understand that part, I'm going to . . .
- I need to change my thinking by . . .
- This means . . . because it says . . .
- I know . . . so . . .
- I think I need to reread because . . .

Example: Fix-Up Strategies Think-Aloud

Think-Aloud for *Fish in a Tree* by Lynda Mullaly Hunt

TEXT	TEACHER
Albert, Keisha, and I get off the bus for our class trip to the Noah Webster House.[1] With no written work today, I'm thinking it will be a silver dollar day.[2]	1. **I'm unsure about** who Noah Webster is and why his house matters. **I think I need to ask someone else** to explain, or I need to do some research. Since it's the subject of the class trip, it must be important. 2. **I know from my own experience** that silver dollars are cool because they're valuable. **I think she's saying** that it will be a good day.
Albert starts collecting acorns from the ground and filling his pockets. I'm tempted to ask why, but I'm afraid the answer will take an hour.[3]	3. **I think** this means Albert talks a lot. **How does it connect** with what I already know about him?
Oliver picks up acorns and whips[4] them at the trees. Max joins in. Max hits a tree every time. Oliver, not so much. Mr. Daniels walks over and says something to them to make them stop.	4. **What does it mean** to whip an acorn at a tree? **I will keep reading** to see if I gain more information that will help me make sense of this statement. Ah, the next sentence makes it sound like whipping is a way of throwing—maybe throwing hard.
I pick an acorn up, too, and it reminds me of a little Frenchman with a pointed chin. Perfectly shaped head with a little beret. I name him Pierre[5] and stick him in my pocket. I decide that I'll do a drawing of him later. Maybe dancing with a lady at the Eiffel Tower. My grandpa always said he was going to take me to see it.	5. Why did she choose this name? **Since I didn't understand**, **I'm going to reread** the earlier part of the paragraph and see if it connects with this part. What does it reveal about her that she names her acorn and keeps it? Does it have anything to do with her grandfather? Since he's mentioned here, I think there might be a connection, but I'll have to read on to be sure.

A flowchart that is a mental model of monitoring and fixing up will provide a useful scaffold to help learners internalize this thought process (see Figure 10.1). This chart could be consulted just before reading to *orient* learners to the task or used as a scaffold while they *extend* and *explore* the skill.

(Continued)

■ FIGURE 10.1: FIX-UP STRATEGIES FLOWCHART

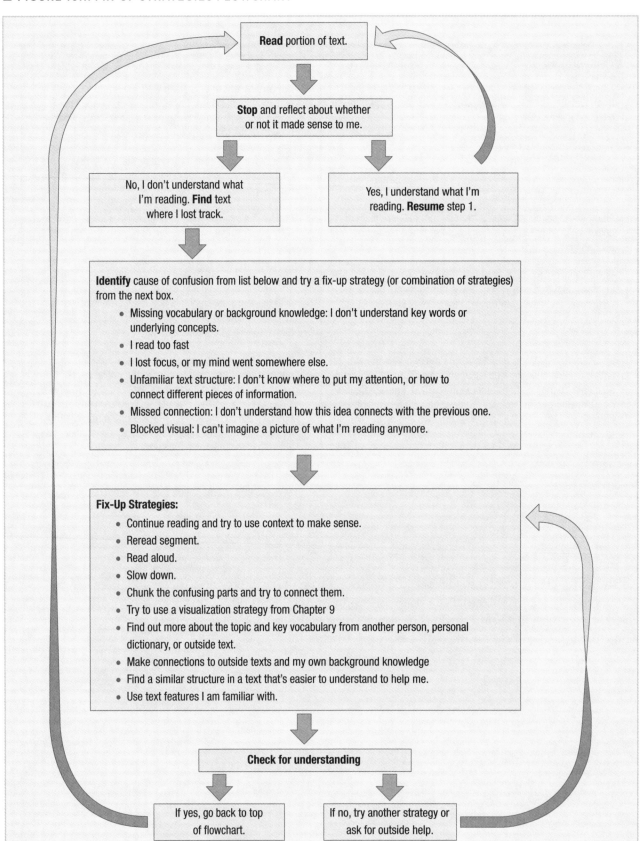

Checklist for Creating Your Own Fix-Up Strategies Activity

❑ The teacher identifies a challenging text or task and some specific fix-up strategies that will help with navigating the challenges. (E-M)

❑ The text excerpt is challenging enough for learners that they have authentic questions and confusions, but not so difficult that they are lost the entire time. (M)

❑ Learners understand that there are different sources of confusion while reading and that these can be navigated by using fix-up strategies. (P-O)

❑ Teachers model and mentor learners by helping them identify when they experience challenges in their reading. (W)

❑ Teachers model and then mentor learners to select and employ appropriate fix-up strategies when they experience confusion, using strategies that best meet the challenges they face. (W-E)

❑ Learners access and use resources—such as an anchor chart or a flowchart representing a mental model or map for using the various fix-up strategies—to help them know how and when to use such strategies. (E)

❑ Learners reflect on what they learned and how they can continue to build and use their repertoire of fix-up strategies in reading and other domains. (R)

THINK-ALOUD MOVE 3: THINK LIKE AN AUTHOR (OR ANY OTHER EXPERT)

Think-alouds are not limited to reading processes. Because think-alouds are useful for making the thinking of experts visible, they are invaluable for *walking through* any composing or problem-solving process. In this strategy, we explore using think-alouds to support the writing process.

Think-alouds can work for a wide variety of powerful purposes. You might conduct think-alouds to do the following:

- Show learners a composing process and solicit feedback on your own writing from your classroom of writers as a way to model composing processes and the application of critical standards about a task to composing and revising.

(Continued)

(Continued)

- Conduct genre-specific think-alouds to model how the features or mental model of a particular kind of narrative, informational text, or opinion piece guides and influences the thought process of a reader or writer.

- Model how you pay attention to a certain writing move in any type of cued think-aloud, highlighting how writers put into a text what they want readers to notice, and how readers notice and make meaning of these details and moves.

- Think-aloud "like an author" to show learners how to attend to organizing and patterning key details, generating descriptive language, describing cause-and-effect relationships, choosing compelling and varied vocabulary, and more. You think like an author any time you write something and share the thinking and moves you make throughout the process with your learners. By doing this often and with different types of writing, you model how to make various expert writing moves and how to write in a variety of different genres.

- Model your writing process for any kind of text or move, in any genre, by using short texts that require specific moves. For example, when composing a timeline for social studies or English, you can think aloud about how you decide on the most crucial events; list them on sticky notes; put them in chronological order; and then identify various relationships, like cause and effect or problem–solution.

- Take something familiar to learners, such as annotations that you've already modeled in front of the class, and revise them into a summary.

- Model productive struggle with a challenge and how you navigate that challenge. This models a growth mindset; resilience in the face of a challenge; and bricolage, or playing around to solve a problem (see Wilhelm, 2012d).

When learners have the opportunity to watch you write and think aloud about a text as it develops, you provide a *walk-through* for an opaque process. You are making the struggle of generating and organizing ideas visible and available to them. Ideally, you will talk while learners watch you write under a document camera or type while projecting the screen to the class. It is important to share how you self-correct and revise *as* you write, so learners see the true process of expert writing or any kind of problem solving. Ongoing revision is an essential component of the writing process; it's normal to make many false starts and ongoing revisions when you write or problem-solve. It is incredibly beneficial for you to navigate trouble and correct errors in front of learners because it models what expert writers experience and do and also provides an opportunity to teach revision in context.

Informational and opinion writing make excellent text types for modeling *thinking like an author* because elementary learners often engage in more narrative writing. The following example focuses on how to write a conclusion to a lab report that compares plants grown with a store-bought fertilizer, plants grown with the class compost pile, and plants grown with soil without anything added (as a control). In this particular example, most of the focus is on the structural features of a conclusion and the work these features do for a reader. The entire think-aloud occurs before learners write up their own lab reports, so they are *oriented* to what they should consider and include in their own writing.

Example: Composing a Science Lab Report

Lab Report, With Think-Aloud in *Italics*

Teacher:　　　*The purpose of a lab conclusion is to review the experiment and the major takeaways, so I'm going to start with the question we wanted to answer because that establishes the purpose for this lab. So I'm going to write,*

My partner and I wondered about how to help our string beans grow as much as possible because we have them in our home gardens.

Teacher:　　　*Next, I'll share our hypotheses because I like how the mentor text for a lab conclusion that we read earlier did the same thing. I'll even use some of the same keywords, such as* hypothesize *and* because.

We hypothesized that store-bought fertilizer would yield the best result because it is developed by professional scientists. We thought the plants grown in compost would be second tallest, and the plants in soil without anything added would grow the least.

Teacher:　　　*I really want to share about whether our answer was right or wrong. Before doing that, I need to briefly share how we conducted the experiment and the results.*

We planted 6 Romano bean seeds in each of the following: soil with a store-bought fertilizer, soil with organic compost, and soil without anything added (control). After 4 weeks, the composted plants on average grew the tallest, with fertilizer second, and the soil control group last.

Teacher:　　　*I have so much data to share, but I'm going to focus on two categories that matter about growth: height and number of leaves. I'm going to avoid using* tallest *and* lots of leaves *and use exact numbers instead, so there are no questions or doubt in the reader's mind and because scientists count and measure things precisely!*

The composted Romano beans grew 2 inches taller than the fertilized seeds and 3.5 inches taller than the control group. They also grew 20% more leaves than the fertilized seeds and 25% more leaves than the control group.

Teacher:　　　*I need to continue to use precise language while I talk about possible causes for data errors. I also need to reference the bean package so I sound credible!*

(Continued)

(Continued)

We used the same amount of soil, light, and water for each group of beans. All of the beans came from the same seed packet. In the compost and fertilizer groups, 5 out of 6 beans sprouted. In the control group, 4 out of 6 beans sprouted. These results were close to the expected germination rate of 70% listed on the seed package.

Teacher: *Now I need to explain why I think the results were different from the hypothesis.*

We believe the composted Romano beans grew the tallest because of the irregularity in the soil and the air pockets that it created. We think the extra air, in addition to the nutrients, promoted better plant growth.

Teacher: *I'm not 100% confident in my explanation, so I'm going to include a proposal for another experiment in the future to answer the new questions this experiment raised. In fact, scientists always look at limitations of their studies and what they will do next to address those limitations.*

The answer was not what we expected, but we believe we succeeded in answering our question about how to help string beans grow. In order to better explain our results and test our new hypothesis, we propose another experiment where we control the amount of air present in the soil.

PLC Connection

Teachers can also usefully engage in a talk-back or a more elaborated process analysis when they engage in lesson planning or lesson study, as they rehearse the map of a lesson plan or reflect back on how a lesson went and what to do next.

After the think-aloud, make sure to discuss the process and to name the text features required in a lab report conclusion so those moves are tangible to learners. One of the best ways to do this is to draw attention to patterns, such as how data and precise language are important to technical and informational writing. In this case, you might focus on the importance of sequencing and how the question leads to the hypothesis, which leads to the experimental design, which leads to testing the hypothesis and the results, and so on. These could be recorded on an anchor chart or reference guide of some kind for learners to use in their own writing afterward. Understanding this kind of patterning of content helps learners develop genre knowledge—in this case, the genre of a lab report.

Just like every other think-aloud strategy, learners can lead this kind as well, as long as you've sufficiently modeled and deliberately practiced this skill beforehand. The first time you ask learners to think aloud about their writing, have them try it with something short and fun, like a response to what they would do if they were magically granted three wishes. Then, the entire class could take turns writing and thinking aloud as each learner writes about a different wish.

Checklist for Creating Your Own Think Like an Author Activity

☐ The teacher determines a few specific expert moves he or she will model based on the purpose of the lesson, the genre of the writing, and the audience for the writing. (E-M)

☐ The purpose and payoff of writing this kind of text or making this kind of move are highlighted for learners. (P-O)

☐ The modeled writing and think-aloud occur authentically in front of the learners, along with all of the productive struggle and self-correction. The teacher models how to find and generate ideas, as well as how to shape and structure his or her expression. (W)

☐ Learners have the opportunity to experiment with their own writing shortly after the think-aloud model and in many future instances. (W-E)

☐ Learners reflect on what they have learned and how to continue using it in new situations. (R)

POWERFUL PLANNING: MAKING INVISIBLE PROCESSES VISIBLE

The versatility and flexibility of think-alouds cannot be overstated; they are a powerful tool to make the invisible processes of experts both visible and available to learners. The think-aloud process allows learners to see inside the minds of experts and then to imitate these skills until they develop and gain independent flexibility with them. Think-alouds also offer incredible opportunities to assess learners' progress toward specific skills by listening to *them* think aloud. There is no better way to get inside the minds of your learners and truly understand what they know and are able to do and to then identify achievable goals, identify next steps, and model ways forward.

One of the many things elementary teachers do very well is read aloud to young learners to model fluency,

share our joy for reading and for books, and use our reading selections as mentor texts. Read-alouds, an excellent strategy in their own right, can easily become think-alouds when the teacher annotates or explains what she or he notices, how she or he notices these details and moves, and how she or he uses what is noticed to interpret and create meaning from the text (e.g., by using the topic-comment strategy to identify main ideas). This easily morphs into the learners creating an ongoing think-aloud commentary about the text. Consider when you might turn a read-aloud into a think-aloud to articulate and model some specific expert moves you make while reading.

As you try these strategies, keep in mind that the examples we provide only scratch the surface of how and where think-alouds can—and should—be used. Any context where you want learners to use an expert thought process is an ideal opportunity for thinking aloud. (For a comprehensive look at the possibilities of thinking aloud, see *Improving Comprehension With Think-Aloud Strategies* [Wilhelm, 2012d].)

Guiding Questions for Designing Think-Aloud Activities

- What is my purpose for conducting this think-aloud? Which specific think-aloud strategy and cues will best support my purpose and the needs of my learners for learning the focal strategy or move? (E-M)

- How will I foreground the purpose and payoff of learning the focal strategy through thinking aloud? (P-O)

- How will I best structure and chunk the think-aloud to promote learner success with the text, task, or skills being taught? (W)

- What specific skills, practices, or moves of expert readers, composers, or problem solvers will I intentionally model in this think-aloud? What are the best ways to do this? (W)

- What opportunities will I provide for my learners to practice the skills or moves modeled in the think-aloud? How will I move from modeling (doing it *for* the learners) to mentoring (doing it *with* learners or having them do it *with* each other) to monitoring (having learners do it *by* themselves)? (W)

- How can I intentionally structure opportunities that require and reward learners to extend and transfer these skills to new texts, tasks, and contexts? (E)

- What opportunities will I structure for my learners to reflect on their learning during and after the think-aloud experience and to consider future opportunities to use what they learned? (E-R)

Lesson: Cued Think-Aloud

Unit: How do I become an expert?

ENVISION the destination
(Where are learners going, and why?)

GOAL *What kind of thinking is targeted?*	EVIDENCE *What product(s) will serve as proof of learning?*	MEASURES OF SUCCESS *What's the standard and quality-assurance tool?*	STAKES *Why will learners buy in?* *What's the why behind the learning?*
✓ Explanation/ reasoning ✓ Application of skill or strategy ✓ Self-assessing or reflecting	✓ Constructed (discrete task, long/short response, graphic organizer) ✓ Structured or unstructured observation	✓ **Checklist**: Assess if product contains essential characteristics or features	Use ESSENCE as a guide for buy-in. Your lesson should have one or more of the following: ✓ ES: Emotional spark or salience (i.e., relevance) ✓ SE: Social engagement (i.e., collaboration) ✓ N: Novelty (i.e., new concepts and skills)
Learners will listen to a think-aloud about the different types of connections that can be made while reading a text, and explain the differences between them.	1. The note taker in each group codes their copy of the text with the type of connection being made (text–self, text–text, and text–world). 2. (Optional) Learners take notes on the rules of notice or sentence frames the teacher uses while reading and then makes use of these in their own think-aloud. 3. Teacher observes small-group practice.	• Learners can explain how textual moves or details connect to other details within this text, to other texts, to the reader, and to the outside world. • Learners can categorize different types of connections and make meaning of the connection.	**ES:** Personal connections with the text make the reading experience relevant. **SE:** Small-group practice and noticing how peers and the teacher connect with a text in similar and different ways supply a social connection. **N:** One or more of the types of connections may be new for learners. Think-alouds and thinking aloud with peers may be new as well.

MAP out the path to expertise/mastery
(How would an expert deconstruct and approach this task, step by step?)

TWITTER SUMMARY *(3 bullets max)*	MENTAL MODELS, PROCESS GUIDES, HEURISTICS	A MODEL OF GOOD WORK LOOKS LIKE . . .	DIFFERENTIATION AND LAYERING
Learners will become more expert readers by having a variety of transactions with their text via learning how to see and interpret different types of connections.	1. *Identify*: Certain details, moves, or parts of a text provide different meanings for the reader. 2. *Connect*: Relate the details in a text to other details in the text, the reader's lived experience, another text, or to the world at large. 3. *Extend*: Use the connections to motivate further reading, understand the main idea, or better understand society and uses of what has been learned in the world. Types of connections 1. Intratextual (within a text)—when a detail connects to other details inside a text to create a pattern of meaning. 2. Text to self—when a reader can relate a section of text to something they've personally experienced. 3. Text to text—when the reader associates an idea, event, or character with something else within the another text. 4. Text to world—when something in the text relates to a larger concept, problem, or question that concerns society at large.	See the example on page 169.	Provide flexible tasks for learners during teaching and modeling. Use different materials appropriate to learners. The duration of the "we do" mentoring stage and the amount of small-group practice will be dependent on learners' needs. Encourage peer conferencing, peer and self procedural feedback, and provide coaching to encourage and invite consolidation and extensions.

(Continued)

POWER through your lesson
(What is the sequence of initial major must-make instructional moves?)

	PRIME	ORIENT	WALK THROUGH (and check for understanding)	EXTEND AND EXPLORE	REFLECT
Leader	Play word association game and categories game to highlight connection-making, how we make connections, and how connection making extends and elaborates meaning. **For word association:** The class forms a circle, and the teacher starts the game by saying a word aloud. For example, teacher says *bird*, learner says *robin*, next learner says *Batman*, and so on. **For categories:** The class remains seated in a circle. The teacher or facilitator names a category. In clockwise order, each person takes turns sharing a word that fits within that category. For example, teacher says *fruit*, learner says *orange*, next learner says *blueberry*, and so on.	FRAME today's lesson: *In the games we just played, we demonstrated how one idea can connect with many other ideas. We also looked at how ideas can be grouped into categories. Today, we're going to do both of those things by making different kinds of connections with the text that we read. These various kinds of connections will help us understand the text in different ways.*	EXPLAIN: Different types of connections (see mental models). CHECK FOR UNDERSTANDING: Ask learners for examples in their own reading experience. Start with inside the text and text–self, then text–text and text–world. MODEL *(I do, you watch)*: Read the text aloud while learners read along. Stop periodically to make different types of connections. CHECK FOR UNDERSTANDING: After experiencing each type of connection, ask learners to guess the type of connection by sharing with a partner first. Then, let them know which type and why. MODEL *(we do together)*: Stop at key passages and ask learners to volunteer a connection of their own. Let them make any type of connection they want. CHECK FOR UNDERSTANDING: Ask learners to guess the type of connection on their own. Have them share their guess by a show of hands for each one. MODEL *(we do together)*: If needed, ask learners to only make a certain type of connection when you stop periodically. CHECK FOR UNDERSTANDING: Ask learners to explain why the connection did or did not fit within the designated category.	DELIBERATE PRACTICE/ ARTICULATE CONSCIOUS AWARENESS: Learners will continue to practice making connections in texts used in other content areas. They can also reflect on self-selected reading with connections of their own choice. Ask learners to consider what a reading experience would be like if they were discouraged from considering what it meant to them or how it connects with other books. How does making such connections deepen meaning, understanding, and use?	Ask learners to write or share reflectively about where they succeeded at making connections and why, as well as their goal for next time. Learners consider how each type of connection changes their thinking about the meaning and use of the text.

POWER through your lesson
(What is the sequence of initial major must-make instructional moves?)

		PRIME	ORIENT	WALK THROUGH (and check for understanding)	EXTEND AND EXPLORE	REFLECT
Learner		**For word association:** In clockwise order, the next person states another word aloud that they can associate with the previous one. The round ends if someone takes more than three seconds to share; a word is repeated; or there is not a clear connection, which can be judged by peers or the teacher. **For categories:** In clockwise order, each person takes turns sharing a word that fits within that category. The round ends if someone takes more than three seconds to share; a word is repeated; or the word does not fit within the category, which can be judged by peers or the teacher.	In partners, learners restate the goals of today's lesson. Then, they discuss how making connections has helped them in the past and how connection-making can help learners to know/think/do in this unit's readings and projects.	GUIDED PRACTICE (*you do in small groups*): Divide learners into groups of three. One learner reads aloud. Another does a think-aloud with different types of connections. The third learner is the notetaker. He or she codes a copy of the text with the type of connections the think-aloud learner shares. Each learner should take a turn at every role, making sure every group changes tasks at the same point in the text. Before rotating, provide all group members a chance to review the text the notetaker coded to make sure they agree on how the connections were categorized. DIFFERENTIATE: If a small group of learners needs more guided practice, work with them while the rest of the class practices in small groups or pairs. Increase or decrease the number of connections learners need to make over a given number of pages. Underline key passages for connections as a way to cue that a connection can be made here. Learners could work in pairs, rather than triads, with the think-aloud learner recording the types of connections. DEBRIEF: Classmates share connections that were challenging to categorize. If using a sentence starter anchor chart, revise and add to it as needed. Poll the class to find out what types of connections they made the most and least frequently. Analyze the results, and ask learners about the connections and which ones were easier or more challenging and why. Ask them how making such connections can lead to interpretations and deeper meanings and understandings.		HOMEWORK EXTENSION: Learners write connections on a copy of the text. Learners write connections on sticky notes they place within a text. Learners are challenged to make a certain number of connections, or a particular type of connection. Learners are challenged to consider how the connection helps them make meaning, and to consider how to use that meaning in the future.

Chapter 11

WALKING LEARNERS THROUGH WITH QUESTIONING

> **ESSENTIAL QUESTION**
> How can we use questioning to promote engagement, curiosity, and deep understanding?

Few of the questions provided in scripted programs or textbooks are the types that we want learners to pose as part of their daily lives and learning. Surveys of such questions show that questions from textbooks and other prepared materials are overwhelmingly on the literal or factual level, and they seldom help learners to notice key details or to ask questions that require higher-level thinking like inferencing, generalizing, critiquing, evaluating, or applying. You, as a teacher, can do a far better job at asking compelling and interesting higher-level questions because you know your learners and their needs. But in the spirit of transformational teaching, the real goal of teaching questioning strategies must be to help learners generate and pursue their own questions.

See *Lesson Plan Canvas* on page 201

How can we expect learners to exercise autonomy and develop the critical skill of asking and answering their own questions if we ask all the questions for them? This is not to say a teacher's questions never have value, but rather, that we want our questions and questioning strategies to be a model for learners that works to apprentice them into the inquiry process. We do this by scaffolding how to ask and answer different kinds of questions, transferring the responsibility and joy of learning to them. When we provide learners support for asking their own higher-level questions, they can successfully *orient* their own learning to pursue an idea, the topic of inquiry, and the culminating project and work they will create within the unit.

The questioning strategies in this chapter provide *walk-throughs* for learners to generate powerful questions that they find personally compelling and then to engage in the thinking necessary to answer these higher-level questions. This process guides learners to deliberately practice and master knowledge and strategies of questioning in ways that promote more expert reading, composing, and problem solving. Most importantly, these questioning strategies are meant to give learners ownership of their learning by *priming* their own interests, curiosities, and meaning-making processes as they use the questions to become *oriented* towards new learning goals.

PLANNING FOR WALKING
LEARNERS THROUGH WITH QUESTIONING

We argue that questioning strategies, to be useful and worthy of the time and energy it takes to teach them, need to be generalizable across texts and situations. (This is in opposition to text-dependent questions, which are only useful for one particular text.) Keep this in mind as you read through the strategies in this chapter and *envision* how they could work with a variety of texts and content areas. The *map* for your unit should include helping learners generate their own questions and guiding them in learning how to find evidence to answer different question types. Questioning schemes should work to connect a text or data to other texts; the wider world; and, most importantly, to the lives of individual learners. These kinds of questions are typically not found in a curriculum guide. Questions that bridge a text or task to the world beyond the classroom ask learners to *extend*, *explore*, and *reflect* on their knowledge and learning (i.e., to work toward high-road transfer).

Before exploring the featured questioning strategies in greater depth, let's consider a checklist of success criteria for planning to promote deep and rich teacher- and learner-generated questioning.

Considerations for Designing and Implementing a Successful Questioning Strategy

❏ The teacher plans when and how to teach different ways to generate and answer different kinds of questions that help to meet unit goals. (E-M)

❏ Learners understand the purposes and payoffs of different ways to generate questions and of various question types and questioning schemes. They understand how these schemes are designed to promote understanding, make meaning, and help solve problems. (P-O)

❏ Teachers and learners sequence questions intentionally to transition from basic and literal comprehension to higher-order thinking that involves inferencing, generalizing, critiquing, and evaluating. (O-W)

❏ Teachers model how to ask and answer questions of different types and how to use questioning schemes for specific purposes. (W)

❏ Learners come to take a major role in classroom questioning, taking over responsibility for generating and using different kinds of questions and questioning schemes. (W-E)

❏ Learners ask and respond to questions that assist them in acquiring threshold knowledge and answering the essential question. (W-E)

- ❏ The questioning strategy provides deliberate practice in reading, composing, and problem solving like an expert, helping learners to develop a mental model for questioning to apply in other contexts and helping them to develop mental models of major concepts and processes necessary for pursuing the inquiry. (E)

- ❏ Learners reflect on how they ask and answer questions and rehearse future uses of different question types in order to transfer those skills to other contexts. (E-R)

QUESTIONING MOVE 1: THREE-LEVEL QUESTIONING

Three-level questioning, a strategy designed by Herber (1978) and further developed by Morris and Stewart-Dore (1984), categorizes questions into three different types or levels—on the lines, between the lines, and beyond the lines—and helps learners move beyond the comprehension of literal, directly stated information to make connections, form inferences, and grapple with real-world applications and evaluations. It is helpful to teach three-level questioning early in the school year because the question types can be used in a variety of contexts. Take care not to conflate these levels with depths of knowledge, Bloom's taxonomy, or other means of gauging higher-level thinking. Rather, these levels refer to the locations of responses to questions within a text and to what needs to be done to answer each question type. As learners internalize the three levels of questioning, they develop an expert mental model of reading that can be transferred across texts and situations. Figure 11.1 walks us through each type of question, as well as sample questions to prompt thinking.

Let's look at the different types of questions in three-level questioning.

ON-THE-LINES QUESTIONS

These are literal-level questions that have a directly stated answer. In the question–answer relationship (QAR) scheme, these questions are referred to as "right there" questions because you can literally point at the text and say, "The answer is right there!" (Raphael, 1982). This is the simplest kind of question. Often, these questions ask about key details, such as the *Who? What? Where? When?* and *How?* from a data set, problem, text, or story. Learners can identify these key details by using rules of notice. (You can download the complete list of rules of notice from **resources.corwin.com/empower-elementary**.) Typically, these kinds of questions are posed earlier in a lesson because they establish a shared understanding of the facts before digging deeper.

online resources

BETWEEN-THE-LINES QUESTIONS

These are questions where the answers are implied by the text or data, requiring learners to make connections and see "between the lines." They are also known as inferential questions, which can be either "think and search" or "author and me" questions according to the QAR scheme [Raphael, 1982]).

(Continued)

(Continued)

- *Think and search*: The reader searches for patterns in the text and then connects the dots and interprets the pattern formed by the different pieces of information.
- *Author and me*: The reader "figures forth" by inferring additional meanings typically from one crucial and revealing piece of information. This requires connecting the detail to personal life experience or world knowledge that reveals the hidden or unstated implications of the details.

With between-the-lines questions, the questioner may be required to

- infer what key details imply but do not directly say;
- connect details from different parts of the text into a pattern that reveals meaning and be able to explain the nature of the connections;
- ask an "author and me" question that requires combining text information with life experience or world knowledge;
- predict or anticipate consequences, what will happen next, endings, or what will happen after an ending;
- state underlying motivations and unstated reasons for problems, events, or actions; or
- make generalizations about a character, setting, problem, or other aspect of text.

Typically, these questions are posed in the middle or near the end of a lesson because they require and build on a shared understanding of the facts.

BEYOND-THE-LINES QUESTIONS

Also known as critical, evaluative, applicative, or inquiry questions, these do not actually require textual details to answer, though the question will be related to a central topic of the text. The reader makes links between a topic of the text and his or her own experience and world knowledge to find the answer. The question is open-ended and promotes rich discussion and deeper understanding. The reader needs to justify the answer with evidence from beyond the text and reasoning about this evidence. The topic of the text and data from the text generally inform the question but will not be absolutely necessary to answering it. Thus, these questions are referred to as "on your own" in the question–answer relationship scheme (Raphael, 1982).

The questioner may be required to

- make generalizations or explain rules that the text or data implies for human behavior in the world;
- make comparisons to different extratextual events, actions, or ideas;
- make judgments, and consider how far the reader wants to accept, resist, or revise major points that apply to the world;
- make recommendations and suggestions;

- make decisions; or
- create alternative endings and explain differences in meaning.

These kinds of questions are typically asked at the outset and closing of a lesson because they are inquiry questions that are not text dependent and that build on learners' prior knowledge and interests and extend their thinking forward to new and novel situations.

■ FIGURE 11.1: THREE-LEVEL QUESTIONING GUIDE

QUESTION TYPES AND DEFINITIONS	EXAMPLES (REHEARSE SAMPLE QUESTIONS HERE, INCLUDING EVIDENCE FROM TEXT OR YOUR LIFE NECESSARY TO CRAFT AN ANSWER.)
ON THE LINES (or Right There questions) TIP: This kind of question should highlight a key detail (cued by rules of notice) that is important to understanding the text at a deeper level. This kind of question should be in service of the higher-level questions that follow it—between and beyond the lines. To ask this kind of question: • Identify a directly stated key detail that conveys deep meaning or that may be important later on, or identify a directly stated point, a generalization/main idea of the excerpt, or what might be a main event or consequential action. **CONFIRM: To confirm this question type, find the answer at one place in the text and point to it in the text.**	**Examples of ON THE LINES question starters, *if the answers are directly stated:*** • What happened . . . ? • How many . . . ? • How did . . . ? • Who . . . ? • What is . . . ? • Which is . . . ? • When did . . . ? • Where was . . . ?
BETWEEN THE LINES (or Think and Search/Author and Me) **Think and Search questions:** Search for patterns in the text and then interpret or explain the pattern formed by the different pieces of information. TIP: This kind of question should connect key details to reveal patterns that express implied meanings. This can also be called a "connect the dots" question. **Author and Me questions:** The reader infers additional meanings from one crucial and revealing piece of information. This requires connecting the detail to personal life experience or world knowledge that reveals the hidden or unstated implications of the detail(s). TIP: This kind of question should help you to interpret the unstated and implied meanings of a detail or event by connecting it to life experience or world knowledge. This involves going beyond what is directly stated to figure out deeper meanings. **CONFIRM: Think and Search questions can be confirmed by pointing to details in different places in the text and explaining how they are connected.**	**Examples of Think and Search question starters:** • Why did . . . ? • What was the deep or hidden reason for/implied meaning of . . . ? • Why might X be important? • What might be the implications or consequences of detail/action/result X? **Examples of Author and Me question starters:** • What do you think about . . . ? • How can you explain . . . ? • What is your theory about why . . . ? • How do you think this was similar to/different from X (from another text or the world)? • How would the character/action/etc. be changed if the text were in a different setting or if the situation was changed to/there was a different narrator (or any kind of change) . . . ? • How does this excerpt extend or complicate our understanding from previous understandings or other texts we have read?

(Continued)

■ FIGURE 11.1: (CONTINUED)

QUESTION TYPES AND DEFINITIONS	EXAMPLES (REHEARSE SAMPLE QUESTIONS HERE, INCLUDING EVIDENCE FROM TEXT OR YOUR LIFE NECESSARY TO CRAFT AN ANSWER.)
Author and Me questions can be confirmed by showing how a detail can be interpreted by connecting it to details and knowledge outside the text, and usually include "you" or "me" in the question.	Examples of Author and Me question starters *(continued)*: • Do you think that . . . should have . . . ? • What else could he/she/you . . . ? • How would you . . . ? • Do you agree . . . ? • What do you think would have happened if . . . ?
BEYOND THE LINES (On Your Own: Evaluation and Application questions) TIP: This is an inquiry question that requires generalizations or rules that can be applied beyond the text (e.g., making a claim that is generally true about the world beyond the text, or setting a rule about behavior applicable in the world beyond the text). CONFIRM: BEYOND THE LINES questions can be confirmed by demonstrating how the question is about the world beyond the text and could be answered without information from the text if needed.	Examples of BEYOND THE LINES question starters: • What is courage, friendship, or leadership (or any other quality or concept definition that applies to the world)? • What makes a good friendship, great leader, or responsible member of the community? • What are your role and responsibilities in the community? • What lesson did you learn that can apply to your life? • What lesson about this topic do you foresee using in the future? • How might major ideas about this topic be used/applied in our lives? • How might . . . ? • What effect does . . . ? • What could be a good solution for . . . ? • How might I use what I've learned in future readings, beyond school, or when I encounter a challenge?

Experts understand that texts or data tell only a small part of the story and that literal comprehension is just the beginning of expert understanding—not the be-all and end-all. Although we begin with on-the-lines questions, we progress quickly to between-the-lines questions, encouraging learners to dig deeper and make the necessary inferences and connections. Initially, it can also be helpful to tell the learners what type of question they are answering, so they know where to search and what to do to reach an answer. However, as learners become proficient in identifying question types, you can remove this scaffold. The process for guiding learners through the three-level questioning guide is as follows:

Step 1: *Prime* learners when you first introduce the three-level questioning guide by asking how they know that they really understand something. Prompt them to think of something they deeply understand and consider how they came to understand it. Point out that understanding has multiple levels. Continue priming by viewing an excerpt of "Questions Only" from *Whose Line Is It Anyway?* or playing a round of twenty questions. Ask learners to reflect on the questions and name which questions generated the most discussion or led to the deepest understanding.

Step 2: *Orient* learners by explaining that expert understanding goes beyond facts to the implications of facts, the connection between details, and the deeper meanings and applications of what has been read. Ask learners to consider how often they ask questions that can be answered with a simple "yes" or "no" or a basic fact. Ask learners to consider when and why they might use deeper, more open-ended questions.

Step 3: The *walk-through* begins by asking learners to write and share questions about a text, video, or activity that you have recently experienced in class. Use the learners' questions to think aloud as you sort them according to the three question types. After grouping several of the questions, explain the three question types and the kinds of work they do for learners and expert readers as they try to make sense of a text, task, or problem. (If a question type is missing, generate an example and explore what unique kind of work this question type gets done.) Display the definitions and criteria for each type of question on an anchor chart. Ask learners to help classify questions when they start to understand the criteria of each question type.

Step 4: Continue the *walk-through* by modeling how to generate questions of each type. The question definitions and stems in Figure 11.1 will serve well here. Quickly move to having learners help you and then to helping each other generate questions of each type. If answering the on-the-lines question primes and helps learners to answer their between- or beyond-the-lines questions, then they have created a questioning sequence. Share and provide procedural feedback about power moves and potential moves used by the learners.

Step 5: Have learners *explore and extend* the use of the questioning guide by applying it independently to their own reading or learning. Peers and teacher can "gut check" the question types with learners and help to revise them as necessary.

Step 6: Throughout, ask learners to *reflect* on the types of questions they used, how the different kinds of questions help them develop deeper understanding, and how they have improved in asking higher-order questions.

■ FIGURE 11.2: EXAMPLE THREE-LEVEL READING GUIDE FOR *ISH* BY PETER REYNOLDS

Part One—Directions: Check the statements that reflect what the author directly tells us. Sometimes, the exact words are used; at other times, other words may be used. Only check the text's literal, directly stated meanings. Explain how you know that the meaning is directly stated by the text. (You can point directly at the answer in the text.)

_____1. Leon burst out laughing. "What is that?" he asked.

_____2. Marisol enjoyed looking at Ramon's drawings.

_____3. Making an Ish drawing felt wonderful.

_____4. Ramon wrote poetry.

Part Two—Directions: Check the statements that you feel represent the text's implied meaning, meaning you have to figure out what a detail or connection between details means. Explain how you know that the meaning is implied, not directly stated. (You figure forth from a detail to its implied meaning, or connect various details to uncover implied meanings.)

_____1. Marisol taught Ramon how to be comfortable with imperfection.

_____2. Leon's comments about Ramon's work were hurtful.

_____3. Ramon overreacted to Leon's comments.

Part Three—Directions: Check the statements that you agree with, and be ready to support your choice with ideas from the text and your own knowledge—this is about evaluating and applying textual meaning. Explain how you know that these meanings are generalizations supported by the text but that can be applied to the world beyond the text. (You use knowledge of the text, but also personal or world knowledge to create meaning that can be applied to the world.)

_____1. We should get rid of grades because they discourage Ramon's "Ish" kind of behavior.

_____2. Grades help us move from "Ish" to exactly what we're trying to create or demonstrate.

_____3. Calling your work "Ish" is an excuse for not doing it correctly.

_____4. Calling your work "Ish" makes sense because nobody's perfect and we learn by improving over time.

online resources ⟋ This figure is available for download at **http://resources.corwin.com/EMPOWER-elementary**

(Continued)

(Continued)

Checklist for Creating Your Own Three-Level Questioning Activity

❑ The teacher introduces the strategy with a text that is comprehensible and easily fosters and rewards the asking of different types of questions. (E-M)

❑ Learners understand the three types of questions and what is required to answer each type, along with the purpose and payoffs of each. (P-O)

❑ The teacher models the creation of on-the-lines, between-the-lines, and beyond-the-lines questions. (W)

❑ The teacher mentors and monitors learners to create and answer their own questions via the gradual release of responsibility. (W)

❑ Learners have access to scaffolds (such as model questions or sentence stems) to help them identify and ask questions at each of the levels. (W)

❑ Learners consider the roles that different types of questions play in developing deep understanding. They consider future uses of the questioning strategy and question types later in the unit, in their lives, and in the future. (E-R)

QUESTIONING MOVE 2: QUESTIONING A MENTOR TEXT

Mentor texts are examples of expert writing that feature moves that we want our learners to emulate in their own writing. Ruth Culham's (2014) *The Writing Thief* makes a compelling case for using more mentor texts in writing instruction and provides numerous examples of mentor texts that are organized by types of writing: information, argument/opinion, and narrative, as well as the 6 + 1 Traits of Writing®: organization, ideas, voice, word choice, conventions, sentence fluency, and presentation.

Building on that approach, *questioning a mentor text* is a tool for conferencing with learners in ways that improve reading and writing. The strategy highlights how different author moves—openings, transition phrases, character descriptions, use of ruptures and surprise, flashbacks, and so on—create meaning and effect. This type of questioning and conferring *orients* learners to the power moves of authors and *primes* learners to employ these moves in their own writing. The approach helps learners become familiar with characteristics of writing craft and learn how to provide procedural feedback to authors in ways that name power moves and what these moves achieve. This strategy utilizes a series of questions that can be adjusted for the types of author moves that you want learners to make use of in their own writing. Take note that *author moves* are what we want learners to think about and use when they write, while *traits* are characteristics teachers (and learners) use to describe and assess writing. When you first use this strategy, make sure you and your learners are aware of the *move or trait* that will be the focus for the lesson. Eventually, learners can decide for themselves which moves or traits to focus on in their reading and writing. If learners are unable to answer a question or respond incorrectly, you can act on that formative data and teach or reteach what a certain move requires of a writer, how an author move works, what a certain trait means, and so forth.

Here are some questions for a mentor text:

- What happened in the text?

- Why did the author write this text?

- Where do you see evidence of [insert writing characteristic or move]?

- What do you think about why and how the author used [insert author move]? What meaning and effect were achieved through the move?

- How does [insert author move] improve the [insert writing trait]?

- How could you use [insert author move] the way this author did to improve [insert writing characteristic] in your own writing? What ideas do you have for using this move in what you are writing right now? In something you plan to write?

Take note that the first two questions can be skipped or briefly reviewed if learners already demonstrated comprehension of the text. They are included in the list because it is essential for learners to understand the basic meaning of the text and the author's purpose for writing before they can understand how various moves serve that purpose, and before they can consider how to transfer the author moves purposefully into their own writing. For the remaining questions, always ask learners to refer to the text to name the move of the expert writer and to provide reference points for future feedback and conferencing.

Following is an example using the children's book *Clemente!* by Willie Perdomo. This book, a biography of Puerto Rican baseball star Roberto Clemente, could be used as a mentor text in our throughline unit about experts. In this example, we focus on the use of voice in writing, which can be confusing and abstract—especially at the elementary level.

(Continued)

(Continued)

Example: Questioning a Mentor Text

Questions for *Clemente!*

Teacher: **What happened in the text?**

Learner A: A family explained why one of them was named after Roberto Clemente.

Learner B: Clemente was really good at baseball and died in a plane crash.

Teacher: **Why did the author write this text?**

Learner A: To inform us about Roberto Clemente's life and why he was such a good person and baseball player. Why he is someone worth being named after!

Teacher: **Where do you see evidence of the author's voice? Please show me in the book.**

Learner A: The author uses Spanish and English words and sometimes mixes them together.

Learner B: Some of the words rhymed, especially in the beginning of the story.

Teacher: **What do you think about how the author made the move of using Spanish words?**

Learner A: I thought it was confusing because I don't speak Spanish! But I do see that the author wanted me to know the family spoke two languages.

Learner B: I liked it because it reminded me of my grandma, who speaks Spanish all the time, and it also reminded me that Clemente spoke Spanish.

Teacher: **What do you think about how the author used rhyme? Show me an example from the book to support your statement.**

Learner A: It was cool to hear when you read it aloud because you knew how to pronounce the Spanish word that rhymes with *Clemente*.

Learner B: Yeah, I liked the line here about hitting curveballs before they drop and the sound of the catcher's mitt—pop.

Teacher: **How did the author move to use rhyme improve the voice?**

Learner A: It was like a Dr. Seuss book; the rhyming helped to keep my attention and helped me remember certain details.

Teacher: **Show us which parts did that.** (Student points to the text)

Learner B: You could tell the author was excited to tell the story of Clemente. The rhyming words reminded me of a cheer.

Teacher: **Show us where you noticed that.** (Student points to the text)

Teacher:	**How could you use rhyme the way this author did to improve voice in your own writing?**
Learner A:	I could keep an eye out for words that happen to rhyme when I'm writing and try to put them together.
Learner B:	I could have people talk in rhyme when they get excited, like the family does in this story. Or I could use rhyme to emphasize an idea that I want people to remember!
Teacher:	**Let's look back at the use of Spanish words because it sounds like we need to deepen our comprehension of them to understand how and why the author switches between two languages . . .**

Although not every conference will go as smoothly as this one, the teacher intentionally uses the question guide to scaffold the learning, and her questions lead to deeper understanding of the author moves and their impact (including how the moves express a trait of powerful writing). The teacher begins with an author move both learners seem to understand. Then, learners consider the effect of the move on the writing, how it promotes voice, and how they could use the move to achieve the same effects. Later, she addresses another author move and recognizes the need to go back to the text to deepen comprehension of the Spanish vocabulary before going further. Whenever possible, select mentor texts that are at learners' independent-reading level, so they can focus on the author's choices and analyze their purpose and payoff.

Notice we took care not to refer to this series of questions as a *script* because you will adapt these questions and their sequence to fit your purposes and the needs of your learners. Although this questioning strategy could work for whole-group instruction, it is particularly effective when used in small groups or conferences because such opportunities allow all learners to dive deep and share their thinking. Of course, learners can take over the use of the questions in their own small-group work and conferencing about mentor texts with other learners.

Provide ample practice opportunities to experiment with different author moves as learners progress with their writing. For example, in the preceding scenario, the teacher could conclude the lesson by asking each learner to experiment with rhyme by writing a dialogue between herself or himself and a friend. This type of writing play allows writers to have fun with writing; provides you with formative-assessment data; and encourages writers to develop their own writing style, which they will later transfer to writing that is more complex.

(Continued)

(Continued)

Checklist for Creating Your Own Questioning Mentor Texts Activity

❑ The selected mentor text showcases specific authorial moves the teacher would like learners to explore. (E-M)

❑ The teacher carefully designs a series of questions specific to the learners in the room and the goals of the lesson for highlighting specific author moves and how to use them. (E-M)

❑ Learners understand the purpose and payoffs of analyzing a mentor text to more deeply understand and appreciate their reading and improve their writing. (P-O)

❑ Learners take time to understand the text before analyzing the author moves and their link to the chosen writing trait. (W)

❑ Learners respond to the series of questions, beginning with the lower-level comprehension questions and building up to the higher-level applicative questions. (W)

❑ Learners experiment with the writing moves they identified in the mentor text in low-stakes writing soon after the discussion takes place. (W)

❑ Learners transfer their learning about effective writing craft to more formal and public writing. (W-E)

❑ Learners apply what they have learned as they read to appreciate how writers compose a text, as well as to their future writing. (E-R)

❑ Learners reflect on their work, considering their command of new moves and how these develop the writing traits, contribute to the overall meaning and effect of a text, as well as how their work resembles that of mentor authors. (R)

QUESTIONING MOVE 3: QUESTIONING IN ROLE

Different perspectives, purposes and contexts call for different types of questions. On the way to the store, for example, you're curious about the weather forecast. When you turn on the radio there's a news story about the effect of weather on this year's strawberry crop. Inside the grocery store, you wonder how the price of strawberries influences your grocery budget. At home, you consider which dish you will prepare with strawberries. The *questioning in role* strategy highlights how different kinds of roles, perspectives, positions, and contexts require and reward different types and lines of questioning and elicit various findings related to these roles, positions, and contexts.

Example: Questioning in Role Using *Ish* by Peter Reynolds

ROLE DESCRIPTION	EXAMPLES FROM *ISH*
The detective: This person is like an officer of the law who just arrived at the crime scene and wants to establish the facts—just the most salient facts. This person deliberately practices noticing and placeholding key details. She or he asks and answers direct, literal-level questions about the text.	• What does each sibling say to Ramon? Why? • What does Ramon do for fun?
The speculator: This person searches for clues and patterns. She or he asks and answers questions that may not have a clear answer. She or he deliberately practices inferencing—both figuring forth from single details and connecting dots to see patterns.	• How might Leon respond to Ramon's poetry? What makes you say so? • How might Ramon treat Marisol in the future? What makes you say so? • What might have inspired Ramon to resume drawing? What makes you say so? • How did writing poetry affect Ramon? • How would you describe what Ramon's parents are like? How do you think they would respond to his artwork?
The researcher: This person searches for helpful background, connections to the inquiry topic or essential question, and potential applications. She or he deliberately practices connecting dots across texts and data sets, to the world beyond the texts, searching for a spirit of transfer. When introducing this role, the topic and extent of research need to be defined to support the researcher getting started and remaining focused.	• Where is there evidence of characters having a growth mindset? What other characters from fiction and nonfiction texts demonstrate this mindset? What effect does this mindset have on characters and on real people? What effect does the growth mindset have on learners? • Where is there evidence of characters having a fixed mindset? What other characters from fiction and nonfiction texts demonstrate this mindset? What effect does this mindset have on characters? • Throughout your experience and reading, what kind of events inspire a change in mindset? In relationships? Classrooms? Families?
The interviewer/commentator: This person is building a personality profile of a potential interviewee. She or he tries to understand a specific character or group of characters. Some of the interviewer's questions may be similar to those of the speculator and the researcher because this role focuses on noticing specific information, figuring forth from this, connecting dots, making generalizations, and searching for applications. Answering these questions requires taking on the role of the character or figure to whom the questions are addressed. This can be done by "hotseating" a learner in the role of the character (Wilhelm, 2012b).	**(Asking Ramon questions)** • What is important to you? What are your greatest commitments and values, and how do they inform your actions? • What are your greatest goals? Future goals? Greatest influences? • What motivates your drawing? • How would you describe your home life? Your relationship with your siblings? How did your home life influence your art? • What advice would you have for people trying to develop a new talent or skill?

(Continued)

ROLE DESCRIPTION	EXAMPLES FROM *ISH*
The learner/futurist: This person has a lust for learning and asks questions for further inquiry. This person deliberately practices extending her or his learning into the future and making connections to the world.	• What are other stories with a similar theme? • To what real-life situations or historical situations does thinking "ish-ly" apply or help me to overcome challenges? • How does "ish-ness" apply to human progress? To the development of expertise? • What would a sequel to *Ish* be like? • What is the origin of the suffix "ish"? How is it used in and outside of this text?
Devil's advocate: This person takes on the opposing perspective, sharing "the other side" of an issue and raising arguments with the text. This person deliberately practices civilly taking on different perspectives and positions and seeing from those points of view.	• Was Ramon being too sensitive to Leon's question? • Could thinking "ish-ly" be used as an excuse for not trying hard? Or not following established rules? • When is "ish" just not good enough?
*For upper elementary and advanced learners: **The critical friend:** An individual who reads the text from a clear position or with a particular point of view in mind to explore a new or silenced perspective. This entire role extends learning because it applies lenses, or a particular position or way of seeing the world to an interpretation of the text (e.g., a power judge lens ([evaluating who has power and who is silenced]), a historian's lens, an environmentalist lens, a coach's lens, a parent lens, a psychologist lens, a movie director lens, etc.). This prepares learners to take on different positions for interpretations, and for critical lenses they will use in high school or college. This could be a role played primarily by the teacher as a means to model expertise. Another option is to have multiple skilled learners take on this role, as different stakeholders. (For example, in a science text about habitats of living things, roles could include an environmentalist and business owner offering their lenses on habitats.)	**(Using the power judge lens)** • How much power does Leon have in the story, and how does he use it? • How much power does Marisol have in the story, and how does she use it? • How much power does Ramon have in the story, and how does he use it? • Who in the story has the least power and the most power, and why is this? • Do some characters lose or gain power through the story? What explains this? • Whose stories are told, and whose stories don't we know? If the silenced characters could speak, what would they tell us? • If Ramon were female, how might the story be different?

Checklist for Creating Your Own Questioning in Role Activity

- ❑ The selected text is appropriately challenging and aligns with and supports the topic and goals of the inquiry. (E-M)

- ❑ The teacher selects specific roles based on the chosen text, learning goals, and subsequent tasks. (E-M)

- ❑ Learners understand the purpose and power of exercising social imagination (seeing from different perspectives and positions) in their own lives. (P)

- ❑ Learners consider the position of each of the selected roles and have the opportunity to consider and practice the role(s) and perspectives they will play with a familiar text or topic. (O)

- ❑ The teacher models the roles, so learners have the opportunity to observe each role and explore its perspective and what can be learned from its position. (O-W)

- ❑ The questions posed in each role build understandings that prepare learners to answer the essential question while considering various perspectives and positions. (W-E)

- ❑ Learners have multiple opportunities to engage in various roles and develop confidence and fluency in playing them, so they can employ these roles in their independent reading and problem solving. (W-E)

- ❑ Learners consider how each role lends itself to seeing from different perspectives, using different kinds of learning strategies, values, commitments, interests, and so on. Learners will reflect on how using different roles fills blind spots. Learners consider how these roles can be helpful in different learning and life situations. (E-R)

- ❑ Learners propose new roles from which to question and respond to a text as they move through the year and justify how each role is appropriate to extending meaning of a particular problem or text. (E-R)

PLC Connection

To encourage adult learners to look at an important educational topic from a variety of perspectives, invite them to take on these or other roles (parent, community member, business owner, future citizen) in a PLC or professional development setting to discuss a text or approach a complex problem. This move is particularly helpful in studying all the angles when considering systems-level change in order to increase buy-in and lead to greater success.

PLC Connection

Use any of these questioning strategies in PLCs or professional development to think deeply about new information, such as standards or curriculum maps, and consider implications and applications of what is revealed to classrooms, school policy, and the world.

POWERFUL PLANNING: LEARNER-GENERATED QUESTIONING TO DEVELOP DEEPER, INDEPENDENT THINKING

Asking questions is an essential element of human conversation, learning, and meaning making. The strategies shared in this chapter help teachers and learners to generate questions that lead to deep understandings, and then to *reflect* on who is asking questions and from what positions, what needs to be done to answer particular kinds of questions, and how these questions apprentice learners into becoming more expert readers, composers, and problem solvers.

All of these questioning strategies mirror and *prime* learners to embrace the purposes and processes of expert reading, composing, learning, and inquiring. Learners crave meaningful work that can develop real-world capacity. They often bring this to our attention when they ask, "Why do we have to read (or do) this?" Questions that connect a text to readers' lives and the world around them provide answers to this valid concern. Questions that unpack the meaning of a text enable readers to transfer the key ideas from the text to their lives and help them consider how they can construct their own texts for various meanings and effects. A questioning sequence builds interest and knowledge because learners will understand what they're reading or studying, what it implies, why it matters, and how to apply what has been learned. Naming question types *orients* both teacher and learners to create their own sequences and balance of question types.

Learner-generated questioning helps learners express curiosity, direct their learning, build internally persuasive understandings, and be fully involved in the EMPOWER process. All of these questioning strategies help learners *explore* new content and *reflect* on what it means to them. We encourage you to teach these skills early in the school year and involve learners in the inquiry process through questioning throughout the year.

Guiding Questions for Designing and Using Questioning Strategies

- What kinds of questions are currently asked in my classroom, and who is asking them? Have I achieved my ideal ratio of teacher–learner, learner–teacher, learner–learner, and learner–self questions? What specific moves might I make and checkpoints might I use to gauge my progress toward more learner-generated questions? (E-M)

- Which questioning strategy best serves the current task and purpose? How will I convey the significance of these tasks and purposes to my learners? (E-M-P-O)

- How will I help learners reflect on their experience with different kinds of questions and how various kinds of questions do different kinds of work, serve different purposes, and yield different results? (P)

- How will I help learners understand the purpose and payoff of the new questioning strategy in the context of this unit? How will learners generate their own questions and seek out answers? (P-O)

- How will learners be assisted to understand the question types, the value of each, and how to appropriately generate, phrase, answer, and sequence questions to build understanding? (W-E)

- How will I help learners identify other contexts and tasks that require and reward the use of the questioning schemes and strategies they have learned? (E-R)

Lesson: Three-Level Questioning

Unit: How do I become an expert?

ENVISION the destination
(Where are learners going, and why?)

GOAL *What kind of thinking is targeted?*	EVIDENCE *What product(s) will serve as proof of learning?*	MEASURES OF SUCCESS *What's the standard and quality-assurance tool?*	STAKES *Why will learners buy in?* *What's the why behind the learning?*
✓ Interpretation ✓ Application of skill or strategy	✓ Performance assessment: open-ended essay/writing; products (i.e., RAFT); concept map	**Simple:** √−, √, √+ on discrete facts/skills	Use ESSENCE as a guide for buy-in. Your lesson should have one or more of the following: ✓ ES: Emotional spark or salience (i.e., relevance) ✓ SE: Social engagement (i.e., collaboration) ✓ N: Novelty (i.e., new concepts and skills) ✓ CE: Critical or creative exploration opportunities
Generate questions at three different levels of cognitive activity: literal recall, inference, and evaluation or application. Learn to sequence related questions from simple to complex.	1. Learners categorize questions by level. They answer each question type and name what resources and actions must be used to answer each type. 2. Learners generate and answer questions at each level for self-selected texts.	√− = Categorize and justify one type of question √ = Categorize and justify two types of questions √+ = Categorize and justify all three types of questions √− = Generate a literal-level question √ = Generate literal- and inference-level questions √+ = Generate literal, inference, and evaluation or application questions	**ES:** Learners generate questions about the text of their choice. **SE:** Learners work together to generate and evaluate questions. They pose questions to each other. They give and receive procedural feedback about the entire process. **N:** Learners generate their own questions, rather than responding to those created by a teacher or textbook. **CE:** Learners apply the strategies to situations in their own lives and in the world.

MAP out the path to expertise/mastery
(How would an expert deconstruct and approach this task, step by step?)

TWITTER SUMMARY *(3 bullets max)*	MENTAL MODELS, PROCESS GUIDES, HEURISTICS	A MODEL OF GOOD WORK LOOKS LIKE . . .	DIFFERENTIATION AND LAYERING
Knowing which types of questions to ask—literal, inferential, and evaluative/applicative—is necessary to develop deep understanding of any text or data set.	• The three levels of questioning model guide corresponds to the trajectory of inquiry: from the literal and factual to the inferential to the evaluative/applicative, moving from the facts, to what facts and combinations of facts reveal, to evaluating and using what has been learned. All three levels of questioning and understanding are necessary to understanding and expertise.	See **pages 189–190.**	Levels of assistance: Assist peers to generate and confirm question types. Use different kinds of groupings. Provide more modeling as needed in the initial categorization step. Provide more scaffolds and stems. Provide continual procedural feedback. Use different levels of texts and data for learners to question.

(Continued)

(Continued)

POWER through your lesson
(What is the sequence of initial major must-make instructional moves?)

	PRIME	ORIENT	WALK THROUGH (and check for understanding)	EXTEND AND EXPLORE	REFLECT
Leader	PLAY a few quick games of twenty questions about an item in the classroom or on the playground to model how a systematic approach of using general to specific questions is useful in refining understanding. Categorize questions by literal, inferential, and evaluative/applicative. Preteach key vocabulary terms, such as *infer*, *explicit*, and *implicit*.	FRAME today's lesson: REFER to the essential question: *How do I become an expert?* Introduce the learning target: "Learners will ask their own questions of different kinds to pursue deep understanding and make meaning." EXPLAIN to learners that individuals are not born with expert knowledge in any field. In order to become an expert, it is critical for someone to know how to ask and answer many different types of questions that move from simpler to deeper forms of understanding. Introduce the text *Ish* by Peter Reynolds. This beautifully illustrated book is appropriate for all age groups because it communicates an important message about the road to expertise and rewards questioning on the literal, inferential, and evaluative/applicative levels.	EXPLAIN: We'll read (or reread) the book *Ish* to learn about expertise and develop our three-level questioning skills. CHECK FOR UNDERSTANDING: Ask learners to list as many questions as possible that relate to the story on individual sticky notes. MODEL: Introduce names of categories: On the Lines, Between the Lines, and Beyond the Lines. Answer questions by modeling and naming what must be done to answer each question type, and categorize the learner questions accordingly. CHECK FOR UNDERSTANDING: Ask learners to make generalizations about how questions for each category were answered—and what resources were needed to generate answers? What type of thinking and understanding was supported? This should lead to a conclusion that On the Lines questions are found explicitly in the text. Between the Lines are found by combining textual details and interpreting the meaning of the connections, or figuring forth from details to what they mean. Beyond the Lines are questions that connect the text with the reader or outside world. Add definitions for each category next to the title of the question type.	DELIBERATE PRACTICE/ ARTICULATE CONSCIOUS AWARENESS AND MENTAL MODELS OF EXPERTISE: Provide learners opportunities to apply the types of questions by asking them to select a children's book of choice and draft their own questions for it. Learners should check with peers and get procedural feedback. Share questions that are challenging with larger groups. Apply this strategy in disciplines such as math, where simple algorithms are On the Lines, story problem questions tend to be Between the Lines, and connections to the contexts of use for the story problems are Beyond the Lines.	ASK learners to check with a peer while you monitor whether or not they are categorizing their questions correctly. POSE the following questions to learners: *Which question type was the most difficult to answer? Why?* *Which answer was the most important to your understanding of the text? Why?* *What kinds of questions most interest you, and why?* *What work does each question type get done?* *What work must you do to answer each question type?* *In what contexts do you think each question type is most important?* *How do you foresee using this questioning technique at school in other classes, at home, when you read or watch movies on your own, or otherwise?* If facilitating literature circles, these questions could be a station facilitated by the teacher while some groups read independently. Ask learners to find connections between the levels and how one answer helps to generate other higher-level questions and answers. If they are comfortable composing their own questions, work on sequencing them effectively so that On the Lines questions help to answer a Between the Lines question that assists with a Beyond the Lines question.

POWER through your lesson

(What is the sequence of initial major must-make instructional moves?)

	PRIME	ORIENT	WALK THROUGH (and check for understanding)	EXTEND AND EXPLORE	REFLECT
Learner	Learners lead a game of twenty questions and note how some objects are more or less difficult to discern, as well as how different questions work together and are helpful in different ways to achieving understanding: After each round, have learners practice categorizing questions as having explicit or implicit answers and identifying when they made inferences.	Learners self-score their current expertise with questioning: 1: I never or rarely ask questions while I read. 2: Sometimes I ask questions while I read. 3: I frequently ask a variety of questions while I read. 4: I can teach someone else to ask a variety of questions while he or she reads.	GUIDED PRACTICE: Examine questions from a curriculum guide or worksheet, and classify them according to question type. In small groups, learners practice coming up with a list of three or four On the Lines questions about *Ish* or another shared class text. As learners become more comfortable with this question type, proceed to Between the Lines and Beyond the Lines. DIFFERENTIATE: Discuss how questions from the curriculum guide should be revised or deleted or new ones added that should be included in future editions. Provide additional practice modeling how to ask different types of questions. DEBRIEF: Small groups share their favorite question with the class. Evaluate as a class how it did or did not fit with the question type criteria and what kind of learning resulted from answering the question.		HOMEWORK EXTENSION: Have learners answer three-level questions about their weekend activities or events at home. Encourage learners to use three-level questions to deepen understanding with self-selected reading. Ask learners to compose three-level questions for family members about favorite TV shows or movies or other shared experiences. They can report out how the questions worked to support discussions and meaning making.

Chapter 12

EXTENDING EXPERTISE WITH COLLABORATIVE GROUP STRUCTURES

ESSENTIAL QUESTION
How can we work together so we are all
better, smarter, and more capable?

"If you want to go fast, go alone. If you want to go far,
go together." —African proverb

See
*Lesson Plan
Canvas*
on page
218

Have you ever been a part of an amazing team? The kind of team where you accomplished things together you never could have dreamed of on your own? Chris and Jackie have had the pleasure of working on such a team in the Idaho Coaching Network, a network of teacher leaders across the state of Idaho who come together monthly to celebrate and empower one another, to deepen their learning of best instructional and coaching practices, and to take their learning forward into their work with students and colleagues. Being part of a team like this is a unique and remarkable experience that requires deep love, respect, trust, mutual support, reciprocal commitments, and transparency for the purpose of doing significant learning together. Ultimately, this is the type of team we all hope to be on *and* the type of team we want and need to create in our classroom: one in which our learners don't just get along but believe deeply in their own and others' potential and then challenge and assist one another to be their best possible learners and selves.

Establishing a collaborative classroom culture is a prerequisite to guided inquiry and high-functioning group work. Chapter 6 focused on how to prime learning by establishing and maintaining a collaborative culture that engages learners in effective and meaningful group work. This chapter builds upon and *extends* this solid foundation, strengthening learners' social skills and helping them meet proficiency standards for collaboration, speaking, listening, and more; develop emotional intelligence and social imagination; participate in the social construction of knowledge; make better decisions; and prepare for college, careers, and their lives. Collaboration skills might very well be the most important set of skills we can teach our learners to prepare them for the innovative and unknown world of tomorrow.

As you likely know from your own experience, successful collaboration does not occur easily, nor by chance. Learners must be explicitly taught skills, such as ways of speaking and listening, offering and respecting diverse perspectives, monitoring one's own participation, honoring all voices and roles, and striving for equitable contributions from all group members. Thus, teachers must intentionally design activities to engage learners in deliberate practice of these skills; provide a multitude of opportunities for procedural feedback and self- and group assessments; and provide space and opportunity for learners to productively struggle, *reflect*, plan, and move forward. When you walk into any room and see learners engaged in successful collaboration, remember to pay homage to all the behind-the-scenes work on the part of both the teacher and the learners to create this magical space.

PLANNING FOR EXTENDING EXPERTISE WITH COLLABORATIVE GROUP STRUCTURES

When planning for *extending* expertise with group structures, teachers should make visible the potential, power, and payoffs of collaboration. One simple way to do this is to share a story about a time you were able to accomplish something collectively that you could not have done alone and then to invite your learners to *reflect* on this same prompt and share their stories. You might end the sharing with a discussion of the essential question, "How can we all be better, smarter, and more capable by working together?"

When you try any new strategy, it's essential to go in with an open mind and a willingness to persevere. As teachers and learners practice and improve at the strategy over time, it will become increasingly more fluid and effective. If you begin the strategy and it starts to fall apart (or your learners do), stop the lesson; repeat the instructions and expectations; provide more modeling or new scaffolds or prompts; and try, try again. And know that you are not alone! A "well-oiled machine" requires a great deal of oil, and that close-to-perfect strategy you saw in the classroom next door definitely blossomed out of many previous approximations, productive struggle, and an unwavering commitment to growth. We hope you will allow yourself and your learners a growth mindset and the gift of time for trying new ideas, making mistakes, and then trying again, because this is the path of all deep and significant learning.

In this chapter, we focus on strategies (which we refer to as *structures* because of the way they are set up and organized) that support, deepen, and *extend* collaboration in order to extend critical thinking and understanding through various kinds of discussions and activities. As we move into these, let's consider what success looks like.

Considerations for Designing and Implementing Collaborative Group Structures in the Classroom

❑ The teacher selects a collaborative activity because learners will benefit from the support of one another to meet the learning goals and accomplish the assigned task. (E-M)

❑ The teacher designs structures and processes to support group formation and productive collaboration through a task. (E-M)

❑ Learners understand the goals and expectations of both the task and the collaboration that will assist in accomplishing it. They understand the purpose and payoff of the task and the collaboration. They understand the responsibilities and roles that group members will play. As deemed appropriate, learners have assigned roles with accountability for each. (P-O)

❑ The collaborative activity engages all learners and capitalizes on each group member's unique strengths, knowledge, and interests and helps all to develop new capacities. (P-O-W-E)

❑ Learners use scaffolds and structures to deliberately practice collaboration in service of developing more expert moves of reading, composing, understanding, and meaning making. (W-E)

❑ Learners reflect on how the structure(s) and moves of collaboration can be used in the future to work with others on significant tasks. (E-R)

❑ Assessment of any deliverable is unbiased and accessible to all learners and recognizes individual and collaborative efforts and accomplishment, as well as new ways forward in a process of continuous improvement. (E-R)

COLLABORATIVE GROUP STRUCTURE MOVE 1: JIGSAW

A jigsaw is a valuable reading, problem-solving, and discussion structure that helps learners to efficiently learn about a new topic by dividing and conquering (or *jigsawing*) parts of the text, problem, or project. It involves what cognitive scientists call **distributed expertise**. In this collaborative structure, learners read different texts

(Continued)

(Continued)

or portions of a text on a particular topic (or address one aspect of a complex task) and are responsible for teaching others about what they have learned. Learners must take seriously their role of becoming an expert on their portion of the learning in order to fulfill their responsibility to teach the larger group. Though this structure can be used for reading any text or data set or pursuing any problem or project, we use the example of reading for main ideas and takeaways.

The jigsaw is structured so that each learner works in two different small groups, a *home group* and an *expert group*, each with a specific task focused on full participation and a clear deliverable. Let's look more closely at the four phases of a jigsaw.

1. *Individual work*: First, the teacher breaks down the text into manageable chunks (perhaps based on headings or other natural divisions) and assigns or lets learners select an excerpt to read. The teacher may number the excerpts or copy them on different colors of paper to distinguish the boundaries of the work and responsibilities for each learner.

Once assigned a portion of the larger text or task, learners work individually (or as needed in pairs or triads) to explore their topic and prepare to share their knowledge with others. Learners should understand that they are expected to teach their peers about their learning (or to make a unique contribution to the overall task completion). This creates high social stakes and prepares learners mentally and emotionally to meet the expectations. Learners should also apply the expert strategies they have learned to this work, such as annotating or highlighting the text or recording *most valuable points* (MVPs) from their reading, using the topic-comment strategy, and so forth (assuming they have had appropriate scaffolding and prior practice with these).

2. *Expert group work*: Next, learners meet together with their expert groups, composed of individuals who have read the same text or excerpt. This expert group discusses and comes to agreement about MVPs, a topic-comment, or a summary to share with their peers who tackled different reading(s). This step is often skipped in many classrooms due to time; however, it is a critical step in apprenticing learners. It ensures all members of the expert group process the information collaboratively; condense their reading or thinking into the most salient takeaways; and feel prepared, comfortable, and confident in teaching their peers. This step is especially important in supporting less confident readers and honoring introverts in the room.

3. *Home group work*: Next, each learner meets with peers that read different sections of the text. Each person represents a jigsaw puzzle piece that brings and shares different learning and unique expertise to this home group; together, they represent all aspects of the whole text or task. As expert

learners take turns sharing their learning, other learners in the group ask clarifying or extending questions of the "expert" and record this information on a note-catcher graphic organizer of some type. Finally, learners may collaboratively complete an overarching task or culminating project that requires and applies every expert's learning about their part of the text or task.

4. *Reconvene with expert groups:* Following the home groups, learners reconvene with their expert groups to reflect on how the teaching went; share new insights and perspectives gained from the mixed home groups; and reconsider their assigned passage or task in light of the whole, reflecting on how their part contributed to the bigger picture (Fisher & Frey, 2018).

Checklist for Creating Your Own Jigsaw Activity

- ☐ The complexity of the text, topic, problem, or project and/or the amount of time allotted requires and rewards a division of labor. (E-M)

- ☐ The text, topic, problem, or project is divided into manageable and complementary parts. (E-M)

- ☐ Learners are organized into expert and home groups for various purposes and pull from previous group experiences to review effective collaboration. (P-O)

- ☐ The teacher provides appropriate scaffolds to support individuals in the expert groups to complete their part of the task. (W)

- ☐ Learners represent the learning to be shared, often through a note-catcher, anchor chart, or application. (W-E)

- ☐ Learners share and listen within a mixed home group so that they develop a sense of the whole task or text and then apply what has been learned from all experts to a new problem or task. (W-E)

- ☐ Learners reflect on their group experience (noting both strengths and opportunities for growth), articulate what they learned from the collaboration, and identify future opportunities to use their new learning. (E-R)

PLC Connection

We recommend using the same jigsaw lesson shown in this chapter's canvas (as well as the picturing themes lesson found in the Chapter 9 canvas) to help teachers explore and make sense of the complex Mathematical Practice Standards (or any other complex policy, practice or requirement that your school or department must implement). This is a perfect example of when teachers should do the task before their students. By engaging in these tasks, the teachers will develop a deeper understanding of the standards, how to implement them in their classrooms, and how to help students internalize them. They will also learn how to effectively use the activity itself to promote student learning.

COLLABORATIVE GROUP STRUCTURE MOVE 2: FISHBOWL

In a fishbowl activity, divide learners into two groups and seat them in concentric circles. All of the learners orient themselves toward the center of the circle; those in the outer circle position themselves directly behind or across from an assigned partner in the inner circle. Learners in the inner circle engage in the discussion, problem-solving task, or activity. Meanwhile, learners on the outside observe and use a protocol or rubric to assess the power moves their "partner" makes, record specific evidence, and prepare to provide procedural feedback (see Chapter 6). Learners swap places with their partner halfway through the activity in order to ensure that everyone has the opportunity to play both the participant and the observer roles. When it is time to swap, learners should share helpful feedback with their partner prior to taking their place in the opposite circle and engaging in the other role. Sometimes, partners confer in the middle of their turn to be "coached" before the completion of it.

The fishbowl makes learners self-aware of their behaviors and moves in a discussion or activity and provides practice with peer assessment and feedback, skills of expert collaborators. The fishbowl structure also limits the number of participants engaged in the discussion or activity at any one time, providing the learners in the group sufficient opportunity to actively contribute or fulfill particular roles while ensuring all learners in the classroom are engaged in meaningful and productive work. After practicing as a whole class, it's possible to set up simultaneous fishbowls in a classroom. When you move to this more elaborate structure, place an empty seat in each of the fishbowls so you (or any other facilitator) can move in and out of these groupings, participating in and monitoring the discussions.

TO PRACTICE MINDFUL PARTICIPATION

A variation of the fishbowl is to give learners in the inner circle a specific number of playing cards in two different colors—for example, each learner may be given two black cards and two red cards. The black cards represent substantive contributions or uptake on another's comment, and the red cards represent questions. Learners must "play" their cards by placing them face up on their desk or in a bowl in the middle of the inner circle in order to make a statement, take up an idea, pose a question, or otherwise. This process ensures that all members participate, no members dominate the conversation, and contributions are strategic. Because learners have fewer opportunities to speak, they are typically more mindful of what they say and when they choose to play their cards. Writing questions and statements prior to or during the discussion prepares all learners, especially those who are more reluctant to share, to make integral contributions. For learners who don't have the chance to play all their cards, they can write a question or statement for each card they did not "play" after the discussion ends. This holds each learner accountable and ensures you hear from and can assess everyone in the group.

TO PROVIDE A MODEL FOR DELIBERATE PRACTICE

Use a fishbowl setup to demonstrate a strategy, an activity, or expectations by asking a model group to showcase an expected way of thinking, doing, responding, or being by role-playing in the inner circle. This can provide a model to the other learners in the room.

Example: Peer Conferencing Fishbowl

Use a fishbowl to model peer conferencing at the beginning of the year in writing workshop. Demonstrate what an expert feedback friend and editor would and would not do by asking a practiced group of exemplar learners (we usually ask them to come in at lunch or another time to practice their "skits" and to provide them feedback in advance of the class presentation) to model the "good," the "bad," and the "ugly" of peer conferencing. As they model each of these conferences in the fishbowl, learners in the outside circle closely watch and record "what expert peer conferencers do" on one side of a T-chart and "what expert peer conferencers avoid" on the other side of the T-chart. As the facilitator, you can also use a "freeze" cue, asking the fishbowl participants to freeze at any point in the conversation so you can provide commentary or lead a discussion among the participants or with the outer circle about the moves they are making and the effect of these moves.

CAROUSEL

A variation known as the carousel provides a useful and efficient structure for pairing learners for discussion or task navigation purposes. Just like the popular ride at many carnivals, the carousel is composed of rotating circles. In this case, learners sit in two concentric circles *facing* one another. Partners sit knee to knee (or stand facing each other) to engage in discussion about the topic of inquiry, answer questions, share resources to complete a task, or present and receive feedback on an artifact they created. You may also set up the carousel so the inside circle plays one role: presenter, detective, interviewer, a character or historical figure, author, or some other role or position, and the outside circle plays a different role such as respondent, interviewee, or other. The teacher may also guide the process by sharing questions or prompts aloud and having the learners tackle them together in their partnerships.

After a designated amount of talk time in one partnership (we make the time short to keep learners on task), the outside circle shifts one position to the left or right, so each learner has a new discussion partner to share ideas with. This continues for the time allotted or until learners have had as many partners as the teacher deems appropriate to promote learning. If learners in the inner and outer circles are playing different roles, they should swap places midway through the entire discussion, so they each have the opportunity to play both roles.

(Continued)

(Continued)

Checklist for Creating Your Own Fishbowl Activity

❑ The teacher has a clear purpose in using a fishbowl structure to promote more powerful collaboration and substantive learning. (E-M)

❑ Learners understand their roles and responsibilities in the fishbowl and are familiar with the protocol and critical standards for completing the inner- and outer-circle tasks. (P-O)

❑ Learners set a goal for how they want to show up and who they want to be in the discussion. (P-O)

❑ The teacher clearly articulates the moves that feedback friends should watch for when observing their partner or the group as a whole during the fishbowl. (O-W)

❑ All outer-circle learners sit in appropriate places to observe and hear their partner's contributions to the discussion. (W)

❑ Learners are familiar with and use scaffolds (such as a note-catcher, graphic organizer, rubric, or feedback sentence stems) to document and provide respectful procedural feedback to one another. (W)

❑ Learners engage in respectful and meaningful discussion or problem solving with one another. (W)

❑ All learners have the opportunity to participate in both the inner and outer circles and to provide procedural feedback and feedforward to each other. (W-E)

❑ Following the discussion, learners reflect on their learning through this experience, their participation in the discussion, and the accomplishment of their goals. Learners consider opportunities to use what they have learned about collaboration, concepts, or strategies later on in the unit or their lives. (E-R)

COLLABORATIVE GROUP STRUCTURE MOVE 3: RECIPROCAL TEACHING

Reciprocal teaching (Palincsar & Brown, 1984) is a highly effective strategy for developing strategic capacity and deeper understanding of texts by dividing up responsibility of central strategies that experts orchestrate when reading. In reciprocal teaching, learners play four roles that mirror general processes of effective reading: the predictor, the questioner, the clarifier, and the summarizer.

It's essential for learners to have a basic understanding of all roles and the skills necessary to perform them prior to participating in reciprocal teaching. Teachers should model each of the skills and provide learners with supports such as cards (see Figure 12.1), bookmarks, props, or graphic organizers that describe their roles and provide prompts. The teacher can assign each learner a specific role once he or she understands the required skills.

You may decide to first group learners by role, so they can practice and learn together (i.e., all predictors together, all questioners together, and so on). Then, learners can form mixed, small groups to practice their roles as they read and discuss a topic or text. Learners should rotate roles over time, gaining practice with each of these integral skills.

■ FIGURE 12.1: RECIPROCAL TEACHING CARDS

Predictor	**Questioner**

Make a good guess about what you think is going to happen based on evidence from the text; expert readers look to confirm or disprove their predictions by continuing to read. Prediction is a form of *figuring forth*, or making an informed guess about future action or meaning based on patterns of key details.	Ask questions along the way that help you better understand the text; expert readers use questions (such as three-level questions) to clarify what is happening in the text, and these questions sometimes require the reader to do additional research to find the answers.
Clarifier	**Summarizer**
To clarify means to make more clear; expert readers use reading strategies to clarify and develop deeper understanding of specific words, phrases, or sections of the text. Clarifiers can also make inferences, share connections, note patterns they see, and use fix-up strategies.	To summarize is to capture the main idea(s) of the text or section; expert readers summarize to remember the most important takeaways of a text. Summaries should be brief and composed of the most important information.

(See questions to promote inferencing in Chapter 11 and prompts and processes for fix-up strategies in Chapter 10.)

The topic-comment strategy can be helpful to summarizers by prompting them to name the topic (general subject and purpose of the text); the key details most essential to understanding; the patterning of those details; and the point or comment about the topic expressed by this patterning of the details. (For more on macro-rules and guides for summarizing, see Wilhelm et al., 2012.)

(Continued)

(Continued)

The goal is to work toward learners using all four of these central strategies simultaneously, just as expert readers do. Note that roles also can change to reflect more complex task- or text-specific goals you are teaching toward (e.g., evidence finder, feedback provider [naming moves of the author], fact checker or fake-news sniffer, or symbol seeker).

Adapt this technique to your learners and the goals and tasks of the moment by adding more specific requirements or adding prompts and guides to their cards. For example, requiring questioners to ask inferential questions makes the role more specific. Prompts and stems for asking inference questions will provide scaffolding. If learners are adept at predicting, you could replace that role with a newer skill, like symbol seeker, main-idea maven, key-vocabulary finder, or inquiry connection maker, adding prompts and guides to the card.

Checklist for Creating Your Own Reciprocal Teaching Activity

❏ The teacher selects a challenging and stimulating text that will require and reward dividing up the strategic work. (E-M)

❏ Learners consider the usefulness of the central strategies in their past experience. They understand the goals, purposes, payoffs, and work to be achieved by playing each role and by reading reciprocally with others playing different roles. (P-O)

❏ The teacher models each featured role in isolation—and, eventually, together—demonstrating how expert readers employ these skills concurrently and at appropriate times when reading. (W)

❏ The teacher provides appropriate scaffolds (such as cards with stems and prompts) to apprentice learners into each role and the expert moves made in that role.

❏ Learners practice each of the strategies (perhaps with others playing that role) prior to practicing them in the reciprocal teaching format while engaging in authentic reading and discussion about topics and texts. (W-E)

❏ Learners in any role provide evidence from the text, from their experience, and from other texts to support their contributions and answers to questions. (WE)

❏ Learners experiment with including more advanced roles (evidence finder, symbol seeker, etc.). (W-E)

❏ Learners reflect on how the strategies work to assist reading and how they might use and extend them in future tasks in reading, math, science, or other areas. (R)

COLLABORATIVE GROUP STRUCTURE MOVE 4: COLLABORATIVE PLACEMAT

A placemat is a graphic organizer or note-catcher learners use to track the thinking and contributions of the entire group with whom they are learning and collaborating. After engaging in some type of learning, such as a discussion, reading of a text, solving of a problem, and so on, learners record their thinking on sticky notes or notecards; this could be a major takeaway, key detail, step in a process, drawing, central insight, or response to a specific question from their teacher or peers. Then, learners contribute to the collaborative placemat by placing their sticky notes in each of the four corners of a designated piece of paper, anchor chart, or poster board. Although this typically works best in groups of four, the collaborative placemat can easily be modified for groups of three or five members. You can combine this activity with a jigsaw so each group member has a different part or phase of a task to share.

Next, learners take turns reading their notes aloud, or the notes can be read silently by all. The group then identifies the most valuable points (MVPs) or most important common ideas or takeaways from the group's contributions. This could be done with a highlighting or coding strategy. The group summarizes the major takeaways on a sticky note and places this in the center of the placemat (see Figure 12.2). In addition to helping learners develop synthesis skills, the limited space on the sticky notes requires them to communicate their ideas concisely and effectively in writing.

■ FIGURE 12.2: COLLABORATIVE PLACEMAT EXAMPLE

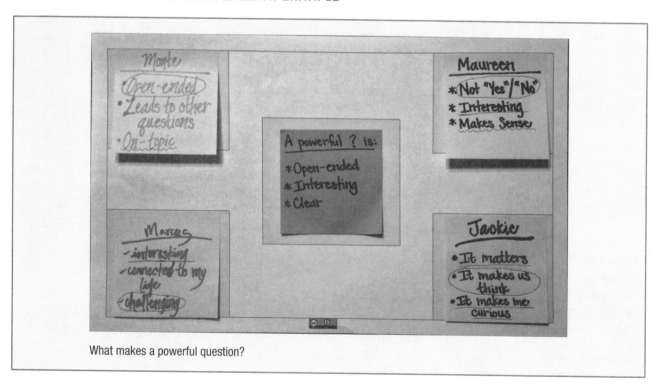

What makes a powerful question?

(Continued)

(Continued)

Sometimes, it might make more sense for learners to create individual placemats—for example, in a jigsaw, learners may fill out one portion of the placemat individually, expand on it when they meet with their expert groups, and then complete it and do the center of the placemat as they learn from their peers in mixed groups. Ultimately, the placemat provides a note-catching structure to support learners in collaborating, determining, and recording important ideas from themselves and others, synthesizing their thinking and reflecting on their learning.

Checklist for Creating Your Own Collaborative Placemat Activity

- ❏ The teacher determines when a placemat might be used during an instructional sequence and for what purpose(s). (E-M)

- ❏ The teacher asks learners when it has been important for them to "placehold" ideas and solicit ideas from others so the ideas can be considered and thought through, checked and expanded on (e.g., a grocery list or a packing list for a trip). (P)

- ❏ The teacher clearly communicates expectations for learners and their placemats, foregrounding the purpose, payoffs, and uses of the placemat in this context and in the future. (P-O)

- ❏ Learners rely on one another, each other's background knowledge, and the different insights gained from the reading or task to successfully complete their placemat and deepen their knowledge of the topic of inquiry. (W)

- ❏ Learners use different ideas to identify major themes and takeaways, thereby synthesizing their learning on the placemat. They identify their individual contributions and what they learned from others and learned by connecting and combining ideas (for reflection and assessment purposes). (W)

- ❏ Learners make connections between their placemats and those of their peers. (W-E)

- ❏ Learners consider real-world applications of structured collaborations and potential applications of what they learned about the topic from collaborating. (W-E-R)

- ❏ Learners assess their collaborative placemat via a rubric or another form of critical standards. They consider what they have learned that can be applied to any future collaborative activity. (R)

PLC Connection

Use one of the moves from this chapter to collaborate on addressing or learning more about a current challenge or initiative undertaken by your team, grade level, or school.

POWERFUL PLANNING: BEING BETTER TOGETHER

This chapter's collaborative structures remind us and our learners that we are better, smarter, and more capable together as we learn to capitalize on the knowledge and strengths of our peers, develop understanding and empathy for one another, and create experiences and products we never could have dreamed up individually. Diversity brings vitality and depth to any situation or kind of learning! Further, we challenge one another's thinking through respectful questioning, build upon one another's ideas, and encourage ourselves and our peers to articulate our knowledge and thinking. This kind of distributed thinking and expertise is central to a community of practice! As learners participate in each of these experiences, they develop not only conceptual knowledge of the topic being studied but also, more importantly, expert procedural knowledge and skills essential for life beyond the classroom, preparing them for the ever-changing and exciting world of tomorrow.

Guiding Questions When Setting Up Collaborative Group Structures

- What is my purpose for using this collaborative group structure? Why is collaborative learning better than independent learning here? How will this collaborative activity promote deeper learning and thinking that extends beyond an individual activity? (E-M)

- What is the best size of group for the activity we will do? (E-M)

- How will I prepare all learners for success with this collaborative activity, particularly considering introverts and learners who are less confident? (P-O)

- What skills will I need to explicitly teach learners (through modeling, mentoring, and monitoring) to help them work together effectively and to be successful with the task? (W)

- How will the collaborative structure model real-world collaborations and assist learners in developing communication and problem navigation skills they will use in future schooling, careers, and life situations? (W-E)

- How will I assess the individual contributions of learners in the group? How will I assess the performance of the whole group? How will I help learners self-assess their personal contributions, as well as those of other group members and the group as a whole? (R)

- How will learners reflect on the experience and plan for continued use and improvement as collaborative members of a community of practice? (R)

Lesson:

Unit: How do I become an expert?

ENVISION the destination
(Where are learners going, and why?)

GOAL *What kind of thinking is targeted?*	EVIDENCE *What product(s) will serve as proof of learning?*	MEASURES OF SUCCESS *What's the standard and quality-assurance tool?*	STAKES *Why will learners buy in?* *What's the why behind the learning?*
✓ Interpretation ✓ Application of skill or strategy ✓ Perspective taking ✓ Empathizing ✓ Self-assessing or reflecting	✓ Constructed (discrete task, long or short response, graphic organizer) ✓ Structured or unstructured observation	✓ **Checklist**: Assess if product contains essential characteristics or features.	Use ESSENCE as a guide for buy-in. Your lesson should have one or more of the following: ✓ SE: Social engagement (i.e., collaboration) ✓ N: Novelty (i.e., new concepts and skills) ✓ CE: Critical or creative exploration opportunities
Learners collaboratively explore content and use expert reading and collaboration skills to build individual and collective knowledge. Learners develop increased ownership, retention, and competence by teaching peers and learning from peers.	Learners become experts on their section of the reading (or task) by annotating the text and creating a representation of their learning to share with their expert groups. Learners share their learning in the expert group and record the most valuable ideas shared by other group members. They revise and rehearse what they will share with their mixed home group.	**Observational data:** ☐ In speaking, learners synthesize by identifying and sharing most valuable points. ☐ In conversation, learners teach their group and answer questions from peers. **Final product:** ☐ The product includes a record of the most valuable points from the individual's assigned section of the reading. ☐ The product includes a record of the most valuable points agreed to by all members of the expert group.	**SE:** Learners collaborate in expert groups to become experts on the content they study and then collaborate in the home group to teach this content to others and to learn from others about different content. **N:** Learners study different material to develop ownership of this new content and then share their learning with others. **CE:** Learners annotate their text, discuss, and synthesize ideas. They explore creative ways to share what they have learned.

MAP out the path to expertise/mastery
(How would an expert deconstruct and approach this task, step by step?)

TWITTER SUMMARY *(3 bullets max)*	MENTAL MODELS, PROCESS GUIDES, HEURISTICS	A MODEL OF GOOD WORK LOOKS LIKE . . .	DIFFERENTIATION AND LAYERING
Learners jigsaw a text and develop understanding of their portion in order to teach others. Learners learn about the entire text when expert peers share about their sections.	Distributed expertise. Creating a community of practice through jigsawing. Learning by doing and teaching others: learners develop expertise by taking responsibility for the content they study, synthesizing the most valuable points, and teaching and learning from their peers.	See jigsaw explanation on pages 208–09.	Learners may be strategically assigned leveled texts based on their reading levels, interests, and needs. Learners access strategies and resources for understanding complex vocabulary. Learners meet in expert groups to compare notes or work with partners prior to sharing the synthesis of their learning in their home groups. The teacher provides models and modeling as needed.

POWER through your lesson
(What is the sequence of initial major must-make instructional moves?)

	PRIME	ORIENT	WALK THROUGH (and check for understanding)	EXTEND AND EXPLORE	REFLECT
Leader	REMIND learners of the essential question for the unit, "How do I become an expert?" and encourage them to reflect on, make connections to, and consider additional questions and inquiries related to this question as they engage in the jigsaw reading and discussion. SHARE the expectation that each learner will become an expert on the topic, text excerpt, task or project section assigned to him or her and that this learning can be effectively and creatively shared with others.	FRAME today's lesson: EXPLAIN to learners that today we will be exploring the guiding question "What do mathematicians do?" in relation to our larger essential question for the unit, "How do I become an expert?" SHARE that we will be using a jigsaw strategy to tackle some complex but important reading about the kinds of moves and practices mathematicians use in the real world and will work together to analyze the text and develop our individual and collective knowledge on the subject. Deconstruct the jigsaw process into specific chunks, so learners have an idea of the overall scope and plan for the lesson. Share the jigsaw process verbally and visually display directions, so learners have a reference.	EXPLAIN to learners that they will read and analyze the Mathematical Practice Standards (we use learner-friendly versions) to gain an understanding of the practices real mathematicians use and that they will employ as learners throughout the year. ASSIGN *each learner a* Mathematical Practice Standard to closely read and analyze. EXPLAIN the close-reading process and note-catcher they will use to record their learning: "For the first read, read your Mathematical Practice Standard silently. Your goal is to get the gist of the overall standard. Then, read the standard a second time, highlighting or boxing keywords essential to understanding the standard. Use your resources (context, dictionaries, etc.) to define these keywords. Next, read the standard a third time (alone or aloud, you choose) using your new understanding of the keywords while thinking about how you might name and describe the processes outlined in the standard. Finally, complete the note-catcher by determining your own learner-friendly title and definition for the standard. Afterward, meet with your expert group to discuss your thinking, learner-friendly title, and definition with peers who have read the same standard."	DELIBERATE PRACTICE/ ARTICULATE CONSCIOUS AWARENESS: When learners finish, invite them to engage in a discussion about all eight mathematical practices and when they have used them before or see them used in the real world. This will provide an extension for learners who finish more quickly and provide more time for groups who need to finish. This discussion is critical to transfer of learning, so all groups should engage in this extending discussion (even though it will likely be for different amounts of time). *Note:* The unit's EXTEND-AND-EXPLORE step will occur primarily in the picturing themes lesson in Chapter 9, but this discussion will prepare them to engage in this application activity.	To conclude the lesson, ask learners to reflect on how the jigsaw process went today. This can be done via a simple exit ticket, such as, "How did you feel about the jigsaw process you engaged in today? What went well for you or your group? What was challenging for you or your group?" Another method for reflection about the process would be to establish a rubric for the jigsaw activity that asks learners to evaluate their own contributions to the group, as well as the effectiveness of the overall group work. This can serve as a powerful formative assessment, as well as feedback to the teacher about how the process went, what may need to be done differently, and what skills still need to be taught to and practiced by the learners to help them be successful.

(Continued)

(Continued)

POWER through your lesson
(What is the sequence of initial major must-make instructional moves?)

	PRIME	ORIENT	WALK THROUGH (and check for understanding)	EXTEND AND EXPLORE	REFLECT
Learner	REFLECT on the essential question by reviewing what you learned and what experts do, and by considering how you can embody these moves as you become an expert on the content you study in the lesson today.	CHECK FOR UNDERSTANDING: REPHRASE the expectations for the jigsaw activity and the roles you will play in the jigsaw.	GUIDED PRACTICE: Learners closely read their assigned standard and take notes via their note-catcher. Learners should discuss their learning with their expert group and prepare to share their learning with a larger group that has not read their text. CHECK FOR UNDERSTANDING: Before learners meet in their home groups, conduct a formative assessment to ensure learners feel comfortable, confident, and prepared to share their expertise in the mixed group. This can be done through a simple thumbs-up or thumbs-down approach. GUIDED PRACTICE (cont.): Learners move into home, or mixed, groups where each member shares their learner-friendly title and definition of the specific standard they studied; while each expert shares, learners record insights about the other Mathematical Practice Standards on their note-catcher. DIFFERENTIATE: Prompt group members to ask follow-up questions, so the expert may clarify ideas or deepen understanding. DEBRIEF: After all experts share about their standard, discuss the level of understanding of all group members and continue discussing the standards as necessary.		EXTENSION OF THIS LESSON: The picturing themes lesson in Chapter 9 provides the specific extension for this lesson for our model unit, "How do I become an expert?" EXTENSION OF THE JIGSAW ACTIVITY: Encourage learners to use a modified jigsaw approach (dividing and conquering the reading or workload) whenever appropriate in collaborative learning activities in the future.

Chapter 13

EXTENDING EXPERTISE BY PROMOTING DEEP DISCUSSION

ESSENTIAL QUESTION

How can we use discussion to promote the most powerful and dialogic learning spaces?

Do you ever talk to yourself? How often do you call up a friend or family member when you need to make a decision or reflect on a life experience? The power of dialogue (including what Vygotsky called *inner speech*—when you talk yourself through a process or problem) is truly remarkable in promoting deeper understanding!

Growing up on a farm, Jackie found that there was always new learning to do, and she would have been completely lost without the apprenticeship of her father and grandfather. Luckily, their experiences, expertise, and willingness to share, combined with her openness to learning, helped her conquer a most any challenge. If you went back in a time machine, you would find a miniature version of Jackie, full of curiosity, as well as mentors patiently listening, answering questions, and asking for her opinion too. You would see the members of her family come together to solve problems by talking them out and considering new or better strategies for getting the job done. Simply put, we are better (and smarter and more efficient) together, and we are better when we deeply listen, consider, and respect the viewpoints, stories, ideas, and questions of those around us.

James Britton (1970) once said that "all writing floats on a sea of talk" (p. 170). Others maintain that in fact all *learning* floats on a sea of talk—and research (and perhaps more importantly, our experiences) shows that this is so. Talk helps us plan, navigate productive struggle, create, and flesh out mental models and processes for complex tasks. That's why thinking aloud, explaining, and talking through our meaning-making and problem-solving processes each constitutes a powerful teaching move of apprenticeship and *walking through*. When learners engage in dialogue, they *extend* and transform their thinking; they challenge, articulate, clarify, and sharpen their thoughts; *explore* new possibilities; see different perspectives; and construct new meanings. Yet research shows that this kind of dialogic discussion rarely happens

See *Lesson Plan Canvas* on page 240

in classrooms (see, e.g., Nystrand, 1997) because high-level discourse doesn't occur naturally. Rather, it must be consciously structured, explicitly taught, scaffolded, continually promoted, and practiced.

PLANNING FOR EXTENDING EXPERTISE BY PROMOTING DEEP DISCUSSION

Learners can only create a mental model of effective discussion if we provide them the opportunity to practice and reflect on what makes discussion effective. This means we must teach our learners the must-make moves so that learners learn to effectively express ideas, listen, restate, uptake, agree and disagree respectfully, question, reflect, and synthesize. And, of course, we focus discussion on the topics of inquiry.

Receptive and careful listening is essential to learning from one another, forming relationships, and establishing a classroom culture where learners feel safe, cared for, and respected. Listening is an essential part of effective discussion; if learners are not yet good listeners, we must teach and assist them (as is the case with any stance or skill). What better place to start doing so than elementary school?

Let's begin with a few standard routines and practical considerations we hope you will find helpful in planning to structure your classroom for dialogue that extends learning and leads to exploration.

STANDARD ROUTINES

The following are routines to prepare learners for any discussion activity in your classroom.

- Use teacher-provided or learner-generated think-alouds, questions, visual creations, or other artifacts, like photos, text, and data, as sources of material to *prime* learners' thinking and stimulate discussion.

- Use pair or small-group discussions to provide learners a practice *walk-through* instead of or prior to whole-group dialogue. This invites all learners to safely share and ensures that everyone's voice will be heard. Further, it honors the introverts in your classroom who feel more comfortable in the small-group setting.

- Prepare your classroom environment for **dialogue** by seating learners in groups of four and numbering the desks 1, 2, 3, 4 so they can quickly talk with a face buddy, elbow buddy, or criss-cross buddy. Another option is *stand and deliver*, where one learner stands and responds to a teacher or learner query or asks a question of the group when you call their desk number. Just standing up sends more blood and oxygen to the brain!

- During a *walk-through* lesson, teach learners how to **uptake** (mirror and use others' ideas), establish and monitor norms, and respectfully disagree. Afterward, learners *explore*, and deliberately practice and monitor these moves.

- Challenge learners to support their thinking and comments with evidence and rationales, and encourage them to build on their own and others' ideas when clarification is needed or confusion occurs. A great way to do this is to make it a common practice in your classroom to ask, "What makes you say so?" This can serve as a powerful *reflection* tool as well.

ACTIVE-LISTENING ROUTINES

We must teach and promote active listening to the messages and perspectives of others. Beforehand, it's important to recognize that our personal filters, perspectives, assumptions, judgments, and beliefs influence what we hear. As a listener, our first role is to understand what is being said—to understand the speaker or author in the ways that they want to be understood. Only then can we meaningfully uptake, disagree, or resist. This requires conscious effort and the capacity to self-monitor, strategically reflect, mirror, ask questions, and provide procedural feedback to others and oneself. In all dialogue and discussion activities, we prompt our learners to do the following:

- Ask questions to clarify certain points.

- Periodically mirror or paraphrase the speaker's comments or deeper points ("What I hear you saying is . . ."). Ask the speaker to confirm the listener's understanding.

- Describe potential meanings, effects, and takeaways of the communicated message once the mirroring has been confirmed. This provides procedural feedback and invites the speaker to respond and engage in further uptake.

- Build on the speaker's ideas to create new meanings. This using and building on others' ideas (even while respectfully disagreeing) is the hallmark of dialogue.

SPEAKING ROUTINES

We must also teach our learners to develop speaking skills, prepare and monitor their contributions, and share the airtime in discussions. We do this by first naming expectations and then providing feedback and feedforward to help learners build awareness of their contributions. In addition, teachers might want to use discussion stems to help learners speak and interact in dialogic ways. Figure 13.1 shows some helpful examples. These can be posted on anchor charts in the classroom or given to learners as an individual resource, such as a laminated bookmark or a flipbook to carry with them to discussions.

We encourage you to consider these success criteria for powerful and effective discussions as you explore the following discussion routines and strategies.

> **PLC Connection**
>
> Lesson study is a way to frame and support meaningful dialogic talk about teaching through co-planning and then reflecting on lessons. Analyzing student work together is another high-leverage discussion activity that promotes dialogic discussion about teaching and learning.

Expressing an idea or opinion

- My opinion is _____.
- I think or believe _____.
- I would like to respectfully offer the idea that _____.
- What would follow/happen if we took the perspective that _____ (offer a new or even controversial perspective).

Mirroring what someone said

- What I'm hearing you say is _____.
- It sounds like you are saying _____. Is that correct?

Uptake/responding to or agreeing with someone

- I hear you saying _____, and I would build on that idea by saying _____.
- I agree with _____ because _____.

Uptake/disagreeing with someone

- I'd like to share a different opinion, perspective, or way of thinking about this. I think _____.
- Another way of looking at this is _____.
- I hear you saying _____; I would say _____.

General uptake

- I'd like to uptake on, add on, or offer a new perspective to what _____ said by _____.
- When you said _____, it made me think of _____.

Asking for clarification

- When you said _____, did you mean _____?
- I'd like to hear more about _____.
- Please tell me more about _____.

Considerations for Designing and Implementing an Effective Discussion Strategy

❑ The discussion strategy is designed to help learners become better at dialogue as they process new learning and extend and transfer this learning. (E-M)

❑ Learners consider when they have felt heard, valued, and helpful in some kind of conversation. What conditions made this happen, and how can we replicate them? (P)

- ❏ Learners understand the purpose and payoff of using the discussion strategy in the context of the current activity and inquiry. (P-O)

- ❏ Learners are provided appropriate scaffolds and deliberate practice with basic speaking and listening skills prior to engaging in a more complex discussion strategy. (O)

- ❏ The strategy motivates learners to share their unique ideas and insights with their peers and to listen to those of others. It provides a safe and encouraging environment for them to do so. (P-O-W)

- ❏ The strategy requires learners to read, write, and/or prepare in some way prior to the discussion in order to serve the purpose of the discussion. (O-W)

- ❏ The strategy builds learners' speaking and listening skills and leads to mastery of the grade-level speaking and listening standards. (W-E)

- ❏ The strategy encourages learners to honor the unique voices and perspectives of others and to challenge their own and others' thinking through respectful dialogue. (W-E)

- ❏ The strategy engages learners in deep learning that can be applied and transferred to new situations. (W-E)

- ❏ The strategy helps learners clarify and reflect on what they are coming to know by asking them to name their learning, monitor their growth, and consider opportunities for future application. (E-R)

PROMOTING DEEP DISCUSSION MOVE 1: GALLERY WALK

A gallery walk is a powerful strategy in which learners share responses to various artifacts posted around the classroom as gallery exhibits. They do this to learn from and respond to others, look for patterns, and participate in discussion. The teacher may display artifacts such as photos, powerful quotes or text excerpts, poetry, or infographics having to do with the inquiry or maybe examples of student work.

Learner creations showcased in a gallery walk may be in response to a question, text, or problem and may be a visual or written explanation of their learning. After learners complete their artifacts, they post them around the room, turning the classroom into a "gallery." All learners then explore the gallery, taking notes about what they are noticing and learning from others' work. Learners may do this observing and note-taking independently, in pairs, or in small groups. Gallery walks should only take ten to fifteen minutes, although the exact time will vary based on the number of exhibits, the number of learners in your classroom, and how the learners are expected to

(Continued)

(Continued)

respond and interact with the exhibits. A few ways learners may respond and interact with the exhibits are as follows:

- Learners carry a notebook, note-catcher, or graphic organizer to record notes of their observations and learning as they explore the gallery. They might look for key details or takeaways, points of connection or disagreement, questions, or ideas that give them a particular emotional charge.

- Learners respond to exhibits on sticky notes and post their feedback, thoughts, additions, or questions on or near the exhibits. Having learners initial their sticky notes allows the creators of the exhibits to follow up with the visitors if they have questions about the feedback or want to continue the conversation in person.

- Learners make connections by looking for similarities, differences, and/or themes as they explore. Learners record notices, thoughts, and wonders (the see–think–wonder strategy in Chapter 9) during this process, or the whole group may highlight these ideas in a follow-up discussion to the gallery walk.

- Learners provide feedforward that will encourage and support revisions and improvements.

Figure 13.2 provides some variations to the traditional gallery walk that you might use in your classroom to provide variety and meet your specific purposes and goals.

■ FIGURE 13.2: VARIATIONS ON THE TRADITIONAL GALLERY WALK

WHAT IS IT?	WHY MIGHT YOU USE IT?
Stay and stray: This gallery walk begins with a group representative staying at the group's exhibit to be a spokesperson about the creation. The remaining group members rotate to the next group's exhibit. The person who stays shares his or her group's creation with the visiting group. The visiting group listens attentively and asks clarifying questions. Then, when it is time to rotate, a person from the visiting group stays at the exhibit to become the new spokesperson, while the rest of the group (including the previous spokesperson) rotates. The new spokesperson presents the exhibit she or he just learned about to the next visiting group. The process continues with groups rotating and new learners taking over the role of spokesperson at each exhibit on each rotation. If time allows, groups will rotate to all exhibits, and all learners will have an opportunity to be a spokesperson.	The stay-and-stray gallery walk allows learners to - teach others about a response related to the inquiry, - strengthen speaking and listening skills, - actively listen so that major takeaways can be remembered and shared, - embrace the responsibility of teaching their peers about the exhibit and content, and - develop a strong classroom community as they interact in diverse groupings.

WHAT IS IT?	WHY MIGHT YOU USE IT?
Mixed group: In this variation, learners explore the gallery in mixed groups (as opposed to exploring with their group that created the artifact). To create mixed groups, have learners number off within the group (1, 2, 3, 4 . . .), having each member join a different group. This move forms mixed groups that include a representative (expert) on each exhibit. As groups explore the gallery, the expert member of the group explains the exhibit she or he helped create.	The mixed-group gallery walk allows learners to • practice their presentation skills as they share their creations with a new audience, and • work in diverse groupings, gaining new perspectives, insights, and appreciation for their peers.
Gallery guides: In this variation of the gallery walk, one creator of each exhibit stays and presents about it. We call this presenter the *gallery guide*. Visitors can either rotate through the exhibits dialoguing with the gallery guides, or each gallery guide can present his or her exhibit to the entire class one at a time. This is similar to a traditional presentation, but the exhibits are still placed on display in a gallery fashion. This can also work when invited guests, such as other classrooms or parents, come to see the gallery. Gallery guides can also be swapped out after one presentation, and the next presenter can present to a new group of visitors so all get a chance to be a guide. **Note:** If you choose this variation, be sure the gallery guides also have the opportunity to explore the gallery.	The gallery guide variation allows learners to • position themselves as experts as they present their creations; • engage in small-group and whole-group discussion around the exhibits in the gallery, leading to deeper understanding of the exhibits and the intention behind them; and • engage in deliberate practice with speaking and listening that models an authentic situation (a museum visit with a docent).

Example: Math Models Gallery Walk

Create a gallery walk of math models with work by learners who completed a problem in diverse ways. For example, a gallery walk for a multiplication problem might include a number line model, a partial products model, an array model, an area model, a tree diagram, a traditional algorithm model, and so on.

As learners walk around the gallery, they post feedback or questions on the models for the learner sharing her or his work. They could focus on the costs and benefits of the approach vis-à-vis other possible approaches. The model creator could also stay to share their technique and answer questions. Learners increase their understanding of different models by engaging in this silent or spoken conversation; it also opens the door for discussions about what's similar and different between models and can lead to a dialogue or debate about the best, most efficient way to solve the problem. Even if learners do not arrive at consensus, they discuss the pros and cons of different approaches, use math vocabulary, and increase their understanding of the various strategies.

(Continued)

(Continued)

Checklist for Creating Your Own Gallery Walk Activity

❑ The teacher defines the purpose of the gallery walk. Consider the following questions: What kinds of learner compositions or knowledge artifacts best suit your unit's goals and promote learning toward these goals? Which variation of the gallery walk strategy best serves your purpose? (E)

❑ The teacher determines how learners will engage in learning during the gallery walk. This could occur through conversation, taking notes, responding to the exhibits with feedback, or a combination of these. (M)

❑ The teacher provides an explanation of the purpose, procedures, and payoffs of the learning. (P-O)

❑ Learners are assisted to create their responses or knowledge artifacts to foreground particular kinds of learning. They are also assisted to usefully respond to and learn from others' responses through the use of note-catchers that guide their observations and thinking, through questioning strategies, and so on. (W)

❑ Learners participate in the gallery walk and extend and explore their own and each other's thinking by viewing, listening, taking notes, responding, or providing feedback on the exhibits they visit. (W-E)

❑ Learners reflect on the gallery walk experience, considering what they learned about the topic as well as what expert discussion skills they used, possibly via a checklist or rubric. (R)

PROMOTING DEEP DISCUSSION MOVE 2: ELEMENTARY SOCRATIC SEMINAR

The Socratic method, derived from Plato's Socratic dialogues and Socrates's belief that lecture was an effective method of transforming understanding, is more than 2,400 years old. A Socratic seminar is a collaborative, intellectual dialogue that allows learners to develop deeper understanding by grappling with open-ended questions and socially constructing their knowledge through the course of the discussion. This formal and highly structured discussion requires learners to think critically; bring background and textual knowledge to the table; assert and support their opinions with evidence and reasoning (see the CREW mental model in Chapter 5); listen attentively to one another; and work to develop deeper understanding of the texts, issues, and concepts under consideration. As you read this, you may be thinking, "I've heard about Socratic seminars, but isn't that a strategy for middle and high schools?" Although more commonly used in upper grade levels, Socratic seminars are not only possible at the elementary level, they are transformational!

A Socratic seminar requires intentional design, setup, and implementation. First, teachers establish discussion protocols to help learners interact and collaborate in meaningful ways. Further, teaching reading and thinking strategies (e.g., see Chapter 10 on think-alouds and Chapter 11 on questioning) in advance of the seminar *primes* and *orients* learners for success. Once learners acquire the necessary skills of close reading, searching for evidence in the text, and asking and answering useful questions, they are ready to engage in a Socratic seminar to *extend* and *explore* their thinking and learning.

The Socratic seminar looks different at different grade levels, likely beginning in the primary grades with a community circle discussion with a talking stick, facilitated by the teacher. In later grades, learners use sentence stems (see Figure 13.1) to help them open the discussion with a question, invite learners into the conversation, and agree and disagree respectfully. With appropriate scaffolding and deliberate practice, learners will internalize the structure, expectations, and process of the Socratic seminar, and by the fourth or fifth grades, they may be able to facilitate the discussion with little to no support, freeing the teacher to monitor the discussion and provide feedback to individual learners and the class as a whole.

PREPARING FOR THE SOCRATIC SEMINAR

1. Provide learners with the appropriate texts (which might include artifacts, videos, etc.) about the inquiry topic to deeply consider prior to the discussion.

2. Ask learners to closely read the texts. Use an annotation or note-taking strategy to help learners attend to important ideas and/or questions they have about the stimuli.

3. Engage learners in partner conversations about the texts, discussing main ideas and key details that support these ideas.

4. Ask learners to write one to two questions they would like to consider in the Socratic seminar.

5. Have learners vote as a whole group on which questions they are most interested in discussing; place questions on the wall and vote with colored dots, write them on the board and have learners raise their hands, or use a technological tool such as Socrative.

(Continued)

(Continued)

6. Invite learners to record the top-two or top-three questions and work in partners to respond to these questions with their own opinions and evidence from the texts.

GETTING STARTED

1. Decide what type of Socratic seminar you will use by considering your purposes for the seminar. There are many options for Socratic seminars, such as these:

   - A single-circle discussion with all learners participating at the same time.

   - A fishbowl (inner and outer circles) with the inner circle engaged in the seminar and the outer group observing. This allows for peer feedback or for back-channelling (when the outer circle silently provides their thinking and contributions in the form of insights, evidence, opinions, and questions via writing; this can be done on a whiteboard, anchor charts, or with a technological tool such as Today's Meet).

   - An empty chair discussion in which you include an empty chair for a member of the outer group to join the discussion. Or a tap-in/tap-out discussion where learners can enter or exit the inner discussion circle as they deem appropriate. Learners in the outer circle can tap the shoulder of an inner-circle member who has already contributed to the discussion to politely request they switch places.

2. Share your expectations for the Socratic seminar, and remind learners of the established discussion norms (see Chapter 6).

3. Ask learners to set a goal for the discussion based on the norms, and record this goal in a place where they will see it throughout the discussion. (In a partner feedback approach, give learners time to share their personal goals with their partners so these can be monitored.)

4. Remind learners to come prepared with all necessary materials: their goal, annotated texts, notes based on the selected questions, additional paper for recording ideas during the discussion, and a pencil.

5. Determine what your teacher role will be in the discussion (facilitator, observational note taker, etc.). If you will not be facilitating, appoint a learner to do so, or let all learners know you will be an observer so they can begin the conversation on their own.

6. Use a timer to monitor the discussion, particularly if you have a tight time frame or you are using inside and outside circles (to provide a cue for learners to switch roles halfway through).

ENGAGING IN THE DISCUSSION

1. Engage learners in the discussion. Serve as an observational note taker, monitor, and/or equal contributor.

- *Optional:* Stop the discussion at a specific point to provide overall feedback to the group. We like using two stars and a wish: two things the group is doing well and one thing you wish to see in the remainder of the discussion. You may also stop the discussion to remind learners of the expectations and discussion norms. Another option is to use a "time out"—to stop and have a participant confer with their observer and peer coach from the outer circle to see how well they are meeting their goals and develop a strategy for what to do next.

2. Encourage participants to mirror and uptake, ask for clarification, and invite other learners into the conversation.

3. Monitor the time, and provide time checks if and when necessary.

AFTER THE DISCUSSION

1. Ask the group to assess themselves as a group, providing procedural feedback guided by a checklist or rubric. Teachers can also provide procedural feedback after learners have done so.

2. If you are using peer guides in the outer circle, have these guides provide procedural feedback and feedforward to the participants they are observing.

3. Prompt learners to reflect on the discussion via a group discussion or in writing.

4. Prompt learners to reflect on their goal for improving discussion, deciding whether to continue focusing on their current goal or to add a new goal for the next discussion.

Socratic seminars have many benefits and are one of the best ways to transition from informational to transformational teaching. These rich and rigorous discussions place learners in the driver's seat. By positioning himself or herself as a facilitator, the teacher steps back and allows learners to step up as leaders. As learners take on responsibility for the discussion, the teacher can provide feedback and assess for success. The teacher may use a checklist or take observational notes to see how learners engage, what moves they try, and the kinds of contributions they make. One way to do this is via a spiderweb discussion (shown in Figure 13.3). During the Socratic seminar, the teacher draws lines between the names of learners to indicate interactions between individuals, and a coding system tracks the types of contributions made. Both of these monitoring tools are invaluable for reflection and goal setting afterward.

For an example of Socratic seminar observation notes, see **resources.corwin.com/ EMPOWER-elementary**.

PLC Connection
Use Socratic seminars in staff meetings to (1) model what this strategy looks like at the elementary level as well as (2) facilitate rich conversations around a central text or a variety of texts on a common educational topic. As you do so, use the spiderweb to map the discussion, and provide teachers an opportunity to reflect on their individual and collective contributions to the conversation, perhaps setting a professional goal for future action as they do so.

(Continued)

(Continued)

■ FIGURE 13.3: EXAMPLE OF A SPIDERWEB DISCUSSION MAP: A TOOL FOR TRACKING PARTICIPANTS' CONTRIBUTIONS TO THE DISCUSSION

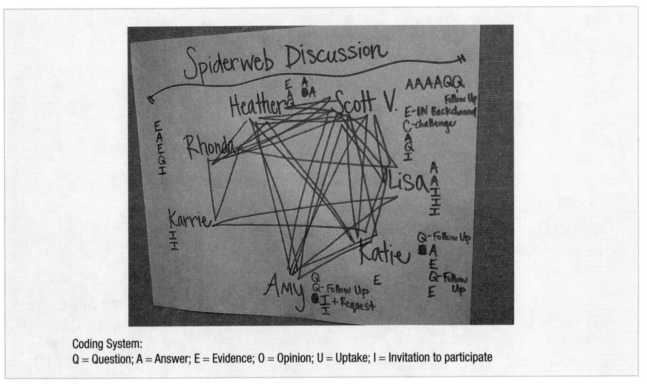

Coding System:
Q = Question; A = Answer; E = Evidence; O = Opinion; U = Uptake; I = Invitation to participate

Source: Wiggins (2017).

Checklist for Creating Your Own Elementary Socratic Seminar

❑ The teacher and/or learners create discussion rules for the Socratic seminar. (E-M)

❑ Learners understand the purpose of the seminar and how it relates to the inquiry. All participants prepare in advance and come to the seminar with supporting materials and a willingness to learn from each other. (P-O)

❑ Appropriate scaffolds, such as discussion stems and note-catchers, are available to learners during the discussion. (W)

❑ The teacher acts as a facilitator (or observer) and intervenes as little as possible, allowing learners to exercise leadership skills. (W)

- ❑ Learners talk to one another, not to the teacher, and use nonverbal and verbal cues to take turns speaking and invite each other to speak. (W)

- ❑ Learners refer to the text and any other supporting material they have brought as they participate in the discussion. (W)

- ❑ Learners express and respect diverse viewpoints and support their viewpoints with evidence from the text or other appropriate resources (personal experience, past study, etc.). (W-E)

- ❑ Learners listen carefully, stay on topic, ask for clarification, uptake, invite other learners into the conversation, monitor their own contributions, and make notes about ideas they would like to return to or share in the future. (W-E)

- ❑ Any observers provide procedural feedback and feedforward on the discussion process, power moves, and potential moves. (W-E)

- ❑ All learners participate in the discussion, are responsible for its success, and reflect on their individual contributions and the success of the discussion as a whole. They set goals for future discussions. (R)

PROMOTING DEEP DISCUSSION MOVE 3: HOTSEATING

Hotseating (Wilhelm 2012a) is a drama technique that puts learners in role and on the spot—in the hotseat. While sitting in the hotseat, learners assume the role of a character, person, or idea other than themselves. They speak from this perspective and answer questions in this role. The learner preparing for the hotseat completes a note-catcher to gather as much information about the role she or he will play and carefully considers that perspective. Teachers model this strategy by first taking a turn in the hotseat themselves. Prior to engaging in a hotseat drama, audience members also prepare by considering the questions they will ask of those who take the hotseat. See Figure 13.4 for an example of how to prepare for a hotseat. Here, we used the character Ramon from Peter Reynolds's story *Ish*, a text we use in our throughline unit (see the three-level reading guide in Chapter 11).

(Continued)

PLC Connection

Different discussion strategies can be used when studying school data or exploring issues important to the community. For example, hotseating can be used to explore perspectives of community members, parents of English language learners, and others and to rehearse ways to consider their concerns.

■ FIGURE 13.4: HOTSEAT PREPARATION EXAMPLE

Hotseating Note-Catcher for *Ish* by Peter Reynolds

For the learner preparing to be in the hotseat

Name of role (character, person, historical figure, or object): Ramon

Your age and physical characteristics: Elementary-school-age boy, curly hair, coffee-colored skin

Your house, city/area, favorite place: Lives in a house with his family. Likes being outside, sitting on a rock in the sun.

Your passions and deepest desires: Drawing and painting pictures

Your main goal: Become an artist and maybe a poet

Your biggest obstacles and problems: My brother, Leon, says mean things about my art sometimes.

Your biggest influences: My sister, Marisol, and brother, Leon

Your greatest strengths: Creativity

Your greatest weaknesses: Lack of self-confidence

What one or two words best describe you? Give examples from the text or personal experiences that demonstrate these traits:
Artist, Ish. I create a lot of pictures in the story. I use the suffix -ish a lot to describe myself.

Consider what questions may be asked of you. How will you respond? How do you know these responses are good ones? What other questions might the audience ask? What will they want to know?

Q: What makes you an artist?

A: I am an artist because I can draw the ideas I have in my mind on paper. If someone gives me a topic, I can turn it into a visual by using my imagination and creativity.

Q: You said your sister and brother are your biggest influences. How do they influence you?

A: My brother, Leon, makes me feel bad about my art when he laughs at it and asks me, "What is that?" I've always looked up to my older brother, so his opinion matters to me. My sister, Marisol, helped me to see my art in a whole new way. It made me think my art does matter and it doesn't have to look in a particular way. She helped me see the power of -ish.

Q: Why do you listen to your brother Leon?

Q: Why do you use -ish to describe you?

For audience members preparing to engage with the learner in the hotseat

What do you want to know about or from the person in the hotseat?

I want to know more about how Ramon sees his artwork and how he became the artist he is today. I also want to know what he plans to create next and what his goals are for the future.

What questions might you ask?

What does -ish mean to you?

How did you become an artist, and what steps might you take to become an even better artist?

If it's important to you for Leon to appreciate your art, how might you help him to see it differently?

Why might this information be important?

This information is important because it will help me better understand what Ramon is thinking and how he can work through his troubles, and it might also give me some tips on becoming an artist myself.

Example: Math—Number Sense Hotseat

- To increase number sense, learners each take on the role of a different number.

- Learners complete the hotseat note-catcher from the perspective of the assigned or chosen number, considering and researching what makes that number special historically or mathematically.

- Learners take turns in the hotseat to interview one another about their qualities, how they might contribute to solving various problems, what jobs they can do, and the like.

- Additionally, learners could wear a nametag throughout the day that displays their number and can introduce themselves to peers and other members of the school community. (For example, a learner might say, "Hi, I'm number 24. I can divide the day into equal segments called hours.")

Checklist for Creating Your Own Hotseating Activity

- ❏ The teacher determines a hotseat activity that will enhance and extend the learning and best serve the purpose and time frame of the lesson. (E-M)

- ❏ Learners consider when they have imaginatively role-played being someone else and what can be enjoyed and gained by doing so. (P)

- ❏ Learners identify and undertake roles in the hotseat (a character, historical figure, concept, process, number, etc.) and understand the purpose and payoffs of exploring the perspective and position of the assigned role. (P-O)

- ❏ Learners prepare by conducting research and rehearsing their role's deepest values, commitments, ways of being and doing things, and how to answer likely questions from others from the perspective of their assigned role. (P-O)

- ❏ Learners practice engaging in the hotseat in pairs or small groups prior to sitting in the official hotseat. (W)

(Continued)

(Continued)

- ❑ Learners engage in the hotseat and speak from the authority of their role, sharing evidence or research to support their opinions, ideas, and perspectives. (W)

- ❑ Learners serve as attentive audience members, asking thoughtful questions and providing procedural feedback and feedforward. (W-E)

- ❑ Learners can consider how responses would be different if provided from the position and perspective of a different role. (E)

- ❑ Learners reflect on their experience the hotseat in order to make revisions and extend their learning from this experience to future work. (E-R)

PROMOTING DEEP DISCUSSION MOVE 4: TALKING BUBBLES

Talking bubbles is a powerful teacher strategy to use with any form of discussion. This strategy (1) helps the teacher maintain the role of facilitator; (2) encourages the teacher to take observational notes that can be used as formative assessments; (3) honors and gives credit to learners as they share ideas; and (4) creates a map of the discussion that learners can use to reflect upon what went well and how to continue improving as speakers, listeners, and dialogic learners.

During a Socratic seminar, gallery walk, literature circle, small group, or any other form of discussion, the teacher listens to learners, recording comments on a clipboard, notebook, or sticky notes. Whenever possible, the teacher records verbatim in order to capture the ideas authentically. Then, the teacher displays the comment on a whiteboard or chart paper for all to see.

In order to emphasize that learners shared these ideas aloud, record the comments in speech bubbles, like in Figure 13.5. Depending on the comment, record learners' thoughts verbatim, summarize them, or name the big ideas. We also recommend including learners' names to give credit to the speakers whenever possible. This requires attentive listening on the part of the teacher. After this strategy has been modeled, a designated learner or small team of learners can do the work of recording and sharing the contributions and quotes of their peers. Following the discussion, it's important to review the talking bubbles as a way to wrap up the conversation and reflect on the learning, citing and thanking people who made major contributions.

During this follow-up discussion, learners

- see and reflect on the ideas they shared and the language they used;

- name insights that helped move their thinking forward, often referring to a comment from a peer that led to an uptake or new thought or new direction for the inquiry;

- review the learning and make connections between ideas, using different colors, shapes, arrows, or symbols to represent evolutions in thinking; and

- perhaps most importantly, recognize and celebrate learner contributions to the learning!

■ FIGURE 13.5: EXAMPLE TALKING BUBBLES CHART

Example Talking Bubbles Chart for a Number Talk

Problem Set:

$1/6 \times 1/4 =$

$1/6 \times 1/5 =$

$1/6 \times 1/6 =$

$1/6 \times 1/7 =$

$1/6 \times 1/8 =$

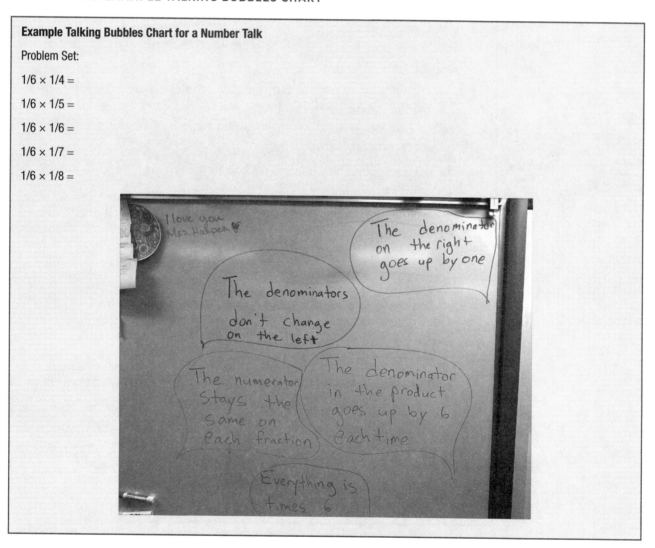

(Continued)

Display talking bubbles as a resource for future discussions and writing. After seeing the teacher model this strategy, a learner or team could take on the role of using thought bubbles as part of "mapping the discussion" for the whole class. Another option is for all learners to contribute a talking bubble or two that captures a classmate's contribution. As they do this work, learners cite and reflect on the valuable contributions of group members, witness and name how learners responded to one another, and provide procedural feedback to their peers. For more information about talking bubbles and discussion maps, check out our secondary companion book.

Checklist for Creating Your Own Talking Bubbles

❑ The teacher considers the ultimate goals of the discussion, mentally noting the kinds of thinking or moves she or he wants to be sure to record in the talking bubbles. (E-M)

❑ Learners understand that the purpose of the strategy is to record substantive contributions or questions about the topic that should be "placeheld" because they can be used to extend thinking and understanding, see new connections, and more. (P-O)

❑ The teacher models the strategy and how to use talking bubbles to note significant contributions and reflect on them. (W)

❑ The teacher monitors the room but does not engage verbally in the discussion. (W)

❑ The teacher records ideas and quotes shared by learners in the discussion. (W)

❑ The teacher records learners' names along with their contributions in order to give credit to the author, as well as to facilitate any follow-up or reflective conversations after the discussion has been completed. (W)

❑ The teacher turns the strategy over to learners, who record significant contributions from other learners so these can be cited and used to further understanding. (W-E)

❑ To wrap up the lesson, the teacher engages the learners in a follow-up discussion about what can be learned from the talking bubbles (learning from others, citing the insights of others, learning as a community of practice, etc.) and plans how to capitalize on these ideas in future discussions, composing, and learning. (E-R)

POWERFUL PLANNING: MEANINGFUL DIALOGUE FOR DEEPER LEARNING

Speaking and listening are two of the most needed and complex skills for learning and for life. As such, it's important for us to recognize our role in teaching our learners through EMPOWER to engage in appropriate, respectful, and meaningful discussions in and beyond the classroom. In this world of talkers, it's critical to teach our learners to listen and respect others' ideas, and even to use, cite, and extend these ideas.

As with every *must-make move* of guided inquiry, these skills extend far beyond your current work in the classroom as you prepare learners to engage in successful and democratic discussions on the playground, at home, at church, in sports, and wherever their lives take them. The power of discussion cannot be underestimated: It helps us outgrow ourselves and expand our perspectives, builds threshold knowledge, promotes social imagination, leads to innovative thinking and products, and creates meaningful interactions and relationships between people. By teaching learners to honor and learn from one another, you may very well be teaching them the most powerful and essential set of skills they will need to be successful and happy in life.

Guiding Questions for Planning for Deep Discussion

- What is my specific purpose for this lesson in terms of unit and life goals, and how does this discussion strategy help fulfill that purpose? (E-M)

- What is the best group size for this particular discussion? What are the benefits and challenges of having multiple discussion groups running simultaneously? How will I structure and monitor the group or multiple groups? (E-M)

- What skills will I need to teach learners in advance to help them see the purpose and payoff of the strategy and to engage effectively in the discussion at hand? (P-O)

- How will I prepare all learners for success, set critical standards and expectations, promote equality in the discussion, and encourage learners to use the thinking of others to extend their thinking? (O)

- What kinds of modeling, gradual release, scaffolding, and supports will I provide to help learners succeed and lead them to independence? (W)

- How will learners consider future applications of their learning and/or the discussion strategy? (E-R)

- How will I assess each learner in the group? How will I assess the group as a whole? How will individuals and groups be accountable for their behavior and contributions? How will all learners be helped to self-assess and share assessments in ways that will help the whole class become more supportive and dialogic? (R)

- How will learners reflect on their progress and create action plans for future improvement? (R)

Lesson: Gallery Walk

Unit: How do I become an expert?

ENVISION the destination
(Where are learners going, and why?)

GOAL *What kind of thinking is targeted?*	EVIDENCE *What product(s) will serve as proof of learning?*	MEASURES OF SUCCESS *What's the standard and quality-assurance tool?*	STAKES *Why will learners buy in?* *What's the why behind the learning?*
✓ Interpretation ✓ Explanation or reasoning ✓ Self-assessing or reflecting	✓ Performance assessment: open-ended essay or writing; products (i.e., RAFT); concept map	✓ **Simple:** √−, √, √+ on discrete facts or skills	Use ESSENCE as a guide for buy-in. Your lesson should have one or more of the following: ✓ ES: Emotional spark or salience (i.e., relevance) ✓ SE: Social engagement (i.e., collaboration) ✓ N: Novelty (i.e., new concepts and skills) ✓ CE: Critical or creative exploration opportunities
Provide learners the opportunity to share the artifacts (e.g., reading strategy posters) they created. Engage learners in using the posters to promote discussion about the reading strategies expert readers use.	1. Learners engage in thoughtful discussion about the reading strategy posters. 2. Learners provide procedural feedback to other groups. 3. Learners revise their reading strategy posters based on feedback.	√− = Learners participate in the gallery walk but have limited conversation about the artifacts. Learners provide limited to no feedback to the original authors. √ = Learners participate in the gallery walk and engage in meaningful conversation about the artifacts. Learners provide feedback to the original authors that furthers understanding of reading strategies. √+ = Learners participate in the gallery walk, engage in extensive conversation about the artifacts, and explain how they use (or could use) the reading strategies shared in their own independent reading. Learners provide kind, specific, and helpful feedback to the original authors to inform revision.	ES: Learners express their ideas via a creative modality (the reading strategy posters) and engage in conversations about moves expert readers make. SE: Learners engage in conversations with their groups as they explore the exhibits in the gallery and provide feedback to the authors. N: Learners deeply consider the exhibits and provide procedural feedback and feedforward. CE: Learners revise their reading strategy posters based on feedback from other groups and/or add examples to clarify their ideas for an outside audience.

MAP out the path to expertise or mastery
(How would an expert deconstruct and approach this task, step by step?)

TWITTER SUMMARY *(3 bullets max)*	MENTAL MODELS, PROCESS GUIDES, HEURISTICS	A MODEL OF GOOD WORK LOOKS LIKE . . .	DIFFERENTIATION AND LAYERING
Gallery walks provide a great opportunity to share and respond to ideas and artifacts, engage in deep discussion, make connections, and encourage feedback.	Learners engage with texts and one another to deepen and challenge their thinking. Learners strive to identify moves and patterns of moves expert readers make, so they can imitate these moves until they internalize them.	See explanation on pages 225–227.	Levels of assistance: Learners receive scaffolded support and practice on noticing key details and providing procedural feedback. The teacher groups learners strategically (see balancing the boat or other grouping ideas in Chapter 6). The teacher provides models and modeling as needed.

POWER through your lesson
(What is the sequence of initial major must-make instructional moves?)

	PRIME	ORIENT	WALK THROUGH (and check for understanding)	EXTEND AND EXPLORE	REFLECT
Leader	REVIEW the expectations for the reading strategy posters (created in the previous lesson), and ensure learners are ready to share these artifacts with the larger group. REVIEW the guiding question, "What do expert readers do?" and explain that in today's lesson, learners will be sharing and learning from one another about expert reader moves. EXPLAIN the structure and plan for the gallery walk. Learners will rotate to each exhibit in groups, discussing the artifacts and providing kind, specific, and helpful procedural feedback and procedural feedforward to inform revisions.	FRAME today's lesson: EXPLAIN to learners that we will be using a "gallery" to display their reading strategy exhibits and that they will engage in a gallery walk, viewing other groups' creations and learning about what expert readers do. EXPLAIN: "Knowing the moves expert readers make can help us imitate and eventually internalize these moves for ourselves as we grow into expert readers. As you explore the exhibits in the gallery, consider what you already know and do as a reader, as well as which moves you'd like to develop. This careful reflection will help you acknowledge your personal strengths as a reader and set goals for the future."	PREPARE for the gallery walk by placing the reading strategy posters around the room with adequate space to move around and discuss without distractions. EXPLAIN to learners the plan for participating in the gallery walk: Learners will explore the gallery with the same groups they worked with to create their reading strategy posters. Groups will begin at the poster to the right of the poster they created and have three minutes to explore and discuss each poster they visit. EXPLAIN the expectation for providing feedback: During the gallery walk, groups will use sticky notes to communicate with the authors of the exhibit. Groups may ask clarifying questions or provide procedural feedback that helps the authors identify strengths and procedural feedforward to identify areas for growing forward. MODEL an example of procedural feedback for one of the reading strategy posters, such as, "Providing multiple examples of how to summarize helps me to see that there are many strategies to use for summarizing. I also appreciate the sentence stem, 'The most important idea in this section was . . .' because this tips me off to the major takeaway." ***Optional scaffold:*** Provide feedback sentence stems that help learners provide kind, specific, and helpful feedback. CHECK FOR UNDERSTANDING: Ask a learner to rephrase the directions for the class to ensure all participants are prepared for the gallery walk. CHECK FOR UNDERSTANDING: Ask learners to use a thumb up, thumb sideways, or thumb down to show how well they understand the expectations for procedural feedback and feel prepared to share such feedback.	DELIBERATE PRACTICE/ ARTICULATE CONSCIOUS AWARENESS: After completing the gallery walk, learners return to the reading strategy poster they created to review the feedback. Using this feedback, groups revise their poster. Once the posters have been revised, display them in the classroom as resources for learners to use throughout the year. ***Optional extension:*** If time allows, have groups share the feedback they received and the modifications this feedback prompted them to make. Learners may use the following sentence stems: • "I used to think . . ." • "Then, I learned . . ." • "Now, I think . . ."	REFLECT: Learners consider what they learned about expert readers. Ask learners to respond to these questions: "What expert reading moves do you already use consistently in your independent reading? What are areas of growth or expert moves you would like to focus on in your future reading?"

(Continued)

(Continued)

POWER through your lesson
(What is the sequence of initial major must-make instructional moves?)

	PRIME	ORIENT	WALK THROUGH (and check for understanding)	EXTEND AND EXPLORE	REFLECT
Learner	PREPARE to engage in the gallery walk by assessing whether the group's artifact is ready to share based on the required criteria. REFLECT on the guiding question, and keep the question in mind throughout today's lesson. ASK any clarifying questions about the structure, and plan for the gallery walk to support success.	CONSIDER: What do you hope to learn from today's gallery walk? REFLECT: What are your personal strengths as a reader now? CONSIDER how you will be a helpful and contributing member of your group and set goals for today's gallery walk.	GUIDED PRACTICE: Learners visit each poster, discuss the reading strategy, and provide feedback and clarifying questions on sticky notes. DIFFERENTIATE: The teacher monitors the class, and learners ask for and receive assistance as needed. The teacher may pause the class in the middle of the gallery walk and provide additional scaffolding for composing procedural feedback. DEBRIEF: Learners reflect as a whole group on how the gallery walk went, discussing what was successful and challenging. Learners could complete a self-assessment based on the checklist.		HOMEWORK EXTENSION: In future reading activities, ask learners to focus on one or more of the reading strategies. Learners should review the strategy prior to reading, deliberately practice the strategy during reading, and reflect on their use of the strategy following the reading. Ask learners to write in a *readinking* (reading and thinking journal) during their independent reading in class or at home. In this journal, they can record what they were thinking while reading, as well as the expert reading moves they made and how these impacted their comprehension of the text.

PART 5: REFLECTING

ENVISION   MAP   PRIME   ORIENT   WALK THROUGH   EXTEND/EXPLORE   REFLECT

Chapter 14

REFLECTING THROUGH FORMATIVE ASSESSMENTS AND TO CULTIVATE A SPIRIT OF TRANSFER

ESSENTIAL QUESTION

How can we use formative assessments and feedback to transform learning?

Do you enjoy spending class time administering traditional summative assessments to your learners? Do your learners get excited when they sit down to take a chapter test? As you read these questions, you likely responded with laughter and an unequivocal, "Of course not!" One of the things that most teachers and learners can agree on is they would rather spend less time on assessment *of* learning (the type of assessment done at the end of something) (Earl, 2003). However, as we all know, assessments have an important purpose, and there are different types of assessment that do different work. Assessments *for* and *as* learning occur naturally through the learning process and have tremendous potential to help teachers and learners achieve the highest levels of success. We need assessment that is **formative** and occurs while we are engaged in our substantive and engaging classroom work. Formative assessments *for* and *as* learning are powerful for preparing learners for success, then for identifying and celebrating progress, planning next steps, and addressing struggles in order to make these struggles productive.

Throughout this text, we have stressed the importance of framing learning as inquiry. EMPOWER is a mental model for *planning* and implementing instruction that requires teachers and learners to inquire into compelling issues (such as our through-line unit inquiry into what it takes to become an expert) but also into the learning process itself and into how to become more expert and strategic in the ways that we develop and apply knowledge. The act of teaching is essentially a form of guided inquiry. One essential question teachers grapple with every day is this: "How can we understand what our learners know and are able to do and help them move forward?" Formative assessments help us understand our learners' level of understanding and learning process and act on what we learn to *map* our next moves.

See *Lesson Plan Canvas* on page 265

Assessing along the journey of learning is essential because it enables teachers to tailor instruction to learner needs, and it prepares learners for the next steps toward expert accomplishment—culminating performances and summative assessments. This preparation for success is what is meant by assessment *for* learning. Another aspect of formative assessment is that learners experience it as an activity that promotes learning. This is what is meant by assessment *as* learning (Earl, 2003). Formative assessment is all about sharing power, promoting growth, and deepening learning. Unlike summative assessments, formative assessments naturally occur through engaging classroom work; the results are not meant to be graded (though they could be recorded as evidence of effort and growth); and, most importantly, they help teachers to teach more effectively and learners to grow and move forward.

Formative assessments used *as* and *for* learning provide the opportunity for something that's sorely lacking in many classrooms: immediately meaningful and usable feedback. They provide descriptive and procedural feedback about current accomplishments and ways to move forward, rather than a final judgment. Teachers can use the results of these assessments to improve instruction for learners—and there will be fewer surprises when you reach the summative assessment. It's also worth noting that sharing and studying formative assessments with colleagues is a quick and powerful way to help us understand our learners and plan together.

CONFERRING: THE MOST POWERFUL FORMATIVE ASSESSMENT

Let's take a few moments to consider one of the most powerful forms of formative assessment and instruction out there: conferring. In the real world, every one of us has a mentor or mentors, trusted colleagues and advisors to whom we look up and who help guide us in our learning by modeling, offering helpful feedback and powerful questions, and helping unveil the next steps in our journey. Having a mentor(s) is essential to guided inquiry and to life itself. In the hero quest archetype, every hero has a mentor! Because conferring is at the heart of both learning and life, there are whole books written about this topic from the area of education to business and everything in between, and it is far beyond the scope of this book to dive too deeply into the conversation around conferring and mentorship. However, we do want to share a few important notes on the subject before proceeding with other ways to use and provide formative assessment.

Conferring is the most powerful form of formative assessment because it is relational, personal, interactive, and authentic and allows teachers to meet each individual learner exactly where he or she is. Further, conferring with learners opens the door for deepening relationships with each individual learner, demonstrating your care, commitment, and love for him or her as a person and as a learner. Conferring acknowledges each child as a person and as a learner and shows how you honor what she or he is doing or producing and the courage, risks, and effort she or he is taking while providing ways forward toward even greater capacity, moving always toward becoming her or his best possible self.

Conferring also models the kind of culture and community we want to establish throughout the classroom, encouraging learners to pay careful attention to each other, to mentor each other into greater being and capacity, and to treat one another in the same humanizing ways we treat them in one-on-one conferences.

However, conferring doesn't come without its challenges. Questions of time and capacity are the first roadblocks that enter our brains when we think about conferring with our learners. What follows are a few tips for setting up conferences with your learners:

1. *Schedule time every day to confer with some learners.* Carl Anderson (2000) writes, "[Conferences] aren't the icing on the cake; they are the cake" (p. 3). Conferring with one or a few learners each day is far better than conferring with none of your learners none of the time. In addition, setting up an intentional schedule can allow you to confer with all learners within the week (or at a maximum, within two weeks). This does require setting aside blocks of time where all other learners in the classroom are able to work successfully at learning stations, with aides, in partners or groups, or independently. However, with intentional planning, classroom management techniques, and high expectations, even our youngest learners can engage in successful work during conference time.

2. *Determine the purpose of the conference.* There are different kinds of conferences for different purposes, and although you may address multiple purposes within the context of one conference, you should have a designated goal(s) and plan when entering a conference with a learner in order to maximize the time for both of you. A conference may serve as a check-in, an opportunity to monitor comprehension or a specific skill, a time for goal setting or offering a challenge, an opportunity for evaluation and reflection, or a discussion of when and how learners are applying their learning to life.

3. *Take careful notes during or after the conference* to record what you have noticed about your learner, his or her needs, and future goals and how to meet them. We recommend keeping a conferring binder with sections for each of your learners, so you can easily take this with you to all conferences and maintain accurate records of learners' progress and efforts from one conference to the next.

4. *Confer with learners throughout the learning process.* Conferring with learners at the beginning of the learning can be one of the most valuable forms of diagnostic assessment. By listening to our learners read, watching them write, and discussing their ideas and problem-solving methods together, we gain some of the most valuable insights on our learners' strengths, needs, gaps, and misconceptions. Conferring with learners at the beginning also helps us to work in tandem with them to set proper goals.

   Conferring with our learners during the learning process helps us assess how to modify, provide feedback, scaffold, and extend instruction in support of their goals. It's truly the best way to personalize learning and meet the needs of all learners.

   Finally, conferring throughout the process and toward the end of the learning progression supports assessment and reflection, skills that do not come naturally to young learners. Through carefully selected prompts, we can lead our learners to increased conscious competence, as they answer questions about how things are going or went, what challenges they are facing or have faced, what new ideas are emerging, what moves they are making and why, and what risks or next steps they'd like to take.

KINDS OF CONFERENCES

Gut checks/check-ins: Quick, personal queries into how things are going and what help might be needed with reading, composing, daily activities, the ongoing inquiry, culminating projects, and more.

Comprehension conferences: To check understanding of reading and the ongoing inquiry.

Nudge or challenge conferences: *Here's something new I want you to try that builds off what you already know and do. . . . What is a next step you can think of to move forward? What's a potential action plan for your project?*

Invitation conferences: *Here's a book I think you might enjoy/a kind of writing/learning activity I think you'd like . . . that you might find challenging but satisfying . . .*

Looking for trouble conferences: *Let's find an area of challenge and look for a way through it.*

Feedback and reflection conferences: *Let's see how well you are meeting critical standards and reflect on how to keep improving and extending learning.*

Connections to inquiry conferences: *What are connections you are seeing to our inquiry in your life, current events, favorite movies and shows, free reading, and other subjects? What future applications do you see?*

Reading life conferences: *When and how much are you reading beyond class? How can I support you?*

Writing life conferences: *When and how much are you writing beyond class? What things are you trying? How can I support you?*

Student-led conferences: For learners to present and justify their learning and to celebrate progress and commit to a plan of next steps for continuous improvement. We often have students do these for parents during parent–teacher conferences or for roundtables of peers to teach others about their learning.

READING CONFERENCES

In reading conferences, we work to invite learners to increase the (1) volume of their reading; (2) variety in their reading; (3) complexity; and (4) ways they identify with authors, genres, ideas, and favorite books. All of this is in service of building reading capacity, a growth mindset (Dweck, 2006), a reading identity, and the habits of expert readers. We ask things like, *How is the reading going? What trouble is brewing in the book (all stories are about trouble)? What big ideas or themes might be emerging? Read aloud a favorite part. Why is this a favorite? Read aloud a challenging part. Why is this a challenging part? How might we navigate that challenge?*

We also prompt learners to tell us about how they are reading and responding, using Jeff's "Tell Me . . ." framework questions and prompts that reflect the dimensions of an expert reader's response from *"You Gotta BE the Book"* (Wilhelm, 2016) by asking questions like, "Tell me, what do you think the author wants you most to notice, and how is your attention drawn to these things?" "Tell me, who is your favorite character and for what reasons?" (For hundreds more Tell Me questions, see Wilhelm, 2016.)

WRITING CONFERENCES

In writing conferences, we use the notion of *order of operations* to focus on what is most important—in other words, first things first. We focus first on ideas and content, then on the form and organization of those ideas, then on voice and other traits, then on conventions and correctness issues. We ask learners to read us a favorite part of their writing and then a challenging part (to explain the power moves or the challenges presented) and then work together to find ways forward. For specific ideas on what to prompt writers to talk about and to try, we use the strategies of narrative composing (see Fredricksen, Wilhelm, & Smith, 2012), the strategies of composing arguments (Wilhelm, Smith, & Fredricksen, 2012), or the strategies for composing specific kinds of informational text structures (Wilhelm, Smith, & Fredricksen, 2012).

GENERAL PROMPTS FOR CONFERENCING

In conferencing, it's important to get the learner to talk. In apprenticeship, we try to get the apprentice to take over doing the work. As we tell our learners, we've already passed second or third or fifth grade. Now it is their turn!

The following prompts help to get learners talking. It's important to get them to talk to us, to each other, and to wider audiences about their learning processes and to share their learning in public spaces, like during parent–teacher conferences or learning celebrations.

> *Tell me about/talk to me about . . . something you are doing or thinking as a writer/ reader/problem solver/citizen scientist. Tell me about how you are working to meet this goal or standard of our unit . . .*

> *Tell me about the favorite part of your book/your writing/the inquiry. . . . Why does that speak to you so much? Why do you find that so powerful?*

> *How does your reading/writing/inquiry connect to your deepest needs, desires, commitments, and goals?*

> **Mirroring:** *What I hear you saying is . . . Do I have that right?*

> *Say/tell me more about . . .*

> *Convince me of . . .*

> *What are some ideas you have for moving forward? What will you do next?*

> *How can we work together to address the challenge of organization/providing more detail (or any other current learning challenge)?*

REFLECTING ON THE CONFERENCE

A crux move in making the most of student–teacher conferences is having learners complete a written self-assessment, such as that shown in Figure 14.1, to promote reflection after any conference meeting.

Student–Teacher Conference Reflection

My conference was helpful and successful in these ways . . . because . . .

The power moves of the conference were . . .

For my next conference, I need to remember to . . .

One of the challenges of my conference was . . .

Ways to prepare for this kind of challenge in the future would be . . .

Things I have learned about my reading/my writing/myself from the conference are . . .

My action plan for using what I learned is . . .

If the conference is led by a student:

Things that I have learned by preparing and holding a conference are . . .

If parents or another audience were present:

The major insights my parents, peers, or other visitors learned about me and my learning from the conference are . . .

PLC Connection

These conferring practices transfer smoothly to peer coaches or instructional coaches as they confer with and use coaching cycles with teachers. Plan how to adapt and use some of these ideas in peer coaching or other instructional coaching situations.

There is no one right way to confer with learners, but one wrong way to go about it is avoiding conferring altogether. Ultimately, our goal is for learners to think aloud and make beliefs, knowledge, and current abilities visible and available to themselves and to us, so we can be reflective and responsive to each learner. We can then probe and prompt them to explore and inquire more deeply; read, write, or problem-solve more consciously and courageously; and believe more profoundly in their own potential.

PLANNING FOR REFLECTING THROUGH FORMATIVE ASSESSMENTS

Any time a learner says, does, writes, or makes anything in a classroom, it can be used as a source of formative assessment to guide instruction if we mindfully *reflect* on the results and *plan* how to provide the necessary supports. Any think-aloud, visual strategy, discussion, or other activity described in this book provides formative-assessment data. In the throughline unit, picturing themes about Mathematical Practice Standards, anchor charts of close-reading strategies, and cued think-alouds about the meaning of *Fish in a Tree* provide snapshots of learner analysis, representation, and publication skills that can highlight what learners are capable of doing and of doing next if we provide supportive instruction. This chapter provides structured formative assessments that help teachers and learners reflect on student learning in ways that inform our teaching.

Assessment *as* learning is the type of formative assessment that is overlooked the most and has the most potential to make learning transformative (Earl, 2003). It can be an inductive and restorative practice because it asks learners to analyze their work, promoting a more positive perspective of school and a dynamic mindset. Assessment *as* learning means the judgments are made *by* the learner, *for* the learner, throughout the learning process. The learner *primes and orients* herself or himself, based on *reflections* about her or his current levels of performance, and *maps* an action plan of next steps.

When we link formative self-assessment to upcoming summative assessments, the *reflection* facilitates a conversation between teacher and learner about where the learning is currently, gaps in understanding, and opportunities for growth. The most inductive and restorative piece of assessment *as* learning is making the assessment process more visible to learners and placing the power to self-assess in their hands. After all, if we want our learners to be inducted into the community of expert practice and reach independence, they have to understand and apply critical standards for expertise to their own work. When learners feel more ownership, they possess more autonomy, purpose, and engagement, which contribute to their ability to master the content. This also prepares learners to assess themselves in the future and set goals for success in learning and in life.

Without formative assessment, we have no idea what learners actually know and what they've learned as a result of our instruction. We can't help learners grow and provide appropriate scaffolding and differentiation if we don't know where they are currently and how they are proceeding. The strategies in this chapter provide you the critical information that guides the instruction of an effective educator. Most importantly, these strategies help you respond to that essential question for educators: "How can I understand what our learners know and are able to do and help them move forward?"

Considerations When Designing Reflective Opportunities and Formative Assessments

❑ The unit or lesson includes intentionally planned, ongoing formative assessments that make current achievement and struggle visible and therefore support the planning of necessary instructional activities throughout the unit. (E-M)

❑ Learners consider and share what kind of feedback and assessment has been helpful to their motivation and learning in the past. (P)

❑ Learners understand the purpose and payoff of each assessment and how they will help them move forward and develop expertise necessary to the culminating project and to life. (O)

❑ The assessment is helpful and supportive of the learner. There is no negative impact on the learner's final grade. The assessment is about learning and moving forward, putting effort into practicing expert strategies and seeing where they currently land so they know what to do next. (W-E)

(Continued)

❑ Learners use the assessment to understand where they succeeded, what contributed to success, and how to proceed to be even more successful. The assessments will name power moves to repeat and potential moves to try. (P-O-W-E-R)

❑ Learners are supported to self-assess and monitor their own efforts and progress toward meeting critical standards. They can extend to offering supportive peer assessments. (E-R)

❑ The overall focus of the assessment is growth—naming where we are and where we need to go next. (R)

PLC Connection

A simple modification of the traditional PQP is the PQW: *praise, questions,* and *ways forward* is a great move to make with colleagues. This move, discussed in our secondary companion book, encourages adult learners to not just consider the possibilities but to set and commit to specific goals that will help them and their learners move forward.

FORMATIVE ASSESSMENT MOVE 1: PRAISE/QUESTION/POSSIBILITIES (PQP)

Praise/question/possibilities (PQP) is one of the most versatile strategies in our formative-assessment toolbox because it can be used in any content area to respond to and confer with learners, to support peer-to-peer feedback, and as a self-assessment. This means PQP can be assessment *for* learning, informing your instruction in a number of ways, as well as assessment *as* learning, supporting learners in identifying and teaching themselves what to do next. The components of PQP are the following:

1. **Praise**: Praise commends the author or creator for what she or he has done well. The feedback should name specific efforts and strategies that were successful or effective in the learning process, presentation, or product and *why* they led to success. By beginning with strengths, we honor what the author or creator has already done and empower him or her to embrace future possibilities.

2. **Questions**: Questions are an essential part of this feedback process because they open the door for discussion and future action. It's helpful to address clarifying questions first. But the ultimate goal for the question portion is to address the *why* and *how* behind certain moves. This promotes conscious competence in learners by asking them to name the purpose behind moves and name the processes and mental models they used.

3. **Possibilities:** Possibilities are a form of feedforward where we focus on what the author or learner did and explore options for revision that would improve the process or product. Framing this as "possibilities" places control in the hands of the author or learner to consider what they will do next time.

The canvas on page 265 in this chapter uses PQP as a tool for peer-to-peer feedback (*feedback friends*). Of course, one of the many concerns about assessment is the *time* it takes for a teacher to respond to every learner. Involving the entire classroom in the feedback process addresses this concern. While it takes time up front to teach, this process helps learners understand critical standards and how to meet them, as well as how to provide feedback to others and to themselves—the independence that is the ultimate goal of all transformational teaching.

The PQP strategy affirms what went well and provides possible future directions in a supportive, learning-centered way. In the throughline unit, we use PQP to provide feedback for the culminating project. However, this feedback protocol could be used with any activity at any point during a unit.

The major principle at play here is to critically examine a learning process or piece of work through multiple lenses: What was effective, and why? What is the audience or reader still thinking about? What's possible next? Answers to these questions help address the larger question: How do we support learners through a process of continuous improvement?

Here are the four main steps of PQP:

1. Briefly share the three different categories of feedback and pass out a handout like Figure 14.2, or ask learners to write those headings on a piece of paper. You can chunk the teaching of the three skills over time.

2. Model providing kind, responsive, specific, and helpful feedback via the PQP to the work of a professional author or problem-solver (based on a shared reading or YouTube video).

3. Give learners opportunities to deliberately practice with you and with peers, also responding to authors you are reading or other experts practicing their craft. Then, practice with anonymous student work that relates to the unit. During this process, discuss how to craft concrete quality feedback that names strengths, surfaces questions, and highlights possible future moves.

4. Give learners continuing opportunities to provide PQP feedback to professional authors, to work samples, to peers, and, ultimately, to themselves. Figure 14.2 gives some sentence starters for each phase of PQP.

Stress the importance of being specific and explaining why and how a move worked for meaning and effect (see Chapter 6 for additional guidance and sentence starters). When multiple learners share similar feedback about a piece, it communicates a pattern to the recipient, which narrows the focus and makes it more likely she or he will remember it during revision. It's ultimately up to authors or composers what feedback they choose to act on. These decisions are an author's prerogative, but the author should be able to articulate a rationale for the choices she or he makes. This allows authors to feel in control of their learning and to make decisions based on a variety of data points.

(Continued)

(Continued)

■ **FIGURE 14.2: PQP SENTENCE STARTERS**

Praise: Something that was successful or effective in the presentation or product and *why* you responded that way.

    a. I felt/thought/understood _____ when you _____ because _____.

    b. When you _____, the effect on me was _____ because _____.

    c. The _____ move made me think _____ because _____.

    d. When you _____, I noticed it was similar to the same move the author made in _____ [text title] because _____.

Questions: Sometimes, it can be helpful to address clarifying questions first. The ultimate goal for the question portion is to address the *why* behind certain moves.

    a. Why did you choose to _____? (*Note:* Tone is important with any *why* question.)

    b. When you _____, what type of response did you want from the audience or reader?

    c. What would you do differently next time, and why?

    d. What was the most successful or satisfying part of your process? Why?

    e. What was the most troubling part of the learning process? How did you navigate the challenge?

    f. What was the most challenging new move you made? How did you navigate the challenge? How do you think it turned out?

Possibilities: Here, we try to focus on what the author or learner did and what they might revise in the current piece or use next time they undertake a similar task.

    a. I wonder what would happen if you moved/changed/added/deleted _____ because _____.

    b. What would happen if you _____ instead of _____?

    c. How could you include _____?

    d. How could you avoid _____?

What follows is an example of PQP in response to a living museum of famous experts, the culminating project of our throughline unit.

Praise: You showed evidence of your research when you quoted Abraham Lincoln and the Gettysburg Address and referenced the Emancipation Proclamation in response to one of our questions. When you told us that joke Lincoln liked, you displayed his personality and humor.

Question: Why did you choose to present as Lincoln when he was President of the United States, rather than a young man or senator? What point in his presidency and the Civil War does your presentation reflect? How did he deal with the stress of being a wartime president and all the death and destruction caused by the Civil War?

Possibilities: I wonder what would happen if you included more information about important individuals in Lincoln's life who helped him on the road to his presidency and during it, because that might help me understand how he became a successful president. I'm also wondering which people provided special challenges to him and his goals.

Checklist for Creating Your Own PQP Activity

❑ The teacher identifies opportunities for feedback and formative assessment that work *as* and *for* learning. (E-M)

❑ Learners reflect on helpful and unhelpful feedback from past experience. They consider how PQP can help them provide powerful feedback and avoid unhelpful feedback. (P)

❑ Learners understand the purpose and payoff of the strategy, how the strategy can prepare them for success on future challenges, and how it can help others with their learning. (P-O)

❑ Both the author or learner—and reader or audience—are primed to work on each other's behalf and come to the feedback conversation honestly and openly as thinking partners willing to help each other. (P-O)

❑ The teacher models and mentors learners in the feedback process, providing appropriate scaffolding and stems as needed. (W)

❑ The teacher (and peers) provide feedback on learners' feedback to help them identify strengths and areas of growth as a feedback friend. (W-E)

❑ Learners have many opportunities to give and receive feedback with their peers throughout the course of instruction so the feedback can truly be formative and deliberately practiced over time. (W-E)

❑ The feedback is kind, specific, growth-oriented, and helpful. (W-E)

❑ The author or creator gains a variety of possibilities to consider for moving forward and creates an action plan for implementation. (R)

❑ The feedback friend reflects on his or her feedback and considers opportunities for growing forward. (R)

FORMATIVE ASSESSMENT MOVE 2: MUDDY/MARVY

When we ask learners if they understand or have questions, most typically sit in silence, afraid to share what they don't understand at the risk of appearing incompetent in front of their peers. This is why it is so important to reinforce that experts are constantly monitoring their understanding and to provide learners continual opportunities to share their level of understanding in a safe space. A thumbs-up or thumbs-down

(Continued)

(Continued)

(or wavering-sideways thumb!) assessment about a particular concept or assignment, for example, gives us a quick pulse check of the class. A written assessment, such as the muddy/marvy strategy, provides us more specific information about what learners understand and don't yet grasp, providing data for our evolving *map* of instruction.

For this strategy, learners create a two-column chart with the column headings *muddy* and *marvy*. In the muddy column, they can list anything that's unclear for them: lingering questions about concepts or skill; confusions about the purpose, payoffs, or applications for the learning; and so on. In the marvy column, learners can list things that are *marvelous*, or what's going well, what they totally get and are ready to do, what inspired or intrigued them, and so forth. This strategy provides invaluable formative-assessment feedback.

This assessment can be used at the outset of a lesson, when you first introduce the learning targets, or at the conclusion to reflect on learners' progress. We prefer to use this assessment on an ongoing basis, especially after something new has been taught. This provides an exit ticket and an opportunity for *reflection*, and we can use the information to plan the next day's lesson. If used as an entrance ticket for the next day, teachers must be flexible with their lesson plan so they can act on the feedback they receive.

We often share some of the muddy/marvy responses to start off the following class. Sharing these responses *orients* learners to the focus for the day. For example, "Half of the class shared that using the number line for negatives was still confusing, so we're going to start today off with a review of that skill and then build on it." This also lets learners know that they are not alone in their struggles. You can also strategically pair learners who struggled with this skill with others who expressed comfort with it. This simple move makes the instructional purpose and plan transparent for learners and helps them to see how their honest feedback is being taken into consideration to help them grow.

You can also use muddy/marvy responses when conferencing. A simple way to do this is to ask learners what they need from you in order to move a concept or skill from the muddy column to the marvy column. Learners may be unaware of how to answer that question for themselves, so you might need to offer them a scaffold, such as a menu of choices. Ultimately, the goal is for the learner to identify the next learning target, as well as the means to get there.

Example: Muddy/Marvy Conference

Teacher:	You listed writing the conclusion to your lab report as "muddy." Which type of practice would move it to the "marvy" column?
Learner:	I'm really not sure. I feel like I've already said everything I want to say before I get to the conclusion.

Teacher:	It sounds like you're unsure of how to use the conclusion to add value to your report and need some guidance about what to include in that section.
Learner:	Yes. I think so.
Teacher:	Some things I could do are give you an extra model or two, provide sentence frames, show you an annotated example, or allow you to create your first draft by using voice-text or a scribe.
Learner:	I think an annotated example would be the most helpful for me because then I could see what the writer did and also see why.

Checklist for Creating Your Own Muddy/Marvy Assessment

❑ The teacher determines the specific focus of the muddy/marvy assessment (content or skill) and the best time to conduct it so that it is actionable by teacher and learner. (E-M)

❑ Learners will understand the mental model of expertise they are progressing towards in order to identify areas of growth and challenge. Learners understand the purpose and payoff of the assessment to identify strengths to build on and challenges to address and to determine what kind of support will help them productively struggle with their challenge. (P-O)

❑ Learners develop confidence and competence in identifying areas of accomplishment that are classified as marvy. Likewise, they feel comfortable sharing areas of confusion or uncertainty and exploring potential causes of struggle. (W-E)

❑ Teachers and learners are challenged to think of ways to support learners to move productively through the struggle, expressing a growth mindset as they do so. (W-E)

❑ The assessment gives the teacher and learners a quick way to reflect on and gauge levels of understanding, as well as to identify confusions, misconceptions, or struggles to address. (R)

❑ The teacher shares with learners the next steps based on the patterns and trends she or he identified from responses, considers together the reasons for the challenges, and negotiates and plans with learners what the next steps should be. (R)

FORMATIVE ASSESSMENT MOVE 3: LEARNING CONTINUUM

The learning continuum serves as a pre-, during-, and post-assessment that encourages ongoing *reflection* on learning and provides valuable information to the teacher and learners about growth, evidence of it, and even reasons for it. It's a perfect strategy for gaining frequent snapshots of learning because it's quick and simple and measures learners on the same scale each time.

Prior to a lesson or unit, ask learners to evaluate what they know and can do in terms of particular unit goals and standards. Prompt them to justify where they place themselves on a continuum by asking, *What makes you say so? How is your work similar to or different from the success criteria?* Return to the same continuum toward the end of the lesson or unit. If the lesson or unit takes place over a long period of time and/or has multiple major learning components, you may also ask learners to evaluate their status on the continuum one or more times at strategic points throughout the learning.

One way to do this is with a line numbered 1 through 10, where 1 represents a total novice and 10 represents someone who could teach the class and provide a model of expert practice. Each learner places a sticky note or colored dot (with their name or initials on it) on the point of the line that represents their level of expertise with a learning target at the start of the lesson. At the conclusion of the lesson, they move their dot or note (or use a different color dot or note) to reflect their new level. Learners provide evidence of their growth from their work during the unit and can be asked to explain what efforts and strategies led to the growth. This evidence and reflection could also be included in a growth portfolio.

Simply placing and moving their dots or notes *primes* learners to the task by connecting to what they already know and offering a target of where they are going; it also provides the teacher with a quick snapshot of learners' notions of their capacity and improvement, what counts as evidence of progress, and overall class understanding. We encourage learners to do reflective writing to accompany their placement and movement along the continuum, in order to make their thinking visible. Furthermore, ask learners what would help them move their dot or note farther down the continuum, and then create action plans together for next steps.

Remember that the indicators of learning (dots or notes) do not always move forward. Learning occurs in fits and starts, with plateaus and breakthroughs. Sometimes, learners move backward or remain where they are during the course of a lesson. Learners should be celebrated when they can honestly assess their learning, understand the highs and lows, make action plans for moving forward, and feel comfortable sharing this with the teacher and/or the rest of the class. We often tell our learners: It will get better, then it will get harder, and then it will get better again!

Remind them (and yourself) that it is deliberate practice with expert strategies *over time* that leads to expertise!

Learners who are familiar with the strategy can reflect on their progress with two learning targets from the same lesson by using a coordinate grid. The following example shows how learners assessed their knowledge of Mathematical Practice Standard 1: Persevere in Solving Problems (*x*-axis) and the content standard of adding and subtracting whole numbers (*y*-axis). The lighter dots are the pre-assessment, and the darker dots are the post-assessment. The resulting coordinate grid provides an overall trajectory for the group's learning, as shown in Figure 14.3.

■ FIGURE 14.3: EXAMPLE OF LEARNING CONTINUUM GRID

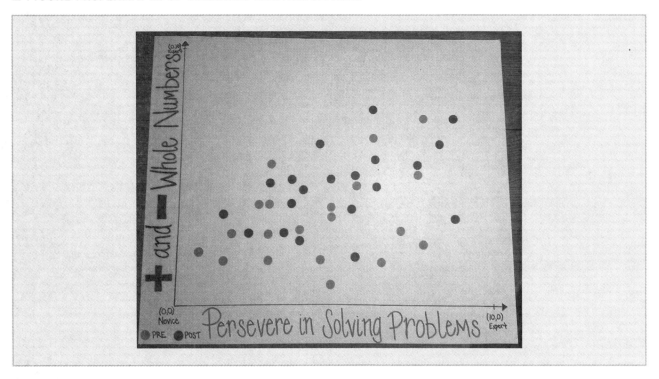

At the elementary level, these continua are helpful for learners to understand the concept of continual growth toward expertise because of the labels that are used, rather than letter grades. The focus is on progress toward understanding and mastery, not on doing assignments or getting a grade.

The simplicity of this strategy also makes it versatile. It can be used as a whole-class check-in to identify trends, or learners can create and revisit personal continua to track progress over time. Personal continua can be a helpful visual to accompany a portfolio, learning log, or journal that demonstrates practice and growth. Seeing one's growth and being able to justify it are powerful components of motivation and of learning (Smith & Wilhelm, 2002, 2006).

(Continued)

(Continued)

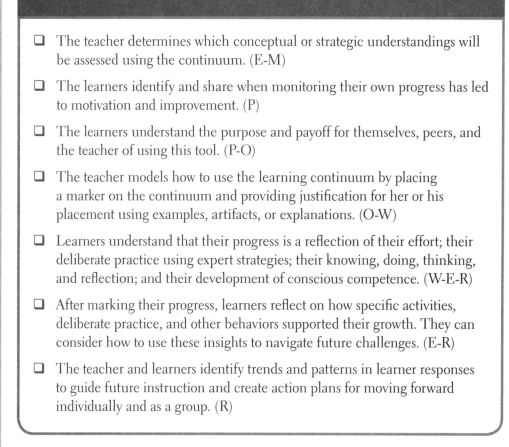

Checklist for Creating Your Own Learning Continuum

- ☐ The teacher determines which conceptual or strategic understandings will be assessed using the continuum. (E-M)

- ☐ The learners identify and share when monitoring their own progress has led to motivation and improvement. (P)

- ☐ The learners understand the purpose and payoff for themselves, peers, and the teacher of using this tool. (P-O)

- ☐ The teacher models how to use the learning continuum by placing a marker on the continuum and providing justification for her or his placement using examples, artifacts, or explanations. (O-W)

- ☐ Learners understand that their progress is a reflection of their effort; their deliberate practice using expert strategies; their knowing, doing, thinking, and reflection; and their development of conscious competence. (W-E-R)

- ☐ After marking their progress, learners reflect on how specific activities, deliberate practice, and other behaviors supported their growth. They can consider how to use these insights to navigate future challenges. (E-R)

- ☐ The teacher and learners identify trends and patterns in learner responses to guide future instruction and create action plans for moving forward individually and as a group. (R)

FORMATIVE ASSESSMENT MOVE 4: SELF-ASSESSMENT

Self-assessment can be a transformative process: It challenges the premise that the teacher is the only one in the room with the expertise to judge the quality of learners' work. It moves teaching and learning from transmission to transformation, from authoritative practice to internally persuasive practice, from *power over* to *power with*, from dependence to independence. Self-assessments give learners practice articulating and applying standards in the context of their own work. If learners cannot judge their own performances and plan ways forward, they haven't yet achieved independence.

One of the challenges of self-assessment is that many learners lack familiarity and practice with the process. As with any new skill, they need a *walk-through* and scaffolding to develop expertise. One of the critical scaffolds is helping learners develop a sense of expert performance by providing questions, a protocol, a rubric, scales, and so forth that express a mental model of expert practice. This *orients* the learner to a clear starting place and end goal and provides some ideas for how to proceed. Naturally, the structures and supports can and should be adapted for your purposes and learning goals. Here are the initial steps:

1. The teacher models a self-assessment based on his or her own writing, reading, or problem-solving process, or a recent lesson or product created along with the class, thinking aloud about how well learning targets have been met and how the evidence demonstrates this. (This is yet another opportunity to use the think-aloud strategies explored in Chapter 10.)

2. After learners see and hear the thought process, the class analyzes a few completed self-assessments (e.g., from former learners). This might be done by ranking examples from most to least helpful to the learner, along with justification for their ranking.

3. Learners are mentored into revising a self-assessment to make it more meaningful. To begin, learners can identify sentence starters or key phrases from the examples provided to them. These phrasings can be posted on an anchor chart in the room for learners to refer to as needed.

4. Learners create or complete self-assessments about their own work and are mentored by peers in pairs or small groups to revise their reflections and provide evidence of their learning.

5. Learners continue to practice self-assessment on an ongoing basis, both formally and informally, through strategies like muddy/marvy and more thorough self-assessments for major learning processes and projects.

Self-assessment is primarily an assessment *as* learning strategy because the learner takes the time to *reflect* on what he or she learned and how. The process promotes and deepens learning. The learner is both the author and the primary audience. Self-assessments are also great artifacts to include in a learner portfolio (which we address in our final chapter, 15). Self-assessments can be used as assessment *for* learning if the teacher analyzes a class set and uses the results to guide instruction. If you decide to go that route, it's best to do so around the middle of the unit so you still have time to act on the results. Figure 14.4 shows a self-assessment that we've used with success; you can find a downloadable version on the online companion as well.

online resources

(Continued)

(Continued)

■ FIGURE 14.4: SELF-ASSESSMENT FORM

My Strengths and Areas for Growth

Artifact (Shorter pieces can be attached to this form): _____

_____

My Opinion

My strengths and areas of growth are: _____

The artifact I included is evidence of this strength/growth because: _____

_____

The actions I took that led to this strength/growth were: _____

_____

My future areas for continued growth are: _____

_____

My action plan for pursuing this next growth area includes: _____

The importance of this future growth to me is: _____

My Teacher's or Classmate's Assessment (Teacher or classmate can fill this out, or learners can write down the feedback)

Strengths/growth areas evident in this artifact are: _____

The evidence for this is: _____

Focal areas for continued growth are: _____

_____

The reasons to grow in this area include: _____

_____

Action plan items for pursuing this growth might include: _____

My Plan

What I will do next is: _____

_____

Next time I will ask for feedback from _____ because _____

_____

Source: Adapted from *Classroom Assessment for Student Learning: Doing It Right—Using It Well* by Stiggins, Arter, Chappuis, and Chappuis (2004).

Checklist for Creating Your Own Self-Assessments

❑ The teacher (or teachers and learners together) determines what kind of self-assessment learners will complete and what scaffolds will help learners succeed. (E-M)

PLC Connection:

All of the formative-assessment moves in this chapter are powerful to use with learners of any age. During a PLC or professional development experience, use one or more of these moves to gauge participants' interest in and/or understanding of a particular topic. For example, the two-way continuum could be used to assess a staff member's *comfort* and *willingness* to make a system-level change the school or district is promoting, and a muddy/marvy exit ticket provides both the learner and PD facilitator with formative-assessment data about what was successful and what needs more clarification or support in a future meeting or as the change is implemented.

- ☐ The teacher and learners develop or review critical standards for success on this task (perhaps expressed in a rubric, checklist, scales, etc.). (E-M-P-O)

- ☐ Learners understand the purpose and payoffs of the self-assessment and will be assisted to identify what a mental model of expert performance looks like. (P-O)

- ☐ Learners view a model self-assessment, noting the author moves they may emulate in their own self-assessment and noting how the critical standards are used to focus the assessment and evaluate growth. (O-W)

- ☐ Learners complete a self-assessment of their own work, using critical standards and evidence from the work to justify their learning progress and to accurately identify areas of focus for the future. (W-E)

- ☐ Learners share their self-assessments and rationale with peers, revising their self-assessments to be more accurate and justifiable based on the feedback they receive. (W-E)

- ☐ Learners use the vocabulary of the content area and of critical standards for success in their writing and thinking about growth and progress toward expertise. (W-E)

- ☐ Learners focus their analysis on where they are in their learning progression and how to move forward, rather than judging their work as a summative assessment. (W-E)

- ☐ Learners reflect on prior self-assessments to see how their assessment capabilities are growing over time and to consider contexts for future use. (R)

POWERFUL PLANNING:
ASSESSMENT FOR AND AS LEARNING

Assessment should always be something a teacher does *for* a learner and never something a teacher does *to* a learner. The Latin root word of assessment (apropos of our focus on conferring) is *assidere*—which means to sit beside. Assessment should be about providing support and promoting growth toward expertise, understanding, and mastery. Formative assessments are the signposts along the road, celebrating effort and progress, deliberate practice, and the passage of mileposts, rather than a traffic ticket issued for a driving violation at the end of a journey. It's often remarkable to see how reflective and knowledgeable even young learners can be about their own learning if they get the proper support. The goal is for our learners to become the world's greatest experts on their own learning so that they can pursue it throughout their lifetimes to transform themselves and their understandings—and even the world.

Guiding Questions for Designing and Implementing Formative Assessments

- What changes do I need to make in my instructional maps to work toward more formative assessment *as* and *for* learning? (E-M)

- How can I alert learners to the "formative assessments" in their personal lives (naturally occurring feedback from their environment about how their are doing, like falling while skiing a certain hill)? How do these assessments influence future actions and learning? How can I promote this same kind of naturally occurring assessment and feedback from learners' work and environment in my classroom? (P-O)

- How can I help learners see the immediate purpose and payoff of each formative-assessment strategy to themselves and their thinking partners? (P-O)

- How will I develop and share a mental model of the process and critical standards for the current task with learners? (O)

- How will I model each strategy? What scaffolding and supports will I provide to help learners succeed and to lead them to independent self-assessment and the creation of action plans for pursuing the next challenges? (W-E)

- How can I help learners consider the influence of ongoing formative and self-assessments on learning and upon supportive relationships (teacher–learner and learner–learner)? (E-R)

- Consider this: What would my school look like if all staff provided one another procedural feedback like the PQP on a regular basis? If all students continually provided peer feedback and participated in self-assessment? (R)

Lesson: Gallery Walk PQP

Unit: How do I become an expert?

ENVISION the destination
(Where are learners going, and why?)

GOAL *What kind of thinking is targeted?*	EVIDENCE *What product(s) will serve as proof of learning?*	MEASURES OF SUCCESS *What's the standard and quality-assurance tool?*	STAKES *Why will learners buy in?* *What's the why behind the learning?*
✓ Explanation or reasoning ✓ Application of skill or strategy ✓ Empathizing ✓ Self-assessing or reflecting	✓ Constructed (discrete task, long or short response, graphic organizer)	✓ **Checklist**: Assess if product contains essential characteristics or features	Use ESSENCE as a guide for buy-in. Your lesson should have one or more of the following: ✓ ES: Emotional spark or salience (i.e., relevance) ✓ SE: Social engagement (i.e., collaboration) ✓ N: Novelty (i.e., new concepts and skills) ✓ CE: Critical or creative exploration opportunities
Use the PQP to provide quality feedback to learners. Teachers and learners use the feedback to make decisions about revisions and next steps and act on these choices. Induct learners into using the PQP to provide peer and self-feedback.	Learners review and use, the feedback to make decisions about their reading, composing, and problem solving, being able to explain the choices they made. Learners provide actionable praise, questions, and possibilities that move their peers and themselves forward. Praise should identify moves and strategies to consolidate and continue using, as well as reasons why to do so. Questions should be useful for other similar situations. Possibilities should provide possible new ways to continue improving and revising, along with justifications.	Refer to criteria of effective feedback: • Kind • Specific • Growth-oriented • Helpful/actionable • Focused on critical standards for the specific learning task or performance • Focused on the product	**ES:** In many instances, learners care about the opinions of their peers as much as or more than the teacher. **SE:** This strategy leverages peer-to-peer collaboration in the revision of products. **N:** Learners will gain new perspectives as they see their products through the eyes of their audience. **CE:** When given the opportunity, learners are adept at identifying the strengths and areas for growth in their work.

MAP out the path to expertise or mastery
(How would an expert deconstruct and approach this task, step by step?)

TWITTER SUMMARY *(3 bullets max)*	MENTAL MODELS, PROCESS GUIDES, HEURISTICS	A MODEL OF GOOD WORK LOOKS LIKE . . .	DIFFERENTIATION AND LAYERING
The PQP feedback strategy is a scaffold for learners to provide themselves and one another formative assessments and feedback that will help them reflect on their product and inform revisions and ways forward.	PQP is itself a mental model of how to provide feedback that can be heard and received, and will be on point and helpful to the learner. Praise acknowledges effort, strategy use, and success. This leads to openness to clarifying questions and to mutual thinking partnerships that explore ways forward.	See example on page 254.	Chunk the types of feedback into praise, questions, and possibilities. These components can be shared separately and eventually combined. Provide sentence stems for how learners could phrase their feedback. Provide a list of criteria for effective feedback. Scaffold the writing of feedback with think-alouds and guided practice. Do work in partners or triads before going it alone.

(Continued)

(Continued)

POWER through your lesson
(What is the sequence of initial major must-make instructional moves?)

	PRIME	ORIENT	WALK THROUGH (and check for understanding)	EXTEND AND EXPLORE	REFLECT
Leader	ASK learners to reflect on helpful and unhelpful feedback. PRESENT a variety of examples of feedback. FACILITATE discussion about criteria of effective feedback. RECORD AND DISPLAY learner-articulated criteria for effective feedback. DISPLAY OR SHARE feedback stems for effective feedback.	FRAME today's lesson: SHARE about the positive or negative effects that feedback can have and how more quality feedback in the classroom will provide everyone more opportunities to learn and improve. SHARE the essential question with learners: *What role does feedback play in our learning?*	SHARE presentation or product and three or four PQP forms already filled out. Guide a discussion about the models and the qualities of effective PQP responses. THINK ALOUD while writing feedback to a new work product with the PQP format. SHARE a new presentation or product for learners to provide feedback. MONITOR learner drafts of PQP feedback until they regularly demonstrate confidence with the skill.	DELIBERATE PRACTICE/ ARTICULATE CONSCIOUS AWARENESS: Have learners provide feedback about topics such as instruction, class behavior, or products they've purchased or used. Have learners use criteria to identify effective and ineffective feedback in real life, such as in online reviews.	ANALYZE trends in feedback from learners and yourself. MODIFY instruction as needed to address learner misconceptions about the qualities of final products. PROVIDE feedback on learner feedback to help them grow as feedback friends.
Learner	ANALYZE what moves make feedback more or less effective. SHARE characteristics of effective feedback. REVISE feedback examples in a way that embodies learner-articulated characteristics.	CONSIDER the role of feedback in their own lives. RESPOND to the essential question.	IDENTIFY evidence of feedback criteria in the PQP model forms completed by the teacher. DISCUSS AND SHARE criteria for effective feedback in learner-friendly terms. LISTEN and take any notes on how the teacher thinks while they use PQP to share their feedback. PRACTICE providing feedback to a teacher or video. REVIEW criteria of effective feedback and analyze whether or not learner drafts fit it. REVISE feedback drafts as needed. WRITE feedback for peer presentation or product.		HOMEWORK EXTENSION Learners provide someone in their household or a character from television or a book with feedback about their actions and feedforward that might inspire future action.

Chapter 15

PUTTING IT ALL TOGETHER

Pursuing Real-World Culminating Projects and Performance-Based Summative Assessments

> **ESSENTIAL QUESTION**
> How can culminating projects, performances, and assessments promote deeper learning and a continuing impulse to learn?

Successful people, in any project or field, possess key mental models and threshold knowledge in terms of concepts and strategic problem-solving processes. For example, doctors must know how to notice the symptoms and potential causes of an ailment, as well as how to interact with their patients and prescribe appropriate treatments. Coffee baristas need to know the ingredients and appropriate temperatures for a drink; the steps to prepare it; and adjustments for special requests, such as an extra hot, skinny, dairy-free hazelnut latte. A good friend remembers the important things about your life, such as your birthday, and knows how to show you appreciation in a way that is meaningful to you. Our lives require that we can know, do, and think around central areas of importance; that we know conceptual content, as well as how to employ that knowledge to do something; and that we can think and reflect on how to keep learning and improving. We must have the knowledge, strategic processes, and mental models for completing the tasks that are central to our lives.

See *Lesson Plan Canvas* on page 285

Authentic culminating projects and summative assessments in our classrooms must require expert understanding and performance from our learners. They should require and reward the use of new mental models and ways of knowing, thinking, and doing that were developed throughout the unit. They must comprise work that is authentic and meaningful and can be applied to problems outside of school. EMPOWER is a mental model that works toward these kinds of culminating projects and assessments because EMPOWER captures how real-world expertise is developed.

Elementary schools tend to make use of projects, but we must continually question the authenticity of these projects. How closely do they match what real experts do in the field? How well do they help learners progress towards this kind of expertise? We also question the ability of individuals or groups of learners to do these projects independently. How do we know we are assessing an individual's abilities, as opposed to those of a "helpful" sibling or parent who steps in on an assignment? Real-world culminating projects are one of the main components of inquiry as cognitive apprenticeship, and they differentiate ICA from many other methods of teaching. In order to prepare our learners for success outside of school, we need to *envision* projects and assessments that meet the real-world test, real-reader test, real-writer test, real-scientist test, and real-mathematician test. This need is why the throughline unit focuses on expertise in a range of fields.

PLANNING FOR PURSUING REAL-WORLD CULMINATING PROJECTS AND SUMMATIVE ASSESSMENTS

Before reading this chapter, we suggest you revisit Chapter 4, where we explored setting critical standards and outcomes and considered measures of success linked to assessment evidence. Although this chapter is positioned at the end of this book and the culminating project typically occurs at the end of a unit, it's important to always begin with the end in mind: *Envision* and *map* out the backward plan of your unit, considering how your culminating project will meet the learning outcomes and performance standards for your unit. This process creates curricular coherence, which is the curricular feature research shows to most help struggling learners (Applebee, Burroughs, & Stevens, 2000).

As you strive to create meaningful culminating assessments for your learners, first position yourself as an inquirer about the current topic of study. Ask yourself these questions to guide your *envisioning* and *mapping*:

- What is my essential question for this unit, and how can my culminating project help learners meaningfully address this question (or part of it)?

- What are the expert strategies, content knowledge, mental models of task completion, and critical standards of success learners need to showcase, and what methods can be used to support and promote this learning?

- What types of products, knowledge artifacts and documents, action plans, and forms of service do experts in this field create? How do these require and reward the development and use of threshold knowledge goals?

- How can I create similar authentic experiences for learners in the classroom to motivate and help them learn and demonstrate learning now and prepare them for encountering these kinds of tasks and challenges in the future?

Ultimately, learners must create products and performances with value beyond school or be asked to solve similar problems as experts in the field in order for the project to pass the ICA test and for learners to be truly apprenticed toward expertise.

If culminating projects are new to you and your learners, consider how you might *envision* small to win big. Rather than examine expertise in a range of fields, as in the throughline unit, your learners might focus on one area. It's most important to dive in and experiment to find out what works for you and your learners. As you engage in teaching through ICA, however small you start, your excitement for and ability to create such projects will grow. More importantly, the enthusiasm and joy of learners will fuel your continued efforts and growth.

If you're concerned about time, we encourage you to first consider how you might spread out the culminating project over time, how learners might divide and conquer the project, whether you can narrow the focus or scope of the project to make it more doable, and how you might differentiate the project for your wide variety of learners.

There are many ways to make things simpler: providing the materials, supplying clear scaffolds and templates, tackling a portion of the task, and making the project shorter. Learners need to experience the work of experts, but they don't need to do all the work in the same way a professional office or job site would function.

Finally, ask yourself if the project you *envision* is something that you're going to be interested in collaborating on or viewing, let alone grading or reviewing. You'll also want to ask yourself, "What are my learners going to think about it?" You want this project to be engaging and joyful. You'll also want to consider your intended audience. In addition to you, who will you share these products with, and why? Most products created or problems tackled outside of school have an authentic audience, whether that be a team, a boss, the public, or another person or group. A key piece to apprenticeship is teaching our learners to consider their audience and to tailor their work accordingly. Having an authentic audience elevates the purpose of the product and provides a unique opportunity for feedback and *reflection*, not to mention a chance to involve members of the community and families in your school culture.

Considerations When Designing Reflective Opportunities and Culminating Projects

☐ Projects are authentic—they correspond to and resemble real-world products in form; require progress towards real expert knowledge; and require grade-appropriate, standards-based skills. (E-M)

☐ Learners are enthusiastic about the project and how it will stake their identity and demonstrate their evolving expertise. They understand the purpose and payoff of the project for themselves

(Continued)

(Continued)

and for others who will experience or use it. They understand how the project reflects real-world expertise. (P-O)

❑ Learners deepen content knowledge and practice high-road transfer by applying the threshold knowledge (new mental models and ways of knowing, doing, and thinking) they've learned in the unit to new contexts and challenges. (W-E)

❑ Learners engage in higher-level thinking skills by creating a usable knowledge artifact, social-action solution, or service-learning project. (W-E)

❑ Projects are shared with or presented to the teacher, peers, and wider audiences, in person or virtually. (W-E)

❑ Learners receive feedback on, reflect on, and self-assess their learning. (R)

❑ Learners reflect on and rehearse how to use what they have learned in their everyday lives and future learning. (R)

REAL-WORLD CULMINATING PROJECT 1: LIVING MUSEUM

Living museum is a drama technique in which learners become a living statue or work together to create a *tableau vivant*, each individual representing a character, historical figure, concept, or part of a process. The classroom transforms into a living literary, history, math, or science museum (Wilhelm, 2012a).

In its simplest form, each learner embodies a role, shares a prepared script from that role's perspective, and interacts spontaneously with questioners or museum visitors. This is a powerful method for representing and extending learning because it asks learners to walk in another's shoes and to articulate knowledge from a specific perspective in a creative and engaging way. The project is real-world in the sense that it requires the social imagination and perspective taking so essential to expertise and everyday life. Learners do much of the same type of work done in theatrical productions, simulations, historical reenactments, impersonations, biography movies, hotseating, and YouTube tribute videos. (In fact, each of these could be projects that extend the living museum technique.) Perhaps even more importantly, learners practice the skills of researching, speaking and listening, presenting, and interacting with an audience—all of which are essential to nearly any job on the planet. Further, this project provides a great opportunity for showcasing and celebrating the creative capacities of learners and involving families and the community in the learning.

The specific goals and content for your living museum will impact who you invite to attend the museum. Family and friends are always invitees. But, for example, if learners research important individuals in the community, invite local community members, whereas if learners embody famous literary characters, you may invite book lovers, authors, and younger learners looking for book recommendations. When *mapping* such an activity, it's important to consider who would actually attend this kind of museum and then plan to invite this audience to a performance.

One of the most important skills for this culminating project is research. Thus, it is important for learners to have strategies for conducting and applying it to the ensuing performance. For the example in our throughline unit, we ask learners to conduct research on a successful person or expert in a discipline. Learners select a person of interest to them and inquire about what made that person successful and how her or his expertise was developed, demonstrated, and used. This could be someone far removed or someone in the local community, perhaps even a relative. Leaving this portion of the project open-ended allows learners a high level of choice, primes their interest, and deepens their understanding of expertise. When learners select their own person to study and demonstrate how that person exemplifies expertise, they express their identity and values. Learners will use a mental model learned during the unit, like the topic-comment strategy for identifying major takeaways from their research and GSAWS for telling the story of how this person achieved expertise.

Examples: Living Museum

Jeff and his colleagues used to do a community night living museum when their middle schoolers studied the Middle Ages. Students researched particular historical figures (for example, Richard the Lion-Hearted or Saladin) or roles (serfs, minstrels, or Templar Knights) and created a museum where they posed as wax statues of these various people. Visitors could ask each student to enact a typical action and recite their name and place in society, describe a typical day or special event, or briefly interview the learner in role.

Students can also play the role of *museum designer* and then *act out roles* in that museum. Students can design an exhibit, a kiosk, or a whole museum. For example, elementary teacher Julie Housum's students created an interactive Egyptian museum. Upon entering, visitors walked down a timeline of the river Nile back into the past. Exhibits were arranged historically and involved Egyptian fashion and makeup, embalming and mummification, and Egyptian religion and gods at various points in time. At the end of the tour, the sphinx would foretell a visitor's future, if he or she wanted. The students played Egyptians from different eras and were well versed in their area of expertise. They could discuss their work, worldviews, and understanding of their exhibit topic at length (see Wilhelm, 2012a).

(Continued)

(Continued)

Checklist for Creating Your Own Living Museum

❑ The teacher and learners plan for and invite an authentic audience to attend the living museum. (E-M)

❑ The teacher thinks critically about the threshold knowledge developed in the unit and how it will be used in the living history performance. (E-M)

❑ The teacher considers the kinds of scaffolds and supports learners will need to be fully prepared to participate in the final living museum and plans for these learning activities and checkpoints throughout the unit. (E-M)

❑ Learners understand the purpose and payoff of the project and how it will demonstrate deep understanding to their audience. (P-O)

❑ Learners have the opportunity to view and analyze historical reenactments, role-plays, or impersonations to identify critical standards of such a performance and to determine what they would like to emulate in their own performance. (O)

❑ Learners have access to a variety of materials and sources for researching and creating their culminating project. In fact, all readings and activities in the unit will, in some way, prepare learners for the culminating project. (W)

❑ Learners are assisted in selecting, researching, and embodying a person (or character, idea, or process) worthy of researching and sharing with others to explore the inquiry topic. (W)

❑ Learners stay in role throughout the performance experience, speaking from their character's or concept's perspective and answering questions from visitors. (W)

❑ The living museum serves as a fun, meaningful, and engaging way for learners to demonstrate and reflect on their knowledge and the process of knowledge construction. As learners respond to audience questions (or promise to do further research to answer the question), they are extending their understanding of the character. (E-R)

❑ Learners understand how they can apply what they have learned about perspective taking, social imagination, research, and role-playing in their everyday lives and future work. (E-R)

(For more on preparing and assisting learners to success with various kinds of role-play, see Wilhelm, 2012a.)

REAL-WORLD CULMINATING PROJECT 2: RANKING MODELS TO ARTICULATE CRITICAL STANDARDS

A necessary first step in pursuing any culminating project is to *orient* learners to the critical success standards they need to master while providing different models of what the project might look like. To clarify, this strategy is not a culminating project; it's included in this chapter because the process articulates success criteria for teachers and learners (a critical step in the *envisioning* and *mapping* stage as well as in *priming*, *orienting*, and apprenticing learners to success through the POWER components). Regardless of your objectives, the ideal way to do this is by inquiring into what makes a knowledge artifact or performance (such as a composition, project, presentation, or service-learning project) excellent by ranking models of the kind your learners will create. This positioning of learners as experts in quality actively involves and values them from the outset. The process helps learners generate ideas for their own projects, deeply understand the critical standards, set individual goals, and take next steps in the creation and improvement of their final products.

The ranking process is also an excellent means of formative assessment because it provides evidence of and insight into learner thinking about a process or product. Ranking requires citing evidence and reasoning about it. Any time experts create something for the first time, they seek out examples to emulate or expand upon. As learners become more familiar with ranking, they too can seek out model performances.

Here are the steps for this process:

1. Begin by providing each group of learners at least three successful products or projects to evaluate. Make sure all shared performances are successful ones so that learners experience three positive models. The models should also show different ways of completing the task so learners get a sense of various ways to be successful. Ask learners to rank the examples from most to least successful and to provide evidence and reasons for their ranking.

   Provide time for each learner to explore the models and record their thoughts independently. Sometimes a simple protocol, such as a see–think–wonder, can be helpful in this process. Another approach is to ask questions to help learners analyze the models using a PQP or other strategy. *What are the strengths in these products? What makes you say so? What makes a product successful? What questions do you have for the people who made them? What are areas of potential growth or improvement?*

2. Ask learners to share their rankings in small groups and come to an agreement about the ranking and the success criteria met by the best example. If consensus cannot be reached, they should understand and share the reasons for their disagreement.

(Continued)

(Continued)

3. In small groups and then as a whole class, record the justifications for the rankings and pull out characteristics of each model that can be considered success criteria. Record these on an anchor chart or whiteboard.

4. Work with learners to create a collaborative rubric or criteria checklist reflecting the success standards. These standards could be posted in the classroom (perhaps alongside the models) as a reference for learners. Limit yourself to the three (or maximum of five) most important criteria. Self-assessing how their work compares to the best model and success criteria will help learners to reflect on what might take them to the next level of success. This process also ensures all learners have voice in and understand the success criteria for their project.

Ideally, learners will rank projects or products created by former learners. However, the first time you unveil a new project, you and your colleagues could create models; it is incredibly powerful to *access* the task by doing the work we ask our learners to do in order to more deeply understand the task, gain empathy for our learners, and anticipate potential challenges or misconceptions. Still another option is to find and share real-world examples. For more complex projects, you may need to break down the project into simpler chunks and articulate the success criteria for each piece of the larger project. For example, if learners are creating a particular kind of art (say, a mosaic or collage) and an artist statement to express how a particular historical concept or era was represented and explored, you may want to have the learners rank models for the art and then separately rank the artist statements, articulating the success criteria for each.

This is a useful exercise for any type of project because it forces you to consider what constitutes excellence for a given product and makes you cognizant of your values and the values of your learners. It also provides different and achievable real-world models of success, and it enables you and your learners to develop a common understanding of what constitutes success. Figure 15.1 shows a note-catcher for ranking projects; a downloadable version is available on the companion website.

■ FIGURE 15.1: EXAMPLE NOTE-CATCHER FOR RANKING

WRITING EXAMPLE A	
NOTICE	**WONDER**
• The author used really strong word choice when describing the porcupine attack. • I'm not sure what happened at the end of the story because it doesn't have a conclusion. • The final draft is neat and doesn't have errors. I bet he got help from a partner.	• I wonder if he used a thesaurus. • Did the author mean to leave us on a cliff-hanger? • Who will I work with during my peer conference?

WRITING EXAMPLE B	
NOTICE	**WONDER**
<ul><li>I liked how the author started with a question. That sparked my interest right away.</li><li>There were a lot of spelling errors. I'm not sure what some of the words are, so it makes it really hard to understand what's happening.</li><li>This looks more like a first draft than a final draft.</li></ul>	<ul><li>I wonder what question or idea I might use to start my writing and hook the reader right away.</li><li>How many drafts will I need to make to get to my final draft?</li></ul>

WRITING EXAMPLE C	
NOTICE	**WONDER**
<ul><li>This story uses GSAWS. There is a character who has a problem. He has a goal. There are high stakes to achieving it. He's in a world or situation that is putting more trouble in his way.</li><li>I noticed that the author used dialogue to help show us what the characters were thinking and saying.</li><li>I was excited by the action at the beginning of the story and just wanted to keep reading and reading. I was sad when it was over.</li><li>The author did a good job using interesting words.</li></ul>	<ul><li>How will I use GSAWS in my writing? How might I use dialogue in my writing to reveal my character's personality and problems?</li><li>What will my story be about? Should I base it on a real experience or make something up totally from my imagination?</li><li>How can I get my readers excited at the very beginning and make them want to keep reading?</li><li>I wonder if we will get to talk with a partner first before trying to put our ideas on paper. It helps me to think through my ideas out loud first.</li></ul>

Ranking

The best project is **Writing Example C** because it engaged us from the very beginning and kept our interest until the very last sentence. We can tell that the author used the writing techniques we've been learning about in class because the author used GSAWS and writing moves like dialogue and interesting and specific word choice.

The next best project is **Writing Example A** because this author used strong word choice to show and not just tell us what was happening. It also was easy to read because there were almost no errors. This is important because we want people to understand the story we are trying to share. This story would be even better if we knew what happened at the end.

The project with the most room for growth is **Writing Example B** because it was really hard to read because of all the spelling errors. It started off well, but then we got lost as readers.

After viewing these examples, I want to be sure to include the following elements and moves in my project:

- A good hook at the beginning to catch my readers' interest
- GSAWS
- Dialogue from the characters
- Strong and specific word choice
- Careful proofreading for correctness in spelling and punctuation, particularly of quotations

 This figure is available for download at **http://resources.corwin.com/EMPOWER-elementary**

(Continued)

PLC Connection

Use *ranking models* as a way to look at models of a culminating project (such as previous students' writing, multimedia presentations, etc.—or by finding a few models online) in order to articulate critical standards and create or revisit a student checklist or rubric. Ranking the models from most to least effective requires articulating critical standards that differentiate more powerful projects from those that are less powerful. This is a kind of work analysis that can inform later student work analysis in PLCs.

(Continued)

Checklist for Creating Your Own Ranking Activity

- ❑ The teacher identifies a culminating project and the threshold knowledge she or he wants learners to demonstrate in their projects; she or he then creates or selects models that showcase how a project requires, rewards, and represents this threshold knowledge. (E-M)
- ❑ The teacher sets the purpose for the ranking by explaining to learners that they will identify critical standards for success with the upcoming project. (P-O)
- ❑ Learners identify how critical standards are addressed within the models and name success criteria for the project. (W)
- ❑ Learners justify their ranking with evidence from the models. (W)
- ❑ Learners engage in high-quality discussion around the products, articulating the strengths and areas for potential growth in each model. (W)
- ❑ The models, learner feedback, and success criteria are displayed in a place where learners can revisit them as they create, revise, and reflect on their own products. (W-E-R)
- ❑ Critical standards and success criteria can be revised as learners continue to learn. (E-R)
- ❑ Learners have opportunities to reflect on how they can use their learning about articulating and using critical standards in their future work. (E-R)

REAL-WORLD CULMINATING PROJECT 3: GROWTH PORTFOLIOS

Helping learners prepare a portfolio is not simply *practice* for the real world, it's the *real deal*! Portfolios are a prime move of ICA because they're used in a wide variety of professions and higher-education settings. They provide evidence of the depth and breadth of one's learning and achievement. They are especially useful for helping learners tell the story of their learning journey in a student-led conference.

Simply put, a portfolio is a collection of learner work that demonstrates growth and accomplishments and tells the story of learning progress. It can be assembled digitally, in print, or as a combination of the two. Unlike an artist's portfolio showcasing his or her best work, learner portfolios can include early attempts with a skill or initial impressions about a concept, as well as a learner's most current level of performance and understanding. Portfolios should demonstrate changes in understanding and performance over the course of the unit and, ideally, over the course of the year.

It's important to introduce portfolios at the beginning of a unit if the portfolio serves as a culminating project or early in the year if the portfolio will serve as a complete portrayal of a learner's progression over the year at that grade level. Provide time throughout the year to curate portfolios and reflect on the pieces learners choose to include. Portfolio reviews and updates allow learners to make learning visible and track their progress over time, as well as to identify how closely they are approaching an expert level in a particular area. This kind of ongoing self-assessment leads to deeper self-understanding and self-efficacy as learners name and reflect on their learning progression throughout the course of the unit or year.

Position learners as the experts about the best evidence of their learning when they curate the contents of their portfolio. This honors their voice and choice and encourages self-reflection because the assessment isn't something that's being done *to* them; rather, it's something the learners do *for* and *by* themselves.

When creating portfolios, it is important to set learners up for success in creating a powerful collection of artifacts that provide evidence of learning and tell the story of that learning, as opposed to being a stack of past work. This means we must teach our learners to curate what they include in their portfolios. The following are a few suggestions to support you in this process:

1. Consider the purposes of the portfolio: to demonstrate effort using expert strategies? To demonstrate growth? To show that particular standards have been met? To provide examples of a learner's best work? To provide archival work for others to learn from or for parents to keep? Then consider how much and what learners should include in their portfolio.

2. Show learners a variety of models, such as your own teacher-generated portfolio, prior learner-generated portfolios, and real-world portfolios from experts in various fields. When looking at examples, start by asking learners something like, "What story does this work tell?" Then ask them to consider how the story changes with the addition or removal of artifacts from the portfolio. Guiding them through the curation process with a portfolio that is not their own allows them to have honest, unbiased discussions about what to include and encourages them to take risks and try things with their own portfolios that they may not have felt comfortable with originally.

(Continued)

(Continued)

3. Mentor learners in articulating clear success criteria for meeting the purposes of a portfolio.

4. Give learners permission to individualize their portfolios to make them relevant and meaningful. Allowing learners this kind of choice and autonomy will make all the difference in motivation and how they value their portfolios now and in the future.

5. Provide time for learners to select examples of learning, and model how to write about the evidence each example provides of productive struggle, deliberate practice, growth, the process one has taken to complete a task, achievement of a standard, and so on. At the elementary level, it will be important to decide if you will ask learners to include specific pieces for specific purposes or let learners select the pieces they believe best demonstrate their learning. When first experimenting with portfolios, we recommend using a combination of these two approaches.

6. After selecting the artifacts, learners reflect on their choices, articulating why they chose each piece, the strengths and areas of growth, and what each piece communicates about them as a learner. Each portfolio entry should have a cover sheet or introduction. Providing a reflection note-catcher (see Figure 15.2; also downloadable as a template from the companion website at **resources.corwin.com/EMPOWER-elementary**) helps learners reflect on their pieces; when learners master this process, they should free-write about the pieces they select. Learners should identify new concepts, strategies, and mental models from the unit that they used, demonstrated improvement with, or achieved mastery of.

7. Learners present their portfolios (or excerpts) to peers at the conclusions of units or learning cycles, to families during parent–teacher conferences, and so forth.

Portfolios function as assessment *as* learning when learners have a chance to select and reflect on individual selections and/or the body of their work. Portfolios serve as assessments *for* learning when they are used to assess a learner's understanding, confer with a learner, or look for patterns among learners' work to inform instructional moves. Portfolios also have a great deal of potential at the grade or building level, as they can be used as the basis for student–parent–teacher conferences, as well as for analyzing student work and discussing and assessing student learning in professional learning communities. When learners create their own portfolios, they develop conscious competence, the ability to name and reflect on what they know and what they don't know *yet*. This allows them to articulate their learning and level of performance to others, whether this be you, as their teacher, or their peers or parents.

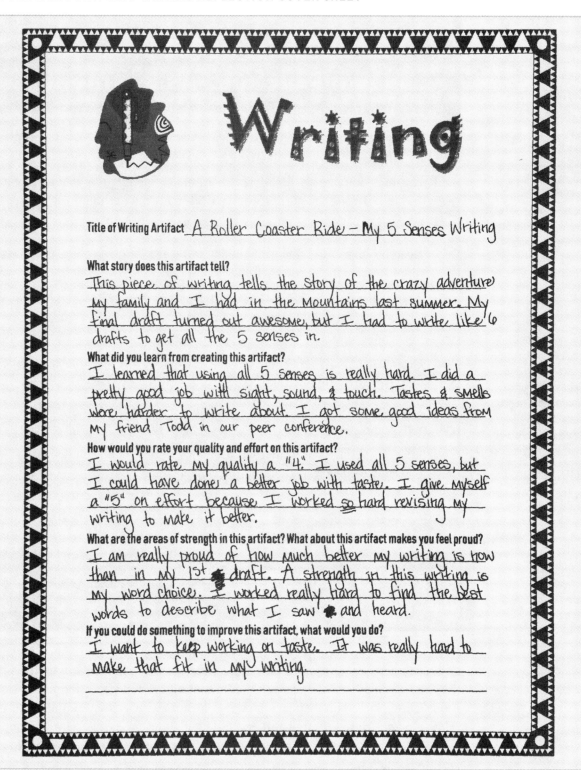

Writing

Title of Writing Artifact _A Roller Coaster Ride – My 5 Senses Writing_

What story does this artifact tell?

This piece of writing tells the story of the crazy adventure my family and I had in the Mountains last summer. My final draft turned out awesome, but I had to write like 6 drafts to get all the 5 senses in.

What did you learn from creating this artifact?

I learned that using all 5 senses is really hard. I did a pretty good job with sight, sound, & touch. Tastes & smells were harder to write about. I got some good ideas from my friend Todd in our peer conference.

How would you rate your quality and effort on this artifact?

I would rate my quality a "4." I used all 5 senses, but I could have done a better job with taste. I give myself a "5" on effort because I worked so hard revising my writing to make it better.

What are the areas of strength in this artifact? What about this artifact makes you feel proud?

I am really proud of how much better my writing is now than in my 1st draft. A strength in this writing is my word choice. I worked really hard to find the best words to describe what I saw and heard.

If you could do something to improve this artifact, what would you do?

I want to keep working on taste. It was really hard to make that fit in my writing.

online resources — A template artifact reflection sheet is available for download at **http://resources.corwin.com/EMPOWER-elementary**

(Continued)

(Continued)

Checklist for Creating Your Own Portfolio Assessment

☐ The teacher (or teacher and learners) designates the scope, learning goals, and content of the portfolio. (E-M)

☐ Learners view and analyze portfolio examples, identifying success criteria and recognizing the purposes and payoffs for using portfolios. (P-O)

☐ Learners have voice and choice in what's included in the portfolio. (P-O-W)

☐ Learners have time, space, and guidance for regularly selecting, reflecting upon, and curating artifacts for their portfolios. (W)

☐ The portfolio includes a variety of artifacts that demonstrate productive struggle, progress, and learner accomplishment in terms of strategic and conceptual understanding. (W)

☐ Learners compose reflections about the artifacts; why they selected them; and their strengths, areas for growth, and next steps. (W-R)

☐ Learners reflect upon their learning journey and portfolio as a whole, as well as how they may use these and other portfolios in the future. (E-R)

☐ Learners periodically share their portfolios with authentic audiences, receiving feedback and considering ways forward. (E-R)

PLC Connection

Encourage teachers to create their own portfolios to show evidence of their professional learning, responsibilities, reflections, and expertise. Specifically, teachers may want to keep artifacts that provide evidence in regards to the domains of Charlotte Danielson's Framework for Teaching or a similar observation or assessment rubric to be used in evaluation conversations with administrators. Such portfolios are also hugely effective in applying for new educational positions, advocating for a leadership role, and more.

REAL-WORLD CULMINATING PROJECT 4: HOW-TO GUIDES

Have you ever watched a video on YouTube to figure out how to do something? There are how-to videos for almost any procedure under the sun, which highlights the authenticity of how-to guides as a real-world culminating project. Chris and his co-teacher, Emily Carter, kicked off their own how-to guide unit with a close reading of the article "How Do You Make a Peanut Butter and Jelly Sandwich? Twitter Has Opinions" by Carolyn Menyes (2018). This prompted students to write their own versions of recipes for PB&J, which were followed to the letter by readers—often with frustrating or hilarious results—and prompted some insight about the importance of clarity, transitions, and sequencing of key details.

Creating an effective how-to guide requires a deep understanding of the process of solving a problem or completing a task. To achieve this, learners need to develop a mental model of task completion, one of the main requirements of expert understanding and performance (Ericsson & Pool, 2016). As a culminating project, learners can be asked to model, think aloud, and/or create a quick reference guide, poster, or flow chart about how to complete a particular task. Learners could also create, record, and share videos, just like real-world YouTube.

How-to guides lend themselves best to the next-generation standards as they are expressed as procedures and strategies. As learners engage in the learning process, they should name and explain the steps they take (as well as possible alternative routes, ways to navigate challenges, etc.), using appropriate content and vocabulary. Thus, how-to guides demonstrate learner expertise in both content and procedural knowledge.

In English language arts or social studies, learners might create a how-to guide explaining how to read a particular kind of text. In math, they could be asked to create a poster explaining how to complete the problem of their choice. In the science classroom, learners could propose how to set up an experiment, demonstrate a scientific principle in action, or apply a scientific understanding to solving a household problem. Regardless of the content area, it's important that these guides are shared with a wider audience, just like those YouTube videos people love to post and watch. An authentic audience provides purpose, meaning, and motivation for the work. An audience could be asked to follow the instructions in the how-to guide and to assess how well it promoted their success and understanding of how to achieve success.

■ FIGURE 15.3: GUIDING QUESTIONS TO ASK WHEN COMPLETING A HOW-TO GUIDE OR PROCESS ANALYSIS

Tips for creating a how-to guide, such as the following, can be useful suggestions to support the work.

Before:

- What is the task? What are you doing or working on?
- How is it similar to other tasks you've completed in the past? How might this prior experience help you?
- How will the task involve reading and composing or other kinds of problem solving?
- How are you feeling about the task?
- How will you get started? What steps will you need to take? How will you divide up the work if this is a group project? How will you monitor progress and navigate challenges?
- What is the purpose of the task? How will you know you have been successful? In what contexts will the product be shared and used? In what situations will it be useful in the future? (This is called *knowledge of purpose and context*, a necessary facet of expert knowledge.)

During:

- Consider what you are doing, the decisions you are making, what seems to be working and not working and why. Consider this and perhaps talk out loud about it or make some quick notes if you are able so you'll have some reminders afterwards when you compose your how-to process analysis.

(Continued)

- How did you get the stuff you needed to do the meaning making, composing, or problem solving?

- (This is called *procedural knowledge of substance,* a necessary element of all expert knowing, doing, and thinking.)

- How did you go about structuring the composition or problem solving on the macro-level?

- What moves did you make to structure the composition or problem solving at the micro-level sentence and word level?

- (This is called *procedural knowledge of form*, a necessary facet of expert knowledge structuring.)

After:

- What did you do, and in what order?

- Why did you do what you did? And in that order?

- What worked? Why did it work?

- What did not seem to work? Why not? What did you do about this?

- What other challenges might people face doing this task, and how can they navigate these challenges?

- How did you feel at various points in the process? How did you manage your feelings to make them productive?

- What options did you have that you did not play out? What could or will you do differently the next time you have this task or are faced with similar challenges?

- To what degree were you successful? How do you know?

- How can you be even more successful next time?

Source: Adapted from Wilhelm, Smith, and Fredricksen (2012).

Learners can name and extend their knowledge by thinking aloud (see Chapter 10) while they demonstrate their how-to guide. This kind of work provides proof of learning, conscious competence, and applicable real-world expertise. If composed or recorded, the how-to guide becomes an archival knowledge artifact that can be used by others. The artifact can go into a portfolio or serve as the basis of discussion in peer or teacher conferences. (For assignment sequences to teach how-to composing, process description, and analysis, see Wilhelm, Smith, & Fredricksen, 2012.)

Example: Analyzing How-To Guides

In preparation for this task, learners can look to their favorite examples as mentor texts: compositions or exemplars that they want to emulate in some way. Chris and his teaching partner, Emily, created the following note-catcher to help learners capture what they learned from how-to guide examples they found online.

YOUR NAME	YOUR SOURCE: WHAT HOW-TO OR PROCESS ANALYSIS WRITING DID YOU FIND? (PASTE YOUR WEBSITE HERE)	WHAT MAKES THIS A GREAT HOW-TO WRITING EXAMPLE?	WHAT MOVES WILL YOU STEAL FROM THIS WRITING TO USE IN YOUR OWN?
Chris Butts	https://www.wikihow.com/Fish	This document is broken down into four parts. This makes it easy for the reader to focus on the information he or she needs, when he or she wants it.	I will add illustrations to my writing for words and concepts that are probably unfamiliar to my reader because when the author of this text did that, it was very helpful.

Checklist for Creating Your Own How-to Guide Activity

❑ The teacher identifies threshold knowledge processes from the unit that learners need to deeply understand and to progress toward expertise. (E-M)

❑ The how-to guide focuses on the larger purposes, processes, and concepts used during the process of completing a particular task, and it is used to support others in addressing similar challenges. (E-M)

❑ Learners reflect on times that they had to learn how to do something and identify what resources and supports were most helpful. (P)

❑ The teacher creates or finds examples of effective how-to guides for learners to analyze and emulate. (P-O)

❑ Learners engage in an activity where they use how-to guides to create something in order to help them understand the purpose and payoff of learning the process, as well as the challenges of creating one. (P-O-W)

❑ Learners supported with various scaffolds to demonstrate the steps in a process and explain how and why they completed these steps and in this particular order. (W)

❑ Learners have opportunities to give and receive feedback throughout the creation process via self-, peer-, and teacher assessments. Learners reflect on how well the how-to guide clearly articulates the process and could be used by a novice audience. (W-E-R)

❑ Learners can name the mental model used to complete the task, how to use it, and applications for future use. (E-R)

❑ Learners reflect on how a specific audience or different contexts or conditions influenced their approach to the task and could influence their future work. (R)

POWERFUL PLANNING: REAL-WORLD PROJECTS DEMONSTRATE REAL-WORLD LEARNING

People create, share, and apply their knowledge in a wondrous variety of unique and interesting ways in the real world. This means that the culminating projects and assessments we offer learners are limited only by our imaginations and what we're able to *envision* and justify as authentic and transferable performances. We know and trust you will develop amazing culminating projects for your classroom.

In the real world, there is seldom a single solution or way of doing things. Experts know there are multiple ways to solve any particular problem and there are various costs and benefits to each choice. This is evident in the number and variety of how-to videos that exist for a single task. The types of projects we've presented in this chapter cultivate learners' abilities to solve nonroutine problems in innovative ways and to communicate what and how they have learned—skills that are quickly becoming the most valuable in today's world. Posing novel problems that require higher-order thinking engenders multiple correct responses, and this requires high-road transfer. This also liberates learners to demonstrate what they know by presenting and justifying their own solutions. By helping our learners to think beyond the box, they develop imagination, creativity, and flexibility. They prepare for the nonroutine analysis and communication challenges that will face them at work and in their personal domains over the course of a lifetime.

Guiding Questions for Planning Powerful Culminating Projects and Performance-Based Assessments

- What kind of projects, products, and problems are encountered in my personal and professional lives that I would want learners to experience in a safe and supportive environment prior to experiencing them in the real world? (E-M)

- What standards need to be met? (E-M)

- What are my intended outcomes? What do I expect learners to know, do, and think to demonstrate proficiency of these outcomes, and how do the outcomes correspond to standards? (E-M)

- What types of learner-created products would learners enjoy pursuing and would I enjoy assessing and providing feedback on? What kinds of products and knowledge artifacts would others benefit from learning about? (E-M)

- What activities can help learners make personal connections to the learning and see the purposes and payoffs of the culminating project? (P-O)

- How will learners see that the culminating project helps them accomplish required learning goals, as well as their personal goals? (P-O)

- How well can learners articulate the success criteria for a culminating project at the outset of the unit? The middle of the unit? The end of the unit? (O)

- How are learners scaffolded in decomposing the task, and how are they supported throughout the unit to prepare for success, complete milestone accomplishments, and deliberately practice expert mental models and moves required by the culminating project? (W)

- To what extent do I encourage creativity, autonomy, and novel thinking with my culminating projects? (W-E)

- To what extent can real-world products demonstrate deep transferable and nameable understanding of how to complete a task? (E-R)

- How do learners and others name and reflect on the process, the mental model at play, and the future applications and contexts of use? (R)

- How can the culminating projects lead to threshold knowledge: changed ways of knowing, doing, thinking, and being that are so generative that they can continue to evolve throughout a lifetime? (R)

Lesson: Living Museum

Unit: How do I become an expert?

ENVISION the destination			
(Where are learners going, and why?)			
GOAL *What kind of thinking is targeted?*	**EVIDENCE** *What product(s) will serve as proof of learning?*	**MEASURES OF SUCCESS** *What's the standard and quality-assurance tool?*	**STAKES** *Why will learners buy in?* *What's the why behind the learning?*
✓ Interpretation ✓ Explanation or reasoning ✓ Application of skill or strategy ✓ Perspective taking ✓ Empathizing ✓ Self-assessing or reflecting	✓ Performance assessment: open-ended essay or writing; products (i.e., RAFT); concept map ✓ Structured/unstructured observation	✓ **Checklist**: Assess if product contains essential characteristics or features ✓ **Holistic**: Assess whole product or response against a rubric with levels of performance	Use ESSENCE as a guide for buy-in. Your lesson should have one or more of the following: ✓ ES: Emotional spark or salience (i.e., relevance) ✓ SE: Social engagement (i.e., collaboration) ✓ N: Novelty (i.e., new concepts and skills) ✓ CE: Critical or creative exploration opportunities
Learners will interpret, take perspectives, and empathize to embody and accurately represent a person they have chosen to research and represent because of his or her expertise in the world. Learners will apply a variety of literacy skills as they research and present knowledge and respond to questions from the chosen person's perspective. They will use what they have learned from the unit (e.g., the topic-comment strategy) to identify major ideas from their research or GSAWS to tell the story of their character.	Learners will integrate researching, reading, writing, speaking, and listening practices to create and present knowledge about a selected person and how they developed expertise. Learners will participate in the museum, as well as observe their peers, ask questions, and provide feedback to help them strengthen their interpretations and presentations. They will make use of strategies they have learned, like questioning strategies and procedural feedback.	Checklist—Learners will create a checklist based on models to support their plan, implementation, and self-assessment. Holistic—A rubric will be designed based on the checklist to assess to what extent learners met the success criteria.	**ES:** Learners will choose to represent a person who is meaningful to them. **SE:** Learners will watch and respond to one another at the living museum. **N:** Learners will take on the persona of their person of interest, presenting and responding in role. **CE:** Learners have many choices in regard to the person they choose to research and how they represent their person.

(Continued)

(Continued)

MAP out the path to expertise or mastery
(How would an expert deconstruct and approach this task, step by step?)

TWITTER SUMMARY (3 bullets max)	MENTAL MODELS, PROCESS GUIDES, HEURISTICS	A MODEL OF GOOD WORK LOOKS LIKE . . .	DIFFERENTIATION AND LAYERING
Learners become the instructors in the classroom when they research and impersonate characters or people in history (past and present) to teach others about how this person developed their expertise, working together to create a living museum.	Learners essentially create a miniature biopic by researching a person they perceive as successful and share about her or his life, the development of her or his expertise, and how this expertise contributes to the world. In order to do this, they work to meet a variety of standards, make use of mental models and threshold knowledge learned throughout the unit, and develop new content knowledge and skills.	An impersonation or historical reenactment you might see at a museum or historical site. The role-player takes on the perspective, dress, voice, and knowledge base of the person portrayed.	• Provide research resources to learners. • Provide a checklist of required elements to ensure learners complete each step throughout the process. • Provide templates for notetaking and organizing research. • Adjust the number and types of sources required for the research. • Adjust the length or expectations of the presentation. • Offer layers of support as learners rehearse and revise their performances.

POWER through your lesson
(What is the sequence of initial major must-make instructional moves?)

	PRIME	ORIENT	WALK THROUGH (and check for understanding)	EXTEND AND EXPLORE	REFLECT
Leader	ASK learners to define *success* and *expertise* and how these ideas are related. ASK learners to generate a list of successful and expert people in their own lives or that they've learned about.	FRAME today's lesson: ASK learners how we can learn to be successful by studying individuals who were successful in their own lives by developing expertise of some kind. *What can we learn by pretending to be someone else or walking in someone else's shoes?* *What can we learn about success and the development of expertise from one another by watching and comparing each other's performances?*	EXPLAIN: We will research individuals who are or have been successful by developing expertise. You will present what you learn by embodying this individual (in spirit, look, and voice) and sharing about her or him in a living museum. We will invite our parents and learners from another grade level to learn from our class about what it means to develop expertise, be an expert, and achieve success. CHECK FOR UNDERSTANDING: Learners can justify how the person they're researching embodies the class definition of expertise and of success. MODEL: The teacher will share examples from past years or their own research project. CHECK FOR UNDERSTANDING: In small groups, learners articulate a checklist of tasks they need to complete in order to be ready to present.	DELIBERATE PRACTICE/ ARTICULATE CONSCIOUS AWARENESS: Learners will consider what and how they share particular findings from their research and how this influences what people learn from their presentation. Learners articulate the most important components of becoming an expert and being successful at something in life. Learners realize how reading, writing, and listening help them become more expert and successful with their own interests and goals.	Learners articulate where they see similarities between themselves and classmates and the person they researched. From there, they can compose a list of goals to work toward in order to become more successful and develop increasing expertise in areas of interest to them. Learners provide feedback to one another on their presentations before they share with a wider audience.

POWER through your lesson
(What is the sequence of initial major must-make instructional moves?)

	PRIME	ORIENT	WALK THROUGH (and check for understanding)	EXTEND AND EXPLORE	REFLECT
Leader				Learners present to an outside audience and receive feedback about the most salient takeaways.	
Learner	SHARE examples and nonexamples of successful people and their behaviors. SHARE examples and nonexamples of expertise. DEVELOP a shared definition of success and of expertise. Have learners write a personal list of individuals they see as both expert and successful.	In role, learners write autobiographically from the perspective of a character they already know about using GSAWS to explain how they became an expert and successful at something in their lives. Learners write a list of traits and areas of expertise they would personally like to develop and select a person who has some of these traits to research. Learners share in small groups about what they hope to learn from others about developing expertise and achieving success.	GUIDED PRACTICE: Learners practice research skills (if not already taught). Learners draft notes to help them memorize information or to serve as a reference during their presentations. DIFFERENTIATE: Provide a variety of materials for learners to read and research, within their ZPD. DEBRIEF: *How do different resources influence what we learn about a person?* *How will the way we are sharing (verbally, in costume) influence what people learn from our presentation?*	Learners anticipate audience questions to their character and rehearse answers. Learners compare the people they have learned about and look for common themes about developing expertise and achieving success. Learners identify what they want to emulate about the person they researched or others they learned about from peer presentations. Learners create an action plan for developing the expertise of the studied person or people. Learners could research another person of interest to see how she or he compares to others they have learned about.	HOMEWORK EXTENSION Learners interview people in their lives or the community to practice learning about others and taking on their perspectives. Learners keep a journal or log where they record how well they embody success traits they learned from experts and set as personal goals.

Concluding Thoughts

WHAT'S NEXT? AN EMPOWERED VISION OF OUR FUTURE TEACHING AND LEARNING

> **ESSENTIAL QUESTION**
> How can we develop systems for continuous improvement in our classrooms and schools?

Aristotle typically evaluated any object, person, or process with respect to *telos*—its ultimate purpose, goal, or end. The telos of a knife is to cut, so a knife that does not cut well is not a good knife. We've argued in this book that the telos of any educational enterprise is learning how to learn. More specifically, the purpose is learning how to deeply engage, understand, and expertly use what has been learned, and we've argued that this learning should be in service of democratic citizenry and social justice.

Learning happens when the learner (whether student or teacher) *is transformed*. Learning happens when learners change their frame of reference by critically reflecting on their prior assumptions. Learning happens when learners consciously make and implement plans that bring about new ways of defining their social worlds and new ways of being and of undertaking action in these worlds (Mezirow, 2000). The shift into deeper learning happens when learners can see why and how their understanding has changed and how this change can be put into action. This kind of transformation is hugely motivating: Developing expertise is empowering. Every human wants to be more competent and powerful, especially when this serves personal growth and is helpful to others or the environment.

It's essential that schools teach skills like critical thinking, problem solving, collaborating, information and data gathering, reflecting, and participatory planning. These are the stances and strategies of disciplinary expertise and democratic work. These include values such as respect for human dignity, equity, freedom, and social responsibility. Guided inquiry not only strongly supports academic learning but also collaborative, dialogic sharing—between teachers, between teachers and learners, and between learners—that leads to improved problem solving, rewarding interpersonal relationships, and deepened understanding. A guided-inquiry approach such as cognitive apprenticeship is exceptionally powerful in promoting engagement and learning because it "integrates academic and social practices that position inquiry as (1) dynamic and dialogic, (2) attentive, probing, and thoughtful, (3) agentive and socially responsible,

(4) relational and compassionate, (5) reflective and reflexive, and (6) valuing multiple and interdisciplinary perspectives" (Jennings & Mills, 2009, p. 1583).

These capacities are certainly worth cultivating in our learners and in ourselves as teachers, learners, and democratic citizens. This is what EMPOWER guides us to do daily as we apprentice learners and each other into more powerful and transformative ways of learning, relating, and being and of democratic working and living.

EMPOWER also helps us to teach specific kinds of threshold knowledge and to do so more deeply over time by helping learners internalize mental maps and models of expert performance. We don't teach opinion writing only once; we don't teach learners how to read for the main idea only once; we don't teach for social imagination and the capacity to see multiple perspectives only once. We teach these kinds of central processes over and over again, lesson after lesson, unit after unit, and year after year. These are throughlines of all curricula and of next-generation standards. EMPOWER helps us to teach these kinds of threshold knowledge in ways that can be named, used, built on, and extended in the future.

ALL MEANS ALL, *EVERY* MEANS EVERY

All committed teachers can become expert planners of instruction who apprentice all learners toward deeper engagement and expertise. Every learner can outgrow her or his current self and become a more competent and even expert reader, writer, mathematician, scientist, and so on—no matter her or his background. We are deeply committed to making this vision possible. When we say that all teachers have the potential to be highly effective and that every learner can become a competent reader and writer, *all* means all and *every* means every. We are convinced by the research on human potential (Bloom, 1976; Vygotsky, 1978), motivation and engagement (Czikszentmihalyi, 1990; Smith & Wilhelm, 2002, 2006), and the development of expertise (Ericsson & Pool, 2016) that this is within our reach.

This is too important a project to leave to chance.

That is why we use EMPOWER as the way to enact the research and practical knowledge of expertise in teaching and learning. It is our calling to actualize the full potential of ourselves and all of our learners. EMPOWER works for inclusion, equity, and social justice. It does so by creating a classroom community that learners find worth belonging to—one that serves their greatest hopes and values, makes compelling personal connections to all learning, is culturally relevant, creates a sense of belonging, requires their active participation from the start, makes the path to expertise clear to all, and provides the necessary assistance and differentiation for all to walk that path. We have found that struggling learners often up their game to amazing levels when they are actively supported in the practices of the expert community (Smith & Wilhelm, 2006).

Here's another major point: EMPOWER offers a way to integrate and situate almost all of the most pressing concerns of schools **through actual instruction**. *Only in* *a context of collaborative guided inquiry* can many powerful features of motivation, flow experience and engagement, social connection and relational learning, social-emotional learning, executive functioning, culturally responsive teaching, inductive and restorative practice, growth mindset and agentive identity, and more be truly achieved. These conditions, attitudes, and capacities must be situated, integrated, and actively cultivated in our daily teaching and learning. These are not goals that can be actualized separately from relationships, complex tasks, and a meaningful context of use. In fact, we argue that guided inquiry is a context that requires and rewards meeting all of these goals for learners and that informational teaching does not meet any of them.

Many schools frame their efforts to meet these goals as separate programs and often as a form of remediation. By integrating these efforts through EMPOWER, we create curricular coherence and situations that support success.

We know that improved teaching is the most powerful avenue to learner engagement and learning (e.g., National Writing Project & Nagin, 2006). Therefore, as teachers, we must serve consciously and consistently the following roles:

- A constant provider of radical invitations to engage in purposeful learning that matters to learners (and to colleagues) right now and in the future

- A constant provider of radical invitations to engage in collaborative and accountable inquiry that serves the self, peers, community, and environment

- A collaborative participant in creating community and caring

- A fellow learner in a community of practice

- A thinking partner who makes others and their developing capacities and potential visible

- A thinking partner who apprentices learners into expert ways of making meaning, working together, being collaborative and compassionate, and so much more

MOVING FORWARD: JUST GET GOING!

If students (or colleagues) need to learn ways of collaborating, repairing relationships, cultivating social-emotional capacity, reading, composing, problem solving, or any kind of learning or way of being, it is up to us to help them. Ours is the most powerful profession in the world because our job is to express faith in the future and work toward its transformation. Our mission is to actualize all potential: to bring what is possible into being. What could be more meaningful than that?

The research on teacher change and development shows that we do not first change our theories and then change our practices (Wilhelm et al., 2001). We change our practices, and then, by reflecting on our innovations, we change our theories, which in turn fuels future change.

In his powerful article "Four Postulates for Teacher Change," Stephen Leinwand (1994) offers four insights for thriving with today's educational challenges, which we recast here:

- We must teach in distinctly different ways from how we were taught. Therefore, we must be mindful about what works and have a map for moving forward.

- The traditional curriculum was designed to meet societal needs that no longer exist. We must therefore design new curricula and instruction that help learners "learn how to learn" and apply this learning to current societal challenges.

- If you don't feel somewhat uncomfortable and inadequate as a teacher, you're probably not doing the job. Just as our learners must lean into productive struggle and move through new zones of proximal development and into a transformed future, so must we. We need to start doing what we can't do yet and use thinking partners and tools like EMPOWER to help us move to the next level.

- Continually revising and refining our instruction demonstrates our professional commitment to growth. It's important to take the next step in the journey and try something new. Every educational experiment is doomed to success (except perhaps on the day before a vacation!) because something is going to be learned and new ways forward will emerge.

Here's our suggestion: Start by planning a lesson using EMPOWER. You'll find that it not only helps your planning but also helps with implementing the plan, reflecting and making decisions while teaching, reflecting afterward, and naming ways to improve the lesson the next time you teach it. Then you can plan a unit using EMPOWER. Once you do so, it will become easier to plan the next unit, and you'll find yourself thinking about how to make the must-make moves even before you get started. It's also helpful to have thinking partners. Just like having a running partner improves your commitment and practice of an exercise routine, so does having a colleague to plan and reflect with. This works well for us even when we plan with someone who teaches a different grade or subject.

Every journey starts with the first step, and every journey *continues* with new moves, reflection, and joining arms with our fellow thinking partners and learners as we go. This is how we engage in the powerful journey of continuous improvement.

We hope you will join us in this journey of EMPOWERment as we collectively seek to transform education and the world for the benefit of our learners and the future. As Nelson Mandela (1990) maintained, "Education is the most powerful weapon you can use to change the world."

REFERENCES

Anderson, C. (2000). *How's it going: A practical guide to conferring with student writers.* Portsmouth, NH: Heinemann.

Applebee, A. N., Burroughs, R., & Stevens, A. S. (2000). Creating continuity and coherence in high school literature curricula. *Research in the Teaching of English, 34*(3), 382–415.

Autor, D. H., Levy, F., & Murnane, R. J. (2003). The skill content of recent technological change: An empirical exploration. *Quarterly Journal of Economics, 118*(4), 1279–1333.

Autor, D., & Price, B. (2013). The changing task composition of the US labor market: An update of Autor, Levy, and Murnane (2003). Retrieved from https://economics.mit.edu/files/9758

Barab, S., & Hay, K. (2001). Doing science at the elbows of experts: Issues related to the science apprenticeship camp. *Journal of Research in Science Teaching, 38*(1), 70–102.

Bereiter, C. (2004). Reflections on depth. In K. Leithwood, P. McAdie, N. Bascia, & A. Rodrigue (Eds.), *Teaching for deep understanding* (pp. 8–12). Toronto: OISE/UT and EFTO.

Bloom, B. (1976). *Human characteristics and school learning.* New York, NY: McGraw-Hill.

Bridgeland, J. M., DiIulio, J. J., Jr., & Morison, K. B. (2006). *The silent epidemic: Perspectives of high school dropouts.* Washington, DC: Civic Enterprises.

Britton, J. (1970). *Language and learning* Coral Gables, FL: University of Miami Press.

Bryk, A., Gomez, L., Grunow, A., & LeMahieu, P. (2015). *Learning to improve: How America's schools can get better at getting better.* Cambridge, MA: Harvard University Press.

Christenbury, L., & Kelly, P. (1983). *Questioning: A path to critical thinking.* Urbana, IL: NCTE.

Collins, A., Brown, J., & Newman, S. (1992). Cognitive apprenticeship: Teaching the crafts of reading, writing, and mathematics. In L. B. Resnick (Ed.), *Knowing, learning and instruction: Essays in honor of Robert Glaser* (pp. 453–494). Hillsdale, NJ: Lawrence Erlbaum.

Csikszentmihalyi, M. (1990). *Flow: The psychology of optimal experience.* New York, NY: Harper & Row.

Culham, R. (2014). *The writing thief: Using mentor texts to teach the craft of writing.* Portsmouth, NH: Stenhouse Publishers.

Dweck, C. (2006). *Mindset: The new psychology of success.* New York, NY: Random House.

Earl, L. (2003). *Assessment as learning: Using classroom assessment to maximize student learning.* Thousand Oaks, CA: Corwin.

Ericsson, A., & Pool, R. (2016). *Peak: Secrets from the new science of expertise.* New York, NY: Houghton Mifflin Harcourt.

Fisher, D., & Frey, N. (2018). Show & tell: A video column / Let's get jigsaw right. *Educational Leadership, 76*(3), 82–83.

Fredricksen, J. E., Wilhelm, J. D., & Smith, M. W. (2012). *So, what's the story? Teaching narrative to understand ourselves, others, and the world.* Portsmouth, NE: Heinemann.

Freire, P. (2013). *Education for critical consciousness.* London, UK: Bloomsbury Academic.

Haberman, M. (2010, October). The pedagogy of poverty versus good teaching. *Phi Delta Kappan, 92*(2), 81–87.

Haskell, R. (2000). *Transfer of learning: Cognition, instruction, and reasoning.* San Diego, CA: Academic Press.

Hattie, J. (2008). *Visible learning.* Thousand Oaks, CA: Corwin.

Herber, H. (1978). *Teaching reading in content areas.* Upper Saddle River, NJ: Prentice-Hall.

Hillocks, G., Jr. (1986a). *Research on written composition: New directions for teaching.* Urbana, IL: ERIC and National Conference for Research in English.

Hillocks, G., Jr. (1986b). The writer's knowledge: Theory, research, and implications for practice. In A. Petrosky & D. Bartholomae (Eds.), *The teaching of writing* (85th Yearbook of the National Society for the Study of Education, Part II) (pp. 71–94). Chicago, IL: National Society for the Study of Education.

Hillocks, G., Jr. (1995). *Teaching writing as reflective practice.* New York, NY: Teachers College Press.

Hillocks, G., Jr. (1999). *Ways of thinking, ways of teaching.* New York, NY: Teachers College Press.

Hunt, L. (2017). *Fish in a tree.* New York, NY: Puffin Books.

Jennings, M., & Mills, H. (2009). Constructing a discourse of inquiry: Findings from a five-year ethnography at one elementary school. *Teachers College Record, 111,* 1583–1618. Retrieved from http://www.tcrecord.org, ID Number 15306

Johnston, P. (2011). *Opening minds: Using language to change lives.* Portland, ME: Stenhouse.

Lave, J., & Wenger, E. (1991). *Situated learning: Legitimate peripheral participation.* New York, NY: Cambridge University Press.

Leinwand, S. (1994, September). Four postulates for change. *Mathematics Teacher, 87,* 392–393.

Lieberman, M. (2013). *Social: Why our brains are wired to connect.* New York, NY: Crown.

Mandela, N. (1990). [Speech, untitled.] Boston, MA: Madison Park High School, June 23, 1990.

McGregor, T. (2018). *Ink and ideas: Sketchnotes for engagement, comprehension and thinking.* Portsmouth, NH: Heinemann.

McTighe, J., Seif, E., & Wiggins, G. (2004). You can teach for meaning. *Phi Delta Kappan, 62*(1), 26–31.

Menyes, C. (2018, June 27). How do you make a peanut butter and jelly sandwich? Twitter has opinions. *Daily Meal.* Retrieved from https://www.thedailymeal.com/eat/how-to-make-peanut-butter-jelly-sandwich-twitter-debate

Mezirow, J. (2000). *Learning as transformation: Critical perspectives on a theory in progress.* San Francisco, CA: Jossey-Bass.

Moore, C. (2016). *Creating scientists: Teaching and assessing science practice for the NGSS.* New York, NY: Taylor & Francis.

Morris, A., & Stewart-Dore, N. (1984). *Learning to learn from text: Effective reading in content areas.* North Ryde, Australia: Addison-Wesley.

National Assessment of Educational Progress. (2019). Retrieved from https://www.nationsreportcard.gov

National Writing Project & Nagin, C. (2006). *Because writing matters: Improving student writing in our schools* (rev. ed.). San Francisco, CA: Jossey-Bass.

The New Teacher Project. (2018). *The opportunity myth.* Retrieved from https://tntp.org/assets/documents/TNTP_The-Opportunity-Myth_Web.pdf

Newmann, F. M., & Associates. (1996). *Authentic achievement: Restructuring schools for intellectual quality.* San Francisco, CA: Jossey-Bass.

Newmann, F. M., Carmichael, D. L., & King, M. B. (2016). *Authentic intellectual work: Improving teaching for rigorous learning.* Thousand Oaks, CA: Corwin.

Newmann, F. M., & Wehlage, G. G. (1995). *Successful school restructuring: A report to the public and educators by the Center on Organization and Restructuring of Schools.* Madison, WI: Board of Regents of the University of Wisconsin System and Document Service, Wisconsin Center for Education Research.

Noguera, P. (2018, May). *Teaching for transformation.* Keynote at Transformative Teaching Summit. King of Prussia, PA: American Reading Company.

Nystrand, M. (1997). *Opening dialogue: Understanding the dynamics of language and learning in the English classroom* (with A. Gamoran, R. Kachur, & C. Prendergast). New York, NY: Teachers College Press.

Paivio, A. (1986). *Mental representations.* New York, NY: Oxford University Press.

Palincsar, A. S., & Brown, A. L. (1984). Reciprocal teaching of comprehension-fostering and comprehension-monitoring activities. *Cognition and Instruction, 1*(2), 117–175.

Perkins, D. N. (1986). *Knowledge as design.* Mahwah, NJ: Erlbaum.

Perkins, D., & Salomon, G. (1988). Teaching for transfer. *Educational Leadership, 46*(1), 22–32.

Raphael, T. (1982). Question answering strategies for children. *Reading Teacher, 36*(2), 186–190.

Seligman, M. E. P. (2002). *Authentic happiness: Using the new positive psychology to realize your potential for lasting fulfillment.* New York, NY: Free Press.

Smith, M. W., & Wilhelm, J. D. (2002). *"Reading don't fix no Chevys": Literacy in the lives of young men.* Portsmouth, NH: Heinemann.

Smith, M. W., & Wilhelm, J. D. (2006). *Going with the flow: Improving literacy learning for boys (and girls too!).* Portsmouth, NH: Heinemann.

Smith, M., Wilhelm, J.D., & Fredricksen, J. (2012). *Oh, yeah? Putting argument to work both in school and out.* Portsmouth, NH: Heinemann.

Stiggins, R., Arter, J., Chappuis, J., & Chappuis, S. (2004). *Classroom assessment for student learning: Doing it right—Using it well.* Upper Saddle River, NJ: Pearson Education.

Vygotsky, L. S. (1978). *Mind in society: The development of higher psychological processes.* Cambridge, MA: Harvard University Press.

Weglinsky, H. (2004). Facts or critical thinking skills. *Phi Delta Kappan, 62*(1), 32–35.

Wiggins, A. (2017). *The best class you never taught: How spider web discussion can turn students into learning leaders.* Alexandria, VA: ASCD.

Wiggins, G., & McTighe, J. (2005). *Understanding by design* (2nd ed.). Washington, DC: Association for Supervision and Curriculum Development.

Wilhelm, J. D. (1995). *Standards in practice, 6–8.* Champaign, IL: NCTE.

Wilhelm, J. D. (2012a). *Action strategies for deepening comprehension* (2nd ed.). New York, NY: Scholastic.

Wilhelm, J. D. (2012b). Cultures of collaboration: leveraging classroom potential. *Voices From the Middle, 20*(2), 60–62.

Wilhelm, J. D. (2012c). *Enriching comprehension with visualization strategies* (2nd ed.). New York, NY: Scholastic.

Wilhelm, J. D. (2012d). *Improving comprehension with think-aloud strategies* (2nd ed.). New York, NY: Scholastic.

Wilhelm, J. D. (2014, May). Moving towards collaborative cultures: Remixing classroom participation. *Voices From the Middle, 21*(4), 58–60.

Wilhelm, J. D. (2016). *"You gotta BE the book": Teaching engaged and reflective reading with adolescents* (3rd ed.). New York, NY: Teachers College Press.

Wilhelm, J. D., Baker, T. N., & Dube-Hackett, J. (2001). *Strategic reading: Guiding the lifelong literacy of adolescents.* Portsmouth, NH: Heinemann.

Wilhelm, J. D., Douglas, W., Fry, S. W. (2014). *The activist learner: Inquiry, literacy and service to make learning matter.* New York: Teachers College Press.

Wilhelm, J. D., & Novak, B. (2011). *Teaching literacy for love and wisdom.* New York, NY: Teachers College Press.

Wilhelm, J. D., & Smith, M. W. (2016). *Diving deep into nonfiction: Transferable tools for reading ANY nonfiction text.* Thousand Oaks, CA: Corwin.

Wilhelm, J. D., Smith, M., & Fredricksen, J. (2012). *Get it done! Writing and analyzing informational texts to make things happen.* Portsmouth, NH: Heinemann.

Wilhelm, J. D., Wilhelm, P., & Boas, E. (2009). *Inquiring minds learn to read and write.* Oakville, Ontario, Canada: Rubicon.

World Economic Forum. (2016). *The future of jobs.* Retrieved from http://reports.weforum .org/future-of-jobs-2016/chapter-1-the-future-of-jobs-and-skills

Zeichner, K., & Tabachnick, P. (1981). Are the effects of university teacher education "washed out" by school experience? *Journal of Teacher Education, 32*(3), 7–11.

INDEX

Because...
ALL TEACHERS ARE LEADERS

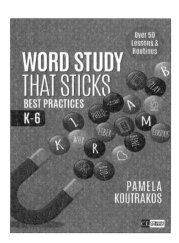

PAMELA KOUTRAKOS

Go back to the source! The book that started it all, *Word Study That Sticks,* delivers challenging, discovery-based word learning routines and planning frameworks you can implement across subject areas.

WILEY BLEVINS

Foremost phonics expert Wiley Blevins explains the 7 ingredients that lead to the greatest student gains. This resource includes common pitfalls, lessons, word lists, and routines.

MARIA WALTHER

101 picture book experiences, a thousand ways to savor strategically—this is the book that shows how to use ANY book to teach readers and writers!

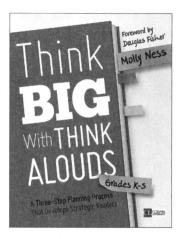

MOLLY NESS

Molly's three-step planning process will help you create dynamic lessons that focus on the five most important think aloud strategies.

Do you have a minute? Of course not.

That's why at Corwin Literacy we have put together a collection of just-in-time, classroom-tested, practical resources from trusted experts that allow you to quickly find the information you need when you need it.

GRETCHEN BERNABEI, KAYLA SHOOK, AND JAYNE HOVER

In 53 lessons centered around classic nursery rhymes, this groundbreaking book offers a straightforward framework for guiding young children in their earliest writing efforts.

PATTY McGEE

Patty McGee helps you transform student writers by showing you what to do to build tone, trust, motivation, and choice into your daily lessons, conferences, and revision suggestions.

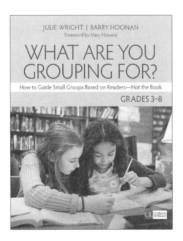

JULIE WRIGHT AND BARRY HOONAN

This book explains the five teacher moves that work together to support students' reading independence through small-group learning—kidwatching, pivoting, assessing, curating, and planning.

NANCY AKHAVAN

With 75 tasks on beautiful full-color pages, this book offers a literacy instruction plan that ensures students benefit from independent effort and engagement.

CORWIN

A SAGE Publishing Company

Helping educators make the greatest impact

CORWIN HAS ONE MISSION: to enhance education through intentional professional learning.

We build long-term relationships with our authors, educators, clients, and associations who partner with us to develop and continuously improve the best evidence-based practices that establish and support lifelong learning.